# HOW TO SELL YOUR HOUSE IN A BUYER'S MARKET

# HOW TO SELL YOUR HOUSE IN A BUYER'S MARKET

**MARTIN M. SHENKMAN**
**WARREN BOROSON**

**JOHN WILEY & SONS**
New York • Chichester • Brisbane • Toronto • Singapore

*Library of Congress Cataloging in Publication Data*

Shenkman, Martin M.
    Selling your house in a buyer's market / by Martin M. Shenkman and
    Warren Boroson.
        p.    cm.
    Includes bibliographical references.
    ISBN 0-471-52508-1.—ISBN 0-471-52507-3 (pbk.)
    1. House selling.    2. Real estate business.    I. Boroson, Warren.
    II. Title.
    HD1379.M474  1990
    333.33′83—dc20                                                    90-31741

Printed in the United States of America

90  91  10  9  8  7  6  5  4  3  2  1

# PREFACE

If you want to sell your house in today's market, you're going to need help. *How to Sell Your House in a Buyer's Market* provides the background information and detailed advice that you'll need to achieve a satisfactory sale—either with or without a broker.

The book covers all aspects of aggressively marketing a house, beginning with the groundwork: an intensive campaign to fix up your house to "creampuff" status. Also included in the critical planning phase is guidance in the careful selection of a broker—and perhaps a lawyer—and the arrangement of a brokerage agreement that will protect your interests and encourage the broker to work for you unstintingly.

If you're selling your house on your own, consult the chapter on the special problems—and advantages—of owner selling, where you'll find advice on the pitfalls to avoid and the best ways to maximize your chances of selling when going it alone.

*How to Sell Your House in a Buyer's Market* leads you through the next stage with pointers on repairs and house inspections. The all-important subject of advertising is covered in depth, with how-to lessons, rules to follow, and sample ads. A special section devoted to fact sheets demonstrates how to put together a fact sheet that emphasizes the best aspects of your house.

When you show your house to potential buyers, the right approach can encourage buyers to seriously consider making an offer; the wrong approach can put off even a good prospect. *How to Sell Your House in a Buyer's Market* gives practical advice for you—and your broker—to follow at this first face-to-face encounter with potential buyers: how to distinguish a serious buyer from a browser, the do's and don'ts of the house tour, and what concerns buyers are likely to have and how you should respond to—or anticipate—them.

The book also illustrates that negotiating the best deal involves a lot more than merely haggling over the selling price. You'll find out how to work the buyer up to the price you want without offending, what accommodations you can and can't make to the buyer, the pros and cons of seller financing, and how to protect yourself if you do decide to help the buyer finance the purchase. The contract is demystified—there are explanations of contract provisions and pointers on what you can give in on and what you must fight for. Sample agreements with explanations and practical tips walk you through typical legal agreements so you'll know how best to work with your lawyer to avoid contract disagreements and keep the deal on track.

The house closing is covered in careful detail. Tips and checklists are provided to help you survive this complex transaction and avoid problems that can derail the deal even at this late stage.

And finally, you'll find advice on keeping your proceeds in your hands and not Uncle Sam's. Sample cases and tax returns, prepared by the accounting firm Ernst & Young, give you practical suggestions on how to keep the money you've received from the sale of your house.

# ACKNOWLEDGMENTS

We would like to thank a number of people who were of considerable assistance with this book: Michael Hamilton at John Wiley & Sons, Inc., who conceived the idea for the project; Louis Chapman, Esq., of Feinman & Chapman, P.A., Wayne, New Jersey, for the review of a number of the chapters and legal agreements; Stanley R. Perla and Arthur I. Gordon, both of Ernst & Young, New York City, for the preparation of the federal income tax returns and accompanying commentary contained in Chapter 27; Irving M. Hyman, I.F.A. Manager of Riotto Associates of Teaneck, New Jersey, for his suggestions and comments; Charles Blumenkehl of Blue Realty Co. of Riverdale, New Jersey, for his advice and assistance with the chapter on broker agreements; Dick Schlott of Schlott Realtors for the use of their fact sheets; René Pabon, Jr., senior vice president and partner in Norman Harvey Associates, Iselin, New Jersey, and Jean Zoller, A.S.I.D., M.I.R.M., senior vice president of JLD, Inc., based in Chicago, Illinois, for their assistance with the Appendix on builder tips. Also, Bill Higgins of Hillsdale, New Jersey; T. J. Gustenhoven of Maywood, New Jersey; Norman Kailo of Wayne, New Jersey; Ferris M. Saydah of Teaneck, New Jersey; and numerous other Realtors who helped us.

MARTIN M. SHENKMAN
WARREN BOROSON

# CONTENTS

# PART FIVE
## WRAPPING UP THE DEAL                                      213

# HOW TO SELL YOUR HOUSE IN A BUYER'S MARKET

# Part One

# INTRODUCTION

# 1 THERE'S A BUYER FOR EVERY HOUSE: SEEING HOW THE PROS DO IT

## DON'T WORRY, BE HAPPY

If you haven't been able to sell your house (or condo, townhouse, cooperative), or you expect to have trouble selling it, don't despair. When it comes to houses at least, the recent popular song advising, "Don't worry, be happy," makes sense.

There are two old sayings in real estate: "There's a buyer for every house," and "The right price sells a house." The reason for the first is the second. If you set a reasonable price on your house, you will make your house exceptional and reduce the competition by 50 percent or more—simply because most homeowners, even in slow times, overprice their houses.

If your house *doesn't* sell for a period of time longer than is normal for your area, even with a reasonable price tag, perhaps it's just the bad luck of the draw. Some common stocks are bargains at their prices, but it can take even professional investors quite a while to discover them. (Shrewd investors have a saying, "You can be right too soon.") Your house just may be an undiscovered gem, and you've just got to give yourself more time and renew your marketing efforts.

Or perhaps your house has problems. It's run-down. It has a structural defect—a roof that leaks, for instance; a flaw in layout or design; not enough bathrooms for the number of bedrooms. Or it's an architectural oddity—a Tudor in a field of colonials and split levels, or maybe a contemporary almost anywhere. But whatever the problem, there are remedies.

3

Your worst nightmare may be that you can't sell your house, even for a ridiculous price, so you must remain there—year after year after year. The house eventually passes into the hands of your resentful children or other heirs, and they bitterly resent their threadbare inheritance.

Relax.

The real estate market always bounces back—just as the stock market always comes back. If you have the time, you can wait out the current malaise. Or you can do your best to sell now, and you'll probably succeed—as long as you don't make the mistakes your competitors are making.

But we must tell the truth: Some people cannot sell their property at all. Slumlords, for example. The plumbing and heating don't work in their apartments. Everything is a wreck, and the taxes are back-breaking. So slumlords walk away.

Yet didn't you yourself once decide to buy your house, because of a combination of the reasonable price and the house's basic appeal? Or did you win it in a raffle? Is your house on the verge of being condemned? Is it located on Tobacco Road? Is it contaminated by radon, asbestos, and urea formaldehyde? Is it in a flood plain? How bad can it be?

So . . . don't worry. Just by virtue of your reading this book, even this single chapter, you'll boost your chances enormously of selling your house for a reasonable price, reasonably quickly.

We'll begin with a look at how the pros do it.


## MEET THE PROS


The services of the vice president of marketing for American Anti-macassar are needed—not in Oshkosh, where she happens to be working now, but in Graustark. So AA asks her to move and at the same time offers to buy her house at a reasonable price.

AA makes this offer for three reasons: (1) AA wants her to agree to move, not to find a job with a competitor in Oshkosh. (2) AA wants the VP to pack up, move to Graustark, and start working right away—without the psychological stress and all the details of selling her house. (3) AA knows that, after it buys her house, it can use a relocation service to sell the house for a reasonable price, reasonably quickly.

How do the relocation services do it? By playing it cool—and smart.

## PRICING

First, relocators set a reasonable, low price on the house. Typically, they hire two independent appraisers to estimate the house's market value, then average the figures. If the two figures are more than 5 percent apart, the relocators hire a third appraiser, then they average the two prices that are closer to each other.

The relocators then ask the transferred executive if he/she will accept that price. The executive has 60 to 90 days to sell the house on his or her own, using a broker or not. Very few people, as you might have suspected, can sell their homes for more than the appraised value. Appraisers are known for being conservative, so when appraisers are used, the house price starts off being reasonable.

Many homeowners, by contrast, think their houses are worth more—usually because they remember all the improvements they paid for. As one real estate authority has said, some homeowners think that their 80 rose bushes are worth a lot, even though the serious buyers are allergic. Or the homeowners may think that the exercise room they installed is valuable, although the most interested buyer is 76 years old.

Homeowners may also overprice their houses because they have heard that a house that's very similar sold for more. (Such rumors, like stock tips, are almost always false.) Or they overprice their houses because their houses were indisputably worth more . . . a few years ago, before the market cooled. Or—and this above all— they overprice their houses because their self-esteem seems to depend on how much they can get for their houses. (One broker has said that homeowners feel about the asking prices on their houses the way parents feel about their kids' Scholastic Aptitude Test scores.)

A rare broker is the overpricer. Some brokers propose an inflated asking price, appealing to the homeowner's desire for a higher price, just to get the listing.

But the relocation service has none of these hangups. It simply, and cold-bloodedly, abides by the appraised value of the house. And then it may put the house up for sale *for a price less than the appraised value.* If a house has been appraised for $300,000, the asking price may be only $296,000.

So that's step one: Set a price on the house that's not just realistic and reasonable, but a bit of a bargain.

## NEGOTIATING

Next, the relocator is willing to haggle. After all, the relocator isn't like the homeowner who may still be living in his or her for-sale house. The corporation that bought the house must pay the existing mortgage, utilities, maintenance, and taxes. That usually amounts to, as a rule of thumb, 1.5 percent of the appraised value every month—which means $4,500 a month in the case of a house appraised at $300,000.

So the relocator is willing to give a bit on the asking price. If the house sells now, and not three months later, that's a savings of $13,500—which means a $282,500 offer would be seriously considered.

Your ordinary homeowner probably put a price of $315,000 or $330,000 on that house—5 percent or 10 percent above the market price. How would he or she feel about a $282,500 offer? Outraged and indignant, of course. Even if he or she had already moved out and was paying that $4,500 extra a month.

Relocation services don't get indignant. They just keep bargaining. No offer is insulting, no offer is ridiculous. And the services can engage in protracted negotiations, making concessions of $1,000 at a time, whereas many home sellers get rattled by back-and-forth haggling.

That's step two: Don't reject any offers at all. Keep negotiating.

## FIX THE PLACE UP

Steps one and two assume an earlier, preliminary step: The house was made shipshape. The relocation service pays for a thorough housecleaning, any repairs, and any redecoration (painting, wallpapering) that's called for. It has inspectors come and check for radon and asbestos. The inspectors also examine the roof, the basement walls, the plumbing, the heating. Then everything is brought up to snuff, at the relocation service's expense.

Just to make sure that nothing is missed, the transferee is asked to fill out a form revealing whatever defects a house has, every wart and blemish. That way, after the house is sold, there's little likelihood that a disgruntled buyer will bring suit. In contrast, quite a few homeowners will try to sell their houses even though they know the 40-year-old roof was leaking a torrent before it was patched, the furnace hasn't been cleaned in years, and the septic-tank system is clearly at the end of its lifespan.

Thus, another secret of the relocators is that their houses have almost no defects—patent or latent. They're freshly painted; their furnaces work noiselessly; neither the roof, the basement, nor the pipes leak.

And you know what it means when you have a spiffy-clean, smoothly working house being sold at a bargain price. You have what real estate agents call a "creampuff."

## CHOOSING AN AGENT

Talking about agents, here's how the relocators choose a broker: They look for a firm with a good reputation, a high ratio of house sales to agents, and lots of local market share. In every area, there seems to be such a firm, and the choice is pretty obvious. The relocators don't hire as a broker the sweet lady across the street, or a brother-in-law, or the broker who hasn't made a sale in six months and who is so desperate for a listing that he or she promises to get the home seller an impossible price.

## MAKE NOISE

Finally, the relocation services keep after the agents. "How's the market? Should the price be reduced? Are buyers coming by? What are they saying? Is there anything that turns them off, that we can repair?" One relocation-service spokesman admits, "We're a squeaky wheel. We push and push—until the house is sold."

And that's all there is to it—well, almost. The fact is that relocation services put lots of houses on the market, so brokers work harder for them than they do for ordinary homeowners. Brokers want repeat business.

But even without that advantage, even in a soft market, relocation services sell their houses fast simply because they do everything right.

They put bargain prices on their houses. They bring them up to tip-top condition, and they redecorate them to beat the band. They hire hard-working, successful brokers and keep pestering them for feedback. And they're willing to listen to all offers without getting insulted.

You can do likewise for success with your house. The remainder of this book will elaborate on these themes and fill in the details.

## CHAPTER SUMMARY

Just about every house can be sold—no matter how soft the real estate market is, no matter what's wrong with the house. You can learn how to do it by studying what relocation services do: (1) They obtain a reasonable market value for a house. Then they offer it for a little less. (2) They have all defects repaired and pretty up the place. (3) They hire the hardest-working, most successful brokerage firm in an area, and (4) they constantly communicate with that broker. (5) They are also willing to consider all offers.

# 2 THE STEPS INVOLVED IN SELLING YOUR HOUSE

The first thing to do when you decide to put your house on the market is this: Start keeping it cleaner than ever before.

Enlist the cooperation of everyone in your family and impress upon them that, from now on, cleanliness and neatness are the passwords.

## GET THE BROOM, GET THE MOP

Everyone must clean out his or her room. They must store away or throw away any rarely used items—or earmark them for the forthcoming garage sale. Impress upon the family that when a real estate agent phones to announce that a buyer will be over in 15 minutes, everyone must go into his or her act—cleaning, straightening, putting away, airing out the place, hiding the pets, and so forth.

While your family is doing its job, you might enlist outside help. Consider hiring cleaning people to work for a week straight, and to come over once a week after that until the house is sold. (You may think this is unneeded advice, but real estate agents report that some homeowners have no idea how messy and grungy their houses are—and how much more they could get if their houses were sparkling.)

At the same time, visit every room in the house—and go around outside, too—with notebook in hand. Mark down everything that needs repair—from the grouting in the bathroom to the ceiling tiles in the basement to the squeaky steps leading to the attic. And begin having everything taken care of, either by yourself or with outside help. (Your local hardware store can probably recommend a jackof-all-trades. Also, check the advertisements in local shopper, or other free newspapers.)

Once your house is clean and neat, and in good operating order, you can put it into play. Keep in mind that you want to make a good impression on real estate agents as well as buyers.

## A DOZEN STEPS

Exactly what steps you take along the way to selling your house, and in which order, aren't etched in stone. But here's a typical, chronological list of what homeowners do to sell a house, *after* having made it presentable.

1. Hire a house inspector to make sure that your place has no major problems that might be discovered only at the last minute— problems that could delay or even cancel a closing, or worse yet, for which an unaware buyer may attempt to hold you liable. If there *are* defects—the roof is at the end of its useful life, the hot-water heater isn't doing its job—try to have them attended to before any buyer comes on the scene. Also, ask the house inspector for advice on having the house checked for asbestos and radon contamination. (See Chapter 10.)

2. Hire a lawyer. While in many areas of the country it's not traditional for sellers to retain lawyers, if you are going to hire one, do it early—before you sign a contract with a real estate broker. (See Chapter 5.)

3. Drop in on some open houses in your area. This will accomplish three things: (1) It will familiarize you with house prices in your area; (2) it will show you what the competition is up to, and should give you some decorating ideas; and (3) it will introduce you to real, live real estate agents at work—and thus start you off on choosing a good agent.

4. If you aren't going to try to sell the house yourself, without a broker, decide which brokerage firm you will list your house with. At the same time, with the help of the agents, you'll decide the asking price to put on your house. (See Chapters 1 and 4.)

5. If you're going to try to sell your house without a broker, consider hiring an appraiser. (See Chapter 9.)

6. Whether you work with an agent or not, develop a fact sheet describing your house and its special virtues. (See Chapter 12.) A fact sheet is sort of a résumé for a house.

7. With the help of your agent, and the guidance of some friends, decide how to add sparkle and flair to your house. (See Chapter 15.)

8. Help your agent sell your house. Cooperate! (See Chapter 8.) Consider buying newspaper advertisements when your broker isn't running any about your particular house. (See Chapter 13.) Blanket the area with your fact sheets. Everyone from the personnel director at a nearby big company to an apartment renter on the other side of town should get one. (See Chapter 14.)

9. If your house isn't selling, or you fear that it won't sell quickly, take remedial steps. If, for example, you have left the house vacant, you might be able to hire a company to provide a caretaker (house sitter) in your absence—free of charge! (See Chapter 18.) Or you could consider leasing out your house to potential buyers, or helping buyers with the financing. (See Chapters 19, 20, 21, and 22.)

10. Even before you begin getting offers, decide how you will deal with them. What if a buyer's offering price is way below your asking price? What if the buyer wants to trade property he or she owns to you, as part of an overall deal? (See Chapters 23 and 24.)

11. When you finally get a preliminary contract ("earnest money," as it's called in some areas), prepare to start moving out. And take measures to prevent any foul-ups at the closing (which usually takes place 45 to 60 days after the signing of the contract, when the deed to the house changes hands). (See Chapter 26.)

12. Finally, decide how to deal with the tax consequences of selling your house so you wind up with the most money possible in your pocket—to buy another house, to retire in comfort, or whatever you choose. (See Chapter 27.)


## CHAPTER SUMMARY

To sell your house, follow certain steps—and in a certain order. Don't hire a lawyer at the last minute, for example, so he or she doesn't have a chance to review any contract you may sign with a broker. And consider hiring your own house inspector, rather than taking a chance that the buyer's house inspector will discover problems at the last minute that quash the sale.

# FOR YOUR NOTEBOOK

## CHECKLIST OF PERSONAL PROPERTY

**TIP:** Before even meeting with a broker or lawyer, walk through each room of your house and complete the form below, specifying exactly what should be included in the sale and what should not be included in the sale. If you're ever uncertain about an item, list it to exclude.

Other advice is as follows: (1) If there are any really important personal items that you don't want to include in the sale, move them out of the house before you begin showing it to prospective buyers. What buyers don't see they can't argue about later. (2) If you can't move out the items you really want to take with you, tell prospective buyers up-front that those items have sentimental value to you and you will take them. (3) Once you get a buyer, carefully list every item of personal property that is to be included and excluded in the sale contract before it goes to the buyer for signature. It's much easier to get a buyer to accept that certain items are excluded if it is in the first contract the buyer sees. In a buyer's market you don't want to end up with hard feelings over an item of personal property—and maybe lose your buyer. It is much harder to get a buyer to agree to let you add something to the excluded list after the buyer has seen the contract.

Don't rely on the broker or your lawyer to know what to include and exclude; they can't read your mind. Prepare the list below. Make photocopies. (Also see Chapter 25.)

| Description of Property | Room | Quantity | Included | Excluded |
|---|---|---|---|---|
| Refrigerator | _____ | _____ | [ ] | [ ] |
| Freezer | _____ | _____ | [ ] | [ ] |
| Electric dishwasher | _____ | _____ | [ ] | [ ] |
| Gas grill | _____ | _____ | [ ] | [ ] |
| Electric/gas stove | _____ | _____ | [ ] | [ ] |
| Oven/broiler | _____ | _____ | [ ] | [ ] |
| Light fixtures | _____ | _____ | [ ] | [ ] |
| | _____ | _____ | [ ] | [ ] |
| | _____ | _____ | [ ] | [ ] |
| | _____ | _____ | [ ] | [ ] |
| | _____ | _____ | [ ] | [ ] |
| Washer | _____ | _____ | [ ] | [ ] |
| Dryer | _____ | _____ | [ ] | [ ] |
| Carpeting/rugs | _____ | _____ | [ ] | [ ] |
| Trash compactor | _____ | _____ | [ ] | [ ] |
| Fireplace equipment | _____ | _____ | [ ] | [ ] |
| Television antenna | _____ | _____ | [ ] | [ ] |

| Description of Property | Room | Quantity | Included | Excluded |
|---|---|---|---|---|
| Microwave oven | —————————— | ———— | [ ] | [ ] |
| Drapes/curtains | —————————— | ———— | [ ] | [ ] |
| | —————————— | ———— | [ ] | [ ] |
| | —————————— | ———— | [ ] | [ ] |
| Air-conditioner units | —————————— | ———— | [ ] | [ ] |
| | —————————— | ———— | [ ] | [ ] |
| | —————————— | ———— | [ ] | [ ] |
| | —————————— | ———— | [ ] | [ ] |
| Storm windows | —————————— | ———— | [ ] | [ ] |
| Workbench | —————————— | ———— | [ ] | [ ] |
| Front-door screen | —————————— | ———— | [ ] | [ ] |
| Back-door screen | —————————— | ———— | [ ] | [ ] |
| Lawn furniture | —————————— | ———— | [ ] | [ ] |
| Window shades | —————————— | ———— | [ ] | [ ] |
| Lawn equipment | —————————— | ———— | [ ] | [ ] |
| Lawn mower | —————————— | ———— | [ ] | [ ] |
| Mirrors | —————————— | ———— | [ ] | [ ] |
| | —————————— | ———— | [ ] | [ ] |
| | —————————— | ———— | [ ] | [ ] |
| Radiator covers | —————————— | ———— | [ ] | [ ] |
| Water softener/filter | —————————— | ———— | [ ] | [ ] |
| Electric garage-door opener | —————————— | ———— | [ ] | [ ] |
| Stove/range in basement | —————————— | ———— | [ ] | [ ] |
| Refrigerator in basement | —————————— | ———— | [ ] | [ ] |
| Freezer in basement | —————————— | ———— | [ ] | [ ] |
| Mailbox | —————————— | ———— | [ ] | [ ] |
| Bookcases | —————————— | ———— | [ ] | [ ] |
| Smoke alarm | —————————— | ———— | [ ] | [ ] |
| Gas alarm | —————————— | ———— | [ ] | [ ] |
| Dehumidifier | —————————— | ———— | [ ] | [ ] |
| Burglar-alarm system | —————————— | ———— | [ ] | [ ] |
| Doorbell and chimes | —————————— | ———— | [ ] | [ ] |
| Intercom system | —————————— | ———— | [ ] | [ ] |
| Awnings | —————————— | ———— | [ ] | [ ] |
| Air-handler covers | —————————— | ———— | [ ] | [ ] |
| Swimming-pool filter | —————————— | ———— | [ ] | [ ] |
| Swing set | —————————— | ———— | [ ] | [ ] |
| Shrubbery, plants | —————————— | ———— | [ ] | [ ] |
| Outdoor statues, planters | —————————— | ———— | [ ] | [ ] |
| Shutters | —————————— | ———— | [ ] | [ ] |
| Lawn/garden shed | —————————— | ———— | [ ] | [ ] |
| Garden hoses | —————————— | ———— | [ ] | [ ] |
| Attic fan | —————————— | ———— | [ ] | [ ] |

(continued)

| Description of Property | Room | Quantity | Included | Excluded |
|---|---|---|---|---|
| Kitchen exhaust fan | _____ | _____ | [ ] | [ ] |
| Shower enclosure | _____ | _____ | [ ] | [ ] |
| Towel racks | _____ | _____ | [ ] | [ ] |
| Sump pump | _____ | _____ | [ ] | [ ] |
| _____ | _____ | _____ | [ ] | [ ] |
| _____ | _____ | _____ | [ ] | [ ] |
| _____ | _____ | _____ | [ ] | [ ] |
| _____ | _____ | _____ | [ ] | [ ] |
| _____ | _____ | _____ | [ ] | [ ] |
| _____ | _____ | _____ | [ ] | [ ] |
| _____ | _____ | _____ | [ ] | [ ] |
| _____ | _____ | _____ | [ ] | [ ] |
| _____ | _____ | _____ | [ ] | [ ] |
| _____ | _____ | _____ | [ ] | [ ] |

# 3 DON'T BUY BEFORE YOU SELL

One of the worst mistakes homeowners can make in a soft real estate market is to buy another house before selling the one they own now. You could wind up with

- two mortgages
- two sets of property taxes
- two hazard-insurance payments
- two sets of expenses for maintenance and repairs—including everything from lawn mowing to repairing leaks.

Unless you're very rich, the expenses may drive you to the poorhouse—even though you own two houses. After all, a house typically makes up 30 percent of your monthly expenses. If those expenses double, your budget will become strained beyond capacity.

Besides, owning two houses will probably be even more expensive than you think. For your new house, you will need new appurtenances: window curtains, appliances, furniture. New homeowners tend to spend thousands of dollars more than other citizens, simply filling in the gaps after they move. As for your old house, with no one on the site to cut the lawn, rake the leaves, shovel the snow, and scout around for problems, you could be faced with sudden high repair costs.

## TEMPTATION

Yet you may be tempted to do the unthinkable—to buy a second house before your first one has sold. Here are the common reasons and rationalizations:

- While your present house is on the market, in looking around for another house, you find a real creampuff—a wonderful house for a bargain price. You don't want to lose it; it seems like a once-in-a-lifetime opportunity.

The fact is, in any soft real estate market there are wonderful bargains. If you buy a good house at a price that's indisputably a bargain, you may have to sell your house for an even greater bargain—to someone else.

- You have confidence that your present house will sell fast— you may even have a deal pending—or, if not, that you can rent it out.

A great many houses that seem sold turn out *not* to be sold. Glitches can arise. For example, a house inspector reports that the roof needs to be replaced for $2,000. The buyer won't pay a nickel toward the expense. You argue that the buyer isn't entitled to a totally new roof, but the result is an undone deal.

Or your house may not sell as quickly as you imagined it would. When you bought the house, you recall, there was a mob of eager buyers, and you were lucky to get your bid in first, and to pay *only* the full asking price. But this is a new market.

As for renting out your house, you can have trouble finding a good tenant—and trouble getting enough rental income to cover your expenses. Remember two things about tenants:

First, if they were very prosperous and had steady incomes, most of them would buy a house instead of renting. Therefore, they may not be prosperous and may not be regularly employed. The result: You have trouble collecting the rent and then trouble evicting them, involving high legal expenses. Be informed that some desperate landlords have wound up paying their tenants to get out. You would have been better off not renting the place, because you wouldn't have to be wasting time and money getting these deadbeats out. Once you do evict them, you'll learn what all experienced landlords know: If you have just one rental property and no rental income from it, you have a 0 percent occupancy rate and a totally negative cash flow.

Second, tenants don't live in a house now, so they may not have lived in houses before. They may not know how to maintain a house properly, especially an upscale house. They may not oil the motor of your hot-water boiler, or check the pressure level; they may not even tell you if the basement or the roof starts leaking. After all, in the past, if something went wrong, they just called the super. And that's not mentioning damage they may do to walls, doors, floors, and plumbing.

Another disadvantage is that you will probably find it harder to sell your house if there are tenants there. The tenants may give you, or your real estate agent, a hard time about when you can show the house to buyers. They may be discourteous to buyers, souring them on your house. They may keep the house messy and dirty, turning buyers off.

Of course, there are many wonderful tenants out there—conscientious bill-payers, conscientious guardians of houses. If you search carefully enough—always get references!—you may find them. But even if you do, considering how high the divorce rate is, their situations can change, and you'll be left in the lurch.

---

**CAUTION:** There are professional deadbeats out there—people who rent houses never intending to pay more than a few months' rent, and then enjoying their landlords' hospitality free of charge. They look for overeager landlords, such as people renting houses they haven't been able to sell. They put on a great song-and-dance: If they like your house and the neighborhood, they say airily, they will probably buy it—they have just sold their business back East (or West) and soon will have a check for several hundred thousand dollars. What they don't say is that years of experience have given them a lawyer's knowledge of the foreclosure proceedings in your area, and a good idea of how long they can remain in your house paying nothing. One professional deadbeat boasted, "I once lived in a sumptuous house rent-free for two years."

It's fairly easy to recognize such characters. They're warm, charming, cheerful, chatty, fun to be with. You really like them on a surface meeting. But when you question them—Who was your previous landlord? What is your bank balance? What is the name of the business you sold?—they tend to give vague answers. Never rent to anyone without getting, and checking, at least three references, including at least one former landlord and one employer.

---

**CASE HISTORY:** A family bought a $380,000 house in 1985. A year later, two of their children moved out, and the family decided to look for a smaller place. They put their house on the market and promptly received an offer for $580,000.

But neighbors told them that new houses were being offered in the $700,000 range. And their bank valued their house at $600,000. Not content with a $200,000 gain in one year, they rejected the offer, to the chagrin of their real estate broker. Meanwhile, they bought another house, in an even ritzier community, for $700,000. Although it was smaller, it had more amenities—pool, Jacuzzi, and so forth.

Then, in 1987, the market rolled over and played dead. They couldn't sell their first house for what they needed and eventually rented it to a woman who took an option to buy. She not only didn't buy; she didn't pay rent. It was a year before they could evict her. Meanwhile, she did horrendous damage to the house.

They fell behind in their mortgage payments on both houses. Interest compounded on interest. Eventually their debt approached a million dollars—more than the equity in their combined houses. They defaulted on both mortgages and lost both houses. They have since moved away from the area.

---

**CASE HISTORY:** A family in the East was eager to move to the Southwest and build a home there. They bought a plot of land and at the same time bought a nearby condo to live in while their new house was being constructed.

But they hadn't sold their old house first, and they still haven't. They started out asking close to $500,000. Although it was a fine house, there was too much competition, and the house didn't move.

The couple already had a home-equity loan (second mortgage on the first house), so now they had a total of four mortgages: one on the plot of land, one on the condo, and two on the home back East. Every month the family reduces the price on the home in the East by $10,000. But even $450,000 has failed to attract a buyer. And every month the family is being forced to pay off their four mortgages, losing $5,000 to $6,000 a month. Says their broker, "Their life savings are going down the tubes."

---

## WHAT TO DO WHEN YOU OWN TWO HOUSES

First, redouble your efforts to sell your old home. Lower its price; spruce it up further; hold frequent open houses; advertise more. After that, consider these additional steps:

- Cut back your spending and sell any overpriced assets you own, like stocks. Then proceed to sell fairly priced assets.
- See if relatives or friends will lend you money to meet all your payments. Or try to refinance and extend your mortgages, in order to lower your monthly payments.

- Consider renting out your first home, or even your new home, for some extra income. Just be *very* careful to whom you rent.
- Think about putting your new house, as well as your old one, up for sale.
- See if you can bow out of buying that second home—even if you lose your deposit.
- As a last resort, check with a bankruptcy lawyer as to whether filing for bankrupcty protection, which may let you keep your first house as long as you pay back your remaining debts within three to five years, is a sensible option.

## WHEN TO BUY BEFORE YOU SELL

In the game of bridge, sometimes you should bid a three-card suit even if you and your partner have agreed never to bid three-card suits; in the stock market, sometimes you should consider buying stocks with high price-earnings ratios, even though basic financial practice warns against it. So let's look at those exceptional times when you *should* seriously consider buying a house in a soft market, even though you haven't sold your old one:

- You're very *very* rich.
- You persuade the seller of the house you want to buy to accept a purchase contract contingent upon your selling your own house at a specified price within a specified period of time. Don't expect much success, though—unless the seller is plain desperate, and doesn't have a good lawyer.
- Your own house is a creampuff and you're willing to put a very reasonable price tag on it; real estate professionals assure you that, even in a soft market, you'll sell quickly; several people have told you, "Let me know if you ever want to sell"; and, the clincher, you like to gamble with your financial well-being. Incidentally, those people who once eagerly told you, "Let me know if you ever want to sell," *never* end up buying your house.

## CHAPTER SUMMARY

Be very wary of buying a second house before you've sold the one you live in, especially in a sluggish real estate market. Only if you're very rich, or if a seller will agree to a purchase contract contingent upon your selling your own home for a specified price, should you even consider it. If you're confident that your house is a creampuff and will sell quickly, or if you're sure you can find good, reliable renters, still think carefully about the pitfalls. Owning two houses in a buyer's market can be financially disastrous.

# 4 THE RIGHT PRICE SELLS A HOUSE

It's a truism that "The right price sells a house." And like most truisms, it's probably 99 percent true.

No doubt there *are* houses that don't sell despite reasonable asking prices—a house condemned by the local board of health, a house on a beach that's eroding away. But even if a house is virtually worthless, the land it's on may be of some value, unless the cost of tearing the place down is astronomical.

But apart from the 1 percent worth of exceptions, a reasonable price will definitely sell a house—if you define "reasonable" to mean "on the low side, but not so low as to give it away."

## HARD SELLS

Certain houses, of course, are harder to sell than others. For example, right now, selling a condominium in the Northeast is murder. Some reasons are the following:

1. The market is glutted. Before the stock-market crash of 1987, investors bought condos like, well, stocks, just to diversify out of the stock market; when the market plunged, these people lost their jobs and their bonuses—and unloaded their condos. Around the same time, the Tax Reform Act of 1986 curtailed the benefits of being a landlord—another reason condo investors sold.

2. Would-be homeowners are afraid to buy condos because they think that, when the time comes, they themselves will have trouble unloading them.

3. Condos have gotten a rotten reputation generally, perhaps because so many tacky old apartments were converted, and they've contaminated the reputation of the new, bright, convenient condos that are also available.

Condos don't deserve their awful reputations. The market for them will revive, just as the stock market marched steadily upward after the crash of 1987.

And then there are other problem houses:

- Any house in a community where the economy is in the dumps. Whenever the local economy is dismal, many people try to move out, in search of new jobs, and very few people try to move in, because new jobs aren't opening up. The inventory of unsold houses climbs up and up. Then you've got what real estate agents call a "buyers market," or, less euphemistically, a seller's disaster. A professor of urban studies who recently sold his house in Austin joked that, when word got around that he had actually found a buyer, "the local TV station sent over a crew."

- Any fancy house in an undesirable area—a mansion in East St. Louis, for example, or a $600,000 house on a block full of $200,000 houses.

- Any unusual house—a contemporary in a flock of colonials; a house painted or decorated or even furnished eccentrically.

- Any house with obvious defects—a wet basement, a leaky roof, a tiny yard, an overflowing septic tank, a kitchen left over from the 1940s.

Granted, such houses will be unusually hard to sell. But with an unusually low price, you will lower the odds enormously. A house in Florida, contaminated from attic to basement with asbestos, recently elicited a serious offer: $5,000. Yes, there's always hope. And, beyond that, there are steps you can take to sell problem houses. (See Chapter 18.)


## WHY A REASONABLE/LOW PRICE SELLS A HOUSE

The answer may seem obvious. Yet some homeowners, discouraged after trying to sell their houses for months or even years, have given up entirely. It can help to explain what is really not so obvious—

the reasons why a low price will sell almost any house, including problem houses in problem communities:

1. By lowering your price, you bring your house into competition with less impressive houses, perhaps smaller or less well designed. In such a context your house becomes more impressive.

Buyers know that it's a buyer's market. That's why they may look at 16 or 20 houses when they go hunting now, whereas they used to look at only 5 or 10. And that means that buyers are better informed about house prices in general than they used to be. If your house is reasonably priced, the buyers who can afford houses in your price range will recognize that it's a bargain. So will real estate agents. They will be more likely to bring buyers to a reasonably priced house, because the chances of their making a sale are greater.

2. When you lower your price, you make your house affordable by a greater number of buyers. There are buyers out there looking for houses costing from $85,000 to $90,000; $91,000 to $94,000; $250,000 to $260,000; $325,000 to $350,000, etc. They know what they can afford—or what they think they can afford.

These buyer-groups overlap ($85,000 to $88,000 and $87,000 to $90,000, say). There may be more in certain cohorts than others—more in the $150,000 to $155,000 group, perhaps, than in the $125,000 to $130,000—depending on the community, the time of year, and a host of other factors. If you lower your price by a reasonable amount, you will obviously make your house suitable not just to your normal cohort of buyers, but to another cohort lower down the ladder.

3. When you lower your price, you begin mollifying any defects your house has. Under the $1 million bracket, few houses are free from defects. They may have small closets, poor layouts, damp basements, animal odors, asbestos-clad pipes in the basement, etc. Buyers rarely see creampuffs for sale, perhaps because owners prefer keeping their creampuffs, or because creampuffs sell so quickly on the rare occasions when they do go on the market.

Let's say your house is badly located (next to a commercial district, for example). When you lower the price, you begin competing with houses that are next to pool halls, or that have only one or two bedrooms, or that don't have fireplaces, or dining nooks in the kitchen. Buyers in that price range have gotten accustomed to defects; they may regard your house's defect as trivial by comparision.

Here's an analogy from the stock market: ABC Corp. is a far better stock than, say, XYZ Corp. ABC Corp. is a sound company paying a good dividend, it's a leader in the health-care field and is almost certain to remain so in the future. XYZ Corp. on the other hand, is a speculative stock, and the company is in trouble. Any sensible person would prefer to buy ABC Corp.

But smart investors would buy XYZ Corp.—*if* XYZ's price fell far enough to make it a bargain, despite its riskiness, and *if* ABC Corp.'s price rose high enough to make it overpriced. That's how many smart investors make enormous profits in the stock market: They sell good stocks when they're overpriced and buy bad stocks when they're incredible bargains.

By the same token, if your house isn't a creampuff, you can find a buyer nonetheless, *if* you just lower the price enough to make the creampuffs, and the other houses like yours, look exorbitant.


## IS A HIGH PRICE EVER RIGHT?

It's possible to overprice your house and yet sell it. You could get lucky.

Perhaps a buyer loves your style of house—colonial, Tudor, contemporary. Perhaps he or she is averse to leaf raking and lawn mowing and wants a small yard just like yours. Perhaps he or she has always lived in houses with small closets, or few bathrooms, just like yours. Perhaps your buyer has a relative or very close friends down the block, or got a job within walking distance of your house.

Perhaps your house has a garage specially built for an oversized recreational vehicle—and guess who has been looking for just such a garage? Or perhaps the buyer is of a certain religious persuasion that forbids driving on certain days of the week, and your house is within easy walking distance of his or her place of worship.

Then again, when you overprice your house, you may sell it in two, five, or ten years.

We don't recommend that you count on luck. And we suspect that, if you're reading this book, you prefer to move out of your house in a matter of months rather than years. That means you shouldn't overprice your house—that is, put an asking price on your house higher than similar ones on the market.

---

**CAUTION:** If you put too high a price on your house at the beginning and it doesn't sell, you eventually may have to lower the price below what you should have asked originally. Unless you're in a depressed area, a house that's been on the market for months and months begins to worry people—buyers as well as brokers. If you're having so much trouble selling it, wouldn't new owners also have trouble when they try to sell? Is there something wrong with your house besides the high price? To remove the curse, you might have to take your house off the market and keep it off for a while, until a new cohort of buyers comes along.

Suppose you don't want to overprice your house, but you do want to get what you think it's worth. Should you price your house fairly? Sure—if (1) it's a creampuff, or (2) you're in no hurry to move. Some houses, even in a slow market, sell fast even when they're not bargain priced. They're so well situated, well maintained, well decorated, and appealing in any number of ways, that they will always stand out—in a word, creampuffs.

Then, too, if you're just testing the waters—say, there's a creampuff that you yourself are interested in, or you're thinking of moving in the next year or two—you might put a fair price on your house. If you used a broker, you're not out any money if it hasn't sold after a few months. (If you were selling it yourself, you would have lost some money on newspaper advertising.) You could take the house off the market for now and wait awhile before offering it again, perhaps at a lower price. (Also bear in mind that inflation may have driven house prices up by the time you put the house up for sale again.)

There may even be benefits: You will have seen your real estate agent in action and can tell if he or she is a live wire or a wet blanket. And now that word has gotten around that your house has been for sale, some buyers may still come by. In fact, someone who didn't buy your house could change his or her mind and months later give you a call.

**CAUTION:** Don't put your house on the market unless you're serious about selling it. If you employ a broker, and if the broker or his or her agent brings around what in legal jargon is called a "ready, willing, and able" buyer, and you decide *not* to sell after all, you may still owe the broker a sales commission, depending on the terms in your brokerage agreement.

## WHEN TIME IS OF THE ESSENCE

Then again, there may be circumstances that force you to sell as fast as possible:

- You lose your job, and you know of an opening far away from your current residence. Or your employer is transferring you elsewhere, without offering to purchase your house from you.
- You lose your job and can no longer meet your mortgage payments or afford the expenses of your house's maintainance and upkeep.
- You need the money that is locked up in your house and don't want to take out a second mortgage.
- You want to retire and move elsewhere.
- You are involved in a divorce, and every day you remain where you are is painful.
- You have already purchased another house, and the two mortgages and other expenses are driving you to the poorhouse. (Owning two houses is, for most people, a bad mistake. See Chapter 3.)

## TIME IS ALWAYS OF THE ESSENCE

Whether or not you're forced to sell fast, selling fast will normally be your goal. You probably want to get on with the rest of your life. So what is the right price to put on your house to sell it within a few months?

Not the same price that other sellers have put on houses like yours. Or, like them, you may wait and wait. You should set your price significantly below the prices of houses similar to yours. "Significantly" doesn't mean $100 or $500. We're talking thousands.

And don't be guided by the *asking* prices of houses similar to yours. Go by the *selling* prices—what the houses are really worth. Let's say that houses like yours have asking prices of $103,000. Houses like yours may actually sell for $99,500.

Therefore, a good price to put on your house is $98,000.

Buyers will see a significant difference between your house and houses like it—which are priced at $5,000 more. And even if you must give a bit during the bargaining process, and you end up with a price of $97,500, how much have you lost? You will have "sacrificed" $2,000, but you will have almost guaranteed the sale of your house and reduced the time you needed to find a buyer.

Besides that, a broker's commission of 7 percent on a $97,500 house is only $6,825, as compared with $6,965 on a $99,500 house. After the broker's fee, you'll get $90,675 instead of $92,535—a difference of $1,860. And the house is sold. The difference is actually 2 percent, but look at it this way: You're getting 98 cents instead of a full dollar. Is that a big deal?

## GETTING HELP WITH PRICING

If you employ a broker, a good broker, you won't have a problem. Tell the broker's agent you want to sell fast—meaning, within a few months, and you're willing to put a reasonable price on your house.

Ask the agent: What are houses like mine selling for? (Remember, not their asking prices, their *selling* prices.) Then ask: How much below the selling prices must I price my house to guarantee a quick sale?

Don't be guided by just one broker's agent, unless you have enormous confidence in that agent. Agents make mistakes. They may overprice your house to inveigle you into listing with them, or drastically underprice it so that they're assured of selling it quickly.

When you're listing your house, ask three brokers or their agents to stop by and answer your questions, and to give you market studies. With three points of view—what houses like yours are priced at, what they're selling for, and what price you should set for an expeditious sale—you're more likely to make the right decision.

If you're selling your house by yourself, you can follow the same technique. Call three brokers or agents in to give you the numbers you need. Explain that you're thinking of trying to sell the house yourself for a while and if you don't succeed, you'll list with the broker who impressed you the most.

The price you set for a house you're selling by yourself shouldn't be as high as the prices the brokers suggested, because you won't have to pay a broker's commission. And, if you're smart, you won't try to hog the savings all to yourself. You'll share them with a potential buyer—perhaps 50-50, or 75-25. (You do deserve some more, because you did the work that agents normally do.)

Let's say that you're going the fizzbo route ("fizzbo" is derived from FSBO, which is derived from For Sale by Owner), and houses like yours, you learn, sell for $120,000. You're saving a 7 percent brokerage fee, or $8,400. You might ask $116,000 for the house, sharing the bounty with a buyer. Or, if you're willing to take a little gamble, ask $118,000. As explained below, particularly in a buyer's market you should carefully evaluate the benefits of using a broker before trying the fizzbo route.

Alternatively, you can pay an appraiser to suggest prices for your house. Call a few local banks for names. The names that keep repeating are the ones to consider; if they have the confidence of the local banks, they must know the local market. Be sure that any appraiser you hire belongs to a reputable national organization.

Appraisers usually charge a few hundred dollars, but some may charge much more. Their charges can be added to your selling costs when you calculate your capital gains if you ever sell your home without rolling over all of the proceeds (See Chapter 27.)

The estimates that appraisers make sometimes tend to be on the low side—for homeowners, at least. When buyers come to your house, show them the appraiser's estimate, providing your price is in line with that estimate. An "official" figure like that can be most reassuring.

As a fizzbo, you generally can nudge buyers along by saying that you're thinking of listing with a broker soon, and once you do that, you're going to boost the price by 7 percent to cover the broker's commission. So the buyers can steal your house for at least 7 percent less than what a broker would be asking now. (You'll have to modify the percentage if your asking price is not 7 percent below going prices for similar houses—because you intended to pass on the commission saved to a lucky buyer.)

## WHY SELLERS DON'T PRICE THEIR HOUSES REASONABLY

---

**CASE HISTORY:** A man bought a house in Mahwah, New Jersey, in 1987, for $800,000. Two years later, when he decided to move, a broker suggested that he ask—at most—$750,000 for the house. Infuriated, the man refused. He wanted at least the $800,000 he paid. The broker told him honestly that his chances of getting $800,000 were, putting it kindly, remote. The man stood firm, and the broker refused to take the listing.

---

Not surprisingly, the house in this story is still for sale. For a broker to turn down a listing, the broker must know whereof he or she speaks.

Why did the man refuse to accept less than $800,000? We all recognize the emotional process. He thought it would indicate that he had been a fool—that a bright person wouldn't have bought the house for $800,000, or wouldn't have bought the house at the tippity-top of the market. And he didn't want his wife, his friends, or the broker to think he had been a fool. Besides, his own exalted view of himself was probably shaky, so that he couldn't stand the blow to his pride.

He was a fool, of course, but not because of his original purchase. Houses in New Jersey in 1987 were at their peak, but it was hard for anyone to know that, or to think that prices wouldn't head higher. At that time, $800,000 for that house was reasonable. All $800,000 houses purchased then took similar hits—and so did houses priced at $100,000 and $500,000 and $1.5 million.

With stocks, you can examine hard evidence to determine whether prices are too high. You can compare a stock's price-earnings ratio to its historical ratio, to the P-E ratio of similar stocks, and to the market as a whole. You can check similar markers to gauge whether the stock market as a whole is overpriced, underpriced, or fairly priced.

But it's not so easy with real estate. The value of real estate depends on so many different factors—the state of the local economy, the influx of new residents, mortgage interest rates. Real estate is simply a far less liquid and far less perfect market than stocks. No one who bought a house in the Northeast in 1987 was a fool. Only someone who bought in 1987 and refused to lower his asking price in 1989, when urged to by a reputable and knowledgeable professional, was a fool.

Here are some other reasons why homeowners don't set reasonable prices on their houses:

1. Homeowners in general are stubborn. It's a good thing, too, because most homeowners don't panic in a soft market, and that helps keep house prices fairly stable. After all, most of them are well aware that they can wait out a real estate slump.

This is not to say that you should panic. We're suggesting that you price your house reasonably, and be a just little less stubborn than other homeowners.

2. Homeowners remember, all too well, the high house prices of the past. A few years ago your house was worth $300,000. How, you ask yourself, can it be worth only $275,000 now? Why must you take a $25,000 "loss"?

Your house may very well be worth only $275,000 now. Perhaps you never invested in the stock market and you're unfamiliar with volatile investments. Maybe you've invested only in certificates of deposit, bonds, and money market funds, where when you lend $1, you always (or almost always) get $1 back if you wait long enough.

As for your $25,000 "loss," did you buy the house at $300,000? Or do you just know it was worth that at that time? If you bought the house at less than $275,000, that means that you have a profit.

3. Homeowners are misled about improvements they have made. Many homeowners, in calculating what their houses are worth, just add the cost of whatever improvements they made—materials and labor—to their purchase prices and the yearly inflation rate. But improvements rarely pay for themselves. You're lucky if you get 50 cents or 60 cents on the dollar for any improvement you made. (See Chapter 11.)

4. Homeowners are occasionaly misled by their agents.

These agents, just to get listings, will tell homeowners what they want to hear: that they can get a lot more for their houses than other agents have been telling them—say, $250,000 instead of $230,000. Wouldn't you be tempted to list your house with a broker who claimed he or she could get you $20,000 more?

Such agents make a desultory effort to sell your house for $250,000, then tell you it's too high and you should drop your house price to $230,000. "Market's softer than we thought," he or she reports with a sigh.

5. Homeowners pay too much attention to small amounts of money. Is $2,000 a small amount of money? Of course not. But when you're dealing with large numbers, the value of $2,000 can be exaggerated. Would you sell your house for $248,000 rather than $250,000, if you knew you could definitely sell your house right now? Do you realize that $2,000 is only 0.8 percent of $250,000?

Sure, everyone would love to have 0.8 percent of $5 million. That's 40 grand. But the point is this: If you're dealing with large figures, a few thousand dollars isn't such a big deal.

Sure, everyone would love to have 0.008 percent of $5 million. That's 40 grand. But the point is this: If you're dealing with large figures, a few thousand dollars isn't such a big deal.

6. Homeowners are misled by their neighbors. Your neighbors or friends may tell you they received a king's ransom where they sold their houses. And maybe they're not exaggerating in order to impress you.

But . . . when did they sell, and when did they buy again? They may have sold when the market was high—and bought when the market was high, too. Perhaps they did receive $300,000 for their house, as they claim. But did they also agree to give the buyer a second mortgage at a bargain interest rate? Or provide the buyer with a flat amount of money to lower their own mortgage interest rate? Or agree to pay $5000 for redecorating and $5000 for new appliances? Or agree to pay most of the buyer's closing costs?

## PSYCHOLOGICAL ADVICE

If you're suffering from anxiety or apoplexy at the prospect of selling your house for a lower price than you could have received a few years ago, ask yourself this: Are you making a profit, considering the price you paid for your house? If you *aren't* making a profit, because you bought your house only a few years ago, ask yourself, are you going to buy another house at a bargain price—one that will make up for your loss?

If you're not making a profit, and you're not buying a bargain house (maybe you plan to retire to a second house you already own), the question is: Which is more important to you, a little extra money or living the life you want to live? As a wise financial planner has said, "Don't let the prospect of a little less money, or a little *more* money, change the way you would prefer to spend the remainder of your days on earth."

The shrewdest investors sell too soon and buy too late. They don't try to buy stocks at their absolute lows or sell them at their absolute highs. That's why they become wealthy. They're content with singles, doubles, and triples. They don't always try for home runs; they know that home-run hitters strike out a lot.

## CHAPTER SUMMARY

Almost any house, anywhere, will sell if it carries a reasonable/low price. When you lower the price, you (1) bring your house into a market group of less formidable competitors—houses offering less to buyers, (2) boost the number of possible buyers, and (3) take some of the sting out of your house's defects.

To set a reasonable/low price on your house, find out what similar houses are actually selling for—not what their owners were asking. And price your house at significantly less than those selling prices.

To arrive at a price, hire a reputable appraiser; or ask three different broker's agents to give you a comparative market analysis, and be guided by the price in the middle.

If you have trouble, psychologically, putting a reasonable/low price on your house, remember that you may still have a hefty profit because you bought the house many years ago, or because you're buying another house very cheaply. Even if you're taking a true loss, don't let relatively small amounts of money determine how you live the rest of your life.

# Part Two

# PREPARING TO SELL

# 5 CHOOSING A COMPETENT— AND SALES-ORIENTED— LAWYER

Until recently, home sellers could have been satisfied choosing a lawyer whose references indicated sufficient competence to handle the closing transaction and whose price seemed reasonable. While these two criteria are still very important, they are no longer sufficient.

When you're trying to sell a house in a soft or declining market, the lawyer's role takes on increased importance. If buyers feel they have the upper hand—because there are 15 more houses to choose from if they don't buy yours—they may be inclined to push you a lot further than in normal market conditions. What you need in this kind of a market is a lawyer who is competent, who can protect your interests, but who can also help and not hinder getting a sale through.

## HIRE A LAWYER WHO HAS A GOOD REPUTATION

How do you know whether a lawyer is good? Ask people who have worked with lawyers extensively (not merely someone who had a lawyer assist with a house purchase a few years ago). This list can include your broker, banker, business associates, and a few selected friends. There is a multivolume legal directory, called *Martindale-Hubbell*, which lists and provides ratings of many lawyers. The ratings are compiled by an independent staff and are based on peer reviews and other procedures. If 20 other lawyers state that a particular lawyer is good, it's a pretty good sign. The highest rating is "av" (a description of the ratings is available in the front of the directory).

The books should be available in most lawyers' offices and at many local libraries. And you can always ask a lawyer if and how well he or she was rated.

You should always ask lawyers how extensive their experience is in real estate matters, how many house closings they've completed, what other real estate work they do, how long they've been practicing, and whether they have lectured or published articles on related topics. Because much of the paperwork in a house closing is standard, lawyers often have secretaries or paralegals prepare the documents for their review. That's fine as long as the lawyer you're hiring properly reviews everything and supervises everyone, is available for questions and to deal with problems, and attends the closing. Ask about the office, review, and other procedures if you're concerned.

## HIRE A LAWYER WHO HAS THE RIGHT ATTITUDE

Lawyers are people, and people have very different personality types. Some personality types are better than others for particular circumstances. A lawyer who is combative or tough may be perfect for suing a recalcitrant creditor or for negotiating a tough business deal. But this personality type is generally far less suited to selling a house.

When it's a buyer's market, a lawyer with an abrasive personality can be a major impediment to getting a sale through. You simply can't afford to be (or through your lawyer appear to be) intransigent or difficult. The buyer may just pick up and go elsewhere. So it's important that your lawyer either be easygoing generally, or be willing to act that way on your instructions.

---

**TIP:** A way to head off trouble is to tell whatever lawyer you hire that (1) the sale is important to you, (2) it's not a great market, and (3) you want him or her to do everything possible to facilitate the closing. Say you don't want him or her to argue for any changes in the deal without first discussing them with you so that together you can decide whether the point is worth fighting for.

This doesn't mean that you want your lawyer to accept unfair changes sought by the buyer's lawyer and not fight for your interests. It simply means that you want to pick your battles. In a better market, you might fight for everything, but in a soft market it may make sense to let some small points go. (See Chapter 26 for more tips on a successful closing.)

---

## HIRE A LAWYER WHO HAS CONTACTS THAT MIGHT HELP YOU

Traditionally, it has been good advice in *buying* a house for you to retain a lawyer active in the local market, who has contacts at local banks and other lending institutions. Now with so many housing markets being soft, it can't hurt as a seller to retain a lawyer who is well connected. Sure, the buyer is likely to have made arrangements, or to have hired an attorney with suggestions, but there may be an opportunity for your lawyer to assist the buyer's lawyer in pushing the deal along. If you have a choice, hire a lawyer who has practiced for some time, who does a substantial amount of real estate work, and who, therefore, has been able to develop good contacts. It's not a critical factor, but it can't hurt.

## FEES AND THE RETAINER AGREEMENT

Fees are always an important issue and, unfortunately, often a sensitive issue between clients and lawyers. If your lawyer is uncomfortable discussing fees before being retained, you can expect problems later.

Although lawyers usually bill by the hour, most charge a flat fee for a house closing. The amount may vary according to whether the lawyer is representing a buyer or a seller, and according to the circumstances. In most cases, competition for house-closing work has kept prices low by comparison with the hourly rates charged by lawyers for most work.

Should you take the lowest-priced lawyer? It depends. The fee for a house closing is negligible by comparison with the value of the house being sold. It's far more important to get the house sold, and to get everything wrapped up cleanly, than to save a few hundred dollars on legal fees. On the other hand, the more expensive lawyer is not necessarily the better lawyer for the job. The only practical solution is to evaluate all the factors discussed in this chapter and try to choose the lawyer who you think will do the best job, as long as the fee is in the same range as other fees you're being quoted.

The main objective is getting the job done right, especially if problems arise. The majority of house closings are straightforward, and you don't encounter unexpected obstacles. Unfortunately, many do run into difficulties. Whatever the source of the problems, you're unlikely to switch lawyers midstream. This is why you have to pick, up front, the lawyer who has the skills you need. You don't want to be involved in one of the minority of closings with problems and find that you've hired an inexperienced lawyer to save $200.

Once you've selected your lawyer, ask for a retainer agreement. This is analogous to what most accountants call an engagement letter. It sets forth what services the lawyer will provide, how much you will be charged, under what circumstances you can be billed for more, and what out-of-pocket costs you'll have to reimburse your lawyer for.

Regarding additional charges and reimbursements, the language of most retainer agreements is open-ended and vague. This is because it's impossible for the lawyer to know in advance what problems will be encountered. However, there should be some reasonable parameters. On reimbursements (for example, the cost of messenger services, overnight-mail shipments, long-distance phone calls, and so forth), some lawyers charge their actual out-of-pocket costs, some charge a small administrative markup, and some lawyers charge substantially more than their out-of-pocket costs and make a profit.

Should you object to paying reimbursements? No, as long as the lawyer incurs only those costs absolutely necessary to serve your interests, doesn't mark them up to make a profit (isn't that what the legal fee is for?), and gives you sufficient detail so that you see what you're being asked to pay for. You shouldn't have to pay for express mail charges, for example, if your lawyer was just slow in getting the work out. On the other hand, you want to keep the deal rolling as quickly as possible.

---

**TIP:** To protect yourself, ask your lawyer to estimate out-of-pocket expenses and to put the estimate in the retainer agreement. The lawyer should also agree to notify you before that amount is exceeded.

---

As for extra charges for work, your lawyer needs a safety net to bill more if major problems occur. But you also need protection. What is extra work and how much should you pay for it? One approach to the issue is to have the retainer agreement say that the lawyer must notify you if he or she believes extra work will be involved, and before any extra time is put in.

Read the retainment letter or agreement carefully and ask questions if you aren't clear about what's involved. If services you expected aren't listed, or provisions don't make sense, ask. If there is no provision for the lawyer to call you before incurring extra expenses, ask for one. If the lawyer is not willing to discuss your concerns, go elsewhere. You're entitled to know in advance exactly what the arrangement is supposed to be. (See the sample retainer agreement in the "For Your Notebook" section of this chapter.)

## CHAPTER SUMMARY

In a tough market, your lawyer has one of the key roles in consummating a house sale. You want a lawyer who can protect your interests, who can handle unexpected problems at the closing, and who has the personality to abet rather than hinder the negotiations with the buyers and their lawyer.

Your lawyer should have the highest professional rating, plenty of experience with house closings, and the willingness to supervise all paperwork carefully. He or she should have a reasonable approach to fees and to the retainer agreement. He or she should be willing to explain any estimated expenses, and to warn you ahead of time about extra charges.

# FOR YOUR NOTEBOOK

## SAMPLE LAWYER'S RETAINER AGREEMENT

**MARTIN M. SHENKMAN**
ATTORNEY AT LAW
420 MADISON AVENUE
NEW YORK, NEW YORK 10017
TELEPHONE (212) 888-6354
TELECOPIER (212) 207-8096

NEW JERSEY OFFICE
537 RUTLAND AVENUE
TEANECK, NEW JERSEY 07666
TELEPHONE (201) 833-4128
TELECOPIER (201) 833-8568

ADMITTED NY, NJ AND WASH. DC

Dear Mr. and Mrs. Smith:

As we discussed, my policy is to obtain an engagement letter from all clients. The primary purpose of this letter is to communicate and explain my billing and other practices. I trust that you will find the enclosed informative and helpful to fostering a good working relationship.

*SCOPE OF WORK:* I would be pleased to assist you with the closing on your house.

*BILLS:*

*Telephone Calls:* No charges will generally be made for brief phone calls where, for example, you inquire as to the status of a matter we are working on, you advise me of an additional point of information, or you make a brief inquiry. It is important for you to feel comfortable communicating openly and regularly in order for us to develop and maintain a good working relationship. To encourage communication I choose not to bill for brief calls of the nature described. However, should calls involve my providing lengthy time, or become frequent, I may then choose to charge for such calls.

The brief, no-charge, conversations referred to above, will generally be entered on bills with a "No Charge" indication so that we will have a record of matters discussed.

*Communication:* Bills are more than simply a means of collection. Bills are an important form of communication, and if properly used will help us maintain a good working relationship. Bills will generally contain detailed descriptions of the work completed, telephone calls made, conferences, and other matters. If you carefully review the bill for its content, it will provide, a valuable summary of most of

40

the matters we have discussed. Where there are still open matters which we have not completed, your bill will often be accompanied by a cover letter mentioning matters upon which we should follow up. Your careful review of both the detailed descriptions in your bill, and any comments in the attached covering letter, will enable you to determine what has and has not been done. I spend a considerable amount of my time preparing bills. I encourage you to spend some time reviewing what you receive and calling me to discuss any open matters, issues or other concerns which you have.

*Frequency:* Bills are generally prepared monthly. However, if a matter is not quite complete at month end, or if the amounts are nominal, I may choose not to send a bill until a later date. If the matter we are working on is completed prior to month end, I may, time permitting, send a bill at that time. If we have discussed the scope of a particular project, and it appears that the work, or costs, will exceed the scope of what we have projected, I will, time permitting, send a bill alerting you to the changes as soon as possible so that you will be apprised of the changes and can keep your account current.

*Rates:* Since we have agreed on a flat fee for the house closing, only extra work done beyond the scope agreed upon for the flat fee will be billed at the rates indicated. Services are billed based on time spent at standard billing rates. My time is billed at $175 per hour. Should others work on your account, you will be advised of their fees and charges in advance.

*Expenses:* Out-of-pocket expenses, which are generally limited to such items as long-distance phone calls, Federal Express charges, messenger costs, photocopying ($.20 per page), facsimile ($2 per page), secretarial overtime, state filing or search fees (at actual cost billed by third parties) and so forth, will be billed to you for reimbursement. I generally retain XYZ Searches, Inc. to effect necessary filings and perform required searches. On occasion, however, I may engage a firm different from that listed. If any other material expenses will be incurred, I will advise you in advance whenever possible, if not I will make whatever decision I feel best serves your interest and will expect reimbursement for the out-of-pocket costs which I incur.

*Due Date For Bills:* The flat fee and any disbursements must be paid at the closing. Bills for any additional work should be paid promptly upon receipt. If bills cannot be paid within thirty (30) days of the date of the bill I would appreciate your phoning me to make special arrangements for payment. If you have any questions concerning a bill, I would appreciate your calling me within the same thirty (30) day period. It will be far easier for both of us to resolve any questions you may have while the work performed is fresh in mind.

*Cost of Billing:* No charges are made for the time or costs incurred in billing. These are treated as overhead costs not allocable to any client.

*RETAINER:* As we discussed, I will not request a retainer at this time. Instead, I will bill you $800.00 payable at the closing of the sale of your house. Should any unusual or extraordinary work be required, I will advise you as soon as possible.

*QUESTIONS:* Should you ever have any questions concerning the work or charges involved, please do not hesitate to call and discuss them with me.

*PLEASE SIGN:* If the above is in accordance with your understanding, kindly sign the enclosed copy of this letter and return it to me with the initial retainer set forth above, if any. The original copy of this letter is for your records.

I look forward to working with you on this and future matters.

Sincerely yours,


Martin M. Shenkman
enc.
MMS:sb

AGREED AND ACCEPTED:

_____

John Smith

_____

Mary Smith

Date: _____

# 6 CHOOSING A CRACKERJACK AGENT

Don't hire your neighbor because you would feel embarrassed if he or she found out that you were using another broker. Don't hire your brother-in-law, your kid's former teacher, or the friendly agent who gave you a bunch of free booklets on how to sell a house.

When you sell your house, you are playing hardball, not Whiffleball. There's big money involved—money that may mean the difference between your having a comfortable retirement, soon, and your having to work years more than you had planned to.

Hire the best broker you can find, a broker who is unlikely to be your neighbor or your brother-in-law.

## THE DIFFERENCE BETWEEN BROKERS AND AGENTS

Actually, you will be hiring two different people: a broker and the salesperson who works for the broker. Brokers have more education and have passed tougher licensing tests than the salespeople who work for them. Both are called "agents," though most people use the term to mean only salespeople. (But here, when we use the word, we mean both brokers and salespeople.) When you list your house with a broker, usually it's just the salespeople who will be out selling your house.

So you want both a crackerjack broker and a crackerjack salesperson who works for that broker. (Realtors are brokers who belong to the National Association of Realtors, a trade organization. Salespeople may be Realtor Associates, or even, in some cases, Realtors.)

## DEFINING A CRACKERJACK AGENT

What you want from an agent is the ability to sell your house. But that's not all. Anyone at all could sell your house—at half-price. And you don't want an agent who's so careless or shoddy that he or she gets you into trouble—someone who tells a buyer that your basement has never leaked when it has, or that your house has passed a radon test when it hasn't. The two of you could wind up in court later on.

You want an agent who will sell your house reasonably quickly, at a good price, and without any foul-ups. And while there are 750,000 agents in the country, they aren't all agents who can accomplish all three objectives for you in a soft market.

In a seller's market, even your sweet, friendly neighbor, the real estate agent, could sell your house quickly at a good price. In a buyer's market, the sheep are separated from the shepherds, and you must be especially discriminating in choosing an agent. Your choice of agent may mean the difference between selling your house in a month, for almost the full asking price, or selling the house (if you sell at all) a year from now, after two or three price cuts. Yes, a good agent can make the difference.


## WHAT TO LOOK FOR IN A BROKER

First, let's look at the brokerage firm. Normally, the best broker to choose is one with lots of agents. The more agents, usually the more contacts they will have, and thus the more buyers under their wing. If a company is relocating employees to your area, the company—or its relocation service—will deal with one of the biggest brokerage firms. And that's what you want: a brokerage firm that can bring around a lot of buyers. A fairly large firm should also have a big budget—big enough to be able to continue advertising in a slow market and not cut back.

The firm should have an office near you. When Bob and Betsy Buyer want to purchase a house in your area, they will more than likely stop off in a local broker's office, whether it's a branch of a national chain or just a small, independent office.

The firm should have a good reputation, not a reputation for pressuring sellers to drastically underprice their houses, or a reputation for fouling up deals.

The broker should be a member of the National Association of Realtors. That organization keeps its members informed; it also sees that they adhere to a strict code of ethics. If you ever have a complaint, you will have someone to complain to. Ask the broker directly if he or she is a Realtor.

The firm should advertise a lot. Check your local newspapers. While some knowledgeable people are skeptical about choosing a broker by virtue of the advertising space he or she buys, let's face it: A broker who advertises houses in Middletown week after week is going to develop an impressive list of people who want to buy houses in Middletown.

Visit any brokerage firm you're interested in. Are there many cars in front? Is the office open at night and on weekends? Are the agents actually working, or are they just chatting around the coffee machine? Telephone a brokerage firm and inquire about a listing. Does the person who answers seem professional? Does he or she try to sell you another house if you say the house advertised is too expensive or not right for you? (The agent should.)

Narrow down your list to three brokerage firms in your area. All of them should belong to the local multiple-listing system, which allows agents from competing firms to cooperate in selling all houses in an area.

Here's how multiple listing works: You "list" your house for sale with a broker. When the broker, or the broker's agents, find a ready, willing, and able buyer for you, you may (depending on the terms of your brokerage agreement) owe the broker a commission—usually 6 percent or 7 percent. The broker and the agent who listed your property share part of that commission—usually half. And the agent who actually brought around the buyer, and his or her broker, share the remainder of the commission. (The agents for brokerage firms you didn't list with, but who show your house anyway, are your subagents, too.)

Generally, brokers will work hardest to sell the properties they themselves have listed, not properties listed by other brokerage firms. It's not just a matter of their trying to win the entire commission. It's a matter of pride. That's why it's important to choose a top-notch brokerage firm in the first place.

What if a firm you're interested in doesn't belong to the local multiple-listing system? Unless the firm can give you a good reason, pass it by. Such a firm won't have access to as many of the serious buyers in your area as will a firm that does belong to the multiple-listing system.

## WHAT TO LOOK FOR IN AN AGENT

A good question is: Which is more important, a good broker or a good salesperson? Answer: a good salesperson. So, while it would be ideal if a top-notch salesperson works for a reputable, prosperous, efficient brokerage firm, pay more attention to the agent. You're far better off using a hard-working, competent agent for a lousy firm than a lazy, incompetent agent for a good firm. A top-flight agent can surmount handicaps.

Here's what to look for in an agent:

- Someone who sells a lot of houses.

    This is first and foremost. And there's a way to find out: Seek out an agent who has been cited for the house sales he or she made recently—someone who is a member of the Million Dollar Club, or whatever it's called in your area. This means someone who sold an unusual number of properties last year. Or, even better, each year for the last few years. In other words, a go-getter.

    Among real estate people, it's accepted that a mere 10 percent of all agents sell the majority of all houses. When you call a broker, ask for the names of his or her salespeople who are members of the Million Dollar Club. And when the salesperson comes over to visit you, ask for proof. After all, the brokerage firm, out of sympathy, may have sent over the person who has been down on his or her luck recently and hasn't sold anything for months. In other words, a loser.

    It's true that these days a great many agents are members of the Million Dollar Club. And it's true that some members of this exclusive group may specialize in underpricing their properties, to sell them quickly. But if you want a go-getter, you are going to have to hunt amidst the ranks of people who have proved themselves to be go-getters.

- Someone charming and reassuring.

    When people have to make difficult decisions, they tend to be guided by extraneous, emotional matters. And if Bob and Betsy Buyer are undecided between your house and the one down the street, which is virtually identical in all respects with yours, they may decide on the basis of which agent they liked more. So be sure that your agent is Prince or Princess Charming—warm, friendly, and pleasant.

He or she should also inspire confidence, but not necessarily by being a fast-talker. If the buyers say, "Hey, this house doesn't have a living room," the fast-talker will say, "One less room for you to clean." The agent who inspires confidence will say, "That's true, and I know you'd prefer a house with a separate living room, rather than a combined living/dining room, but that's why this house is so reasonably priced. You might pay $40,000 more for a house like this if it had a separate living room. That would make your monthly payments a lot higher, wouldn't it?"

Agents who inspire confidence are relaxed, frank, and honest. And they obviously know their stuff. If the buyers ask, "What are the taxes?" these agents don't guess. If they don't know off the top of their heads, they look it up.

- Someone who is full-time.

We once asked Mort Walker, who draws the comic strip "Hi and Lois," why Lois never sells any houses. His answer: She works only part-time. (Actually, Lois occasionally *does* sell a house, but as Walker said, in the comics you can forget such things.)

You want someone to be available whenever buyers have any questions, or whenever there are job transferees scouting around in your area for just a few days.

- Someone who has advanced designations.

Advanced certifications mean that the agent has pride in what he or she does and is exceptionally well informed. Among the most impressive designations: graduate of the Real Estate Institute, or—even better—a certified residential specialist.

- Someone who gives you good advice.

An agent should tell you what to do to spruce up your house, how to eliminate the odors from the pet you have, and so forth.

- Someone ethical.

Good advice is also ethical. You don't want an agent who recommends that you hang pictures to conceal cracks in the wall. An agent should caution you not to conceal any defects from the buyers—especially if the defects cannot readily be seen (not that the house needs a paint job, but that the basement leaks in a bad storm, or there's a building going up next door, which will block off your view of the lake). You may be halfway across the country, happily settled in your new house, when you learn that the buyers have brought suit against you.

An ethical agent doesn't suggest an unrealistically high asking price for your house, just to inveigle you into listing with him or her. Nor does the agent propose a fire-sale price, just so he or she can pocket a quick commission, or sell your house to a good friend looking for a bargain. The agent will probably suggest an asking price in the middle range of the prices other agents have proposed.

- Someone imaginative.

An agent proves his or her mettle at the negotiating table. What if the buyers want you to pay for a new roof, because the house inspector says that the roof is nearing the end of its life? A sharp agent will propose that the buyers pay half—because you never promised them a totally new roof.

What if the buyers, at the last minute, insist that you throw in the lawn furniture, the freestanding bookcases, and the expensive fireplace equipment? A good agent won't immediately say no, or say yes, either. A good agent will think about it, weighing how likely your house is to sell quickly to someone else, at the same price, before he or she recommends a decision.

What if the buyer also wants an expensive painting and is willing to pay $25,000 for it, but the seller won't part with it? An imaginative agent will suggest that they flip a coin. (It happened—with a Gilbert Stuart painting of George Washington. The buyer won the coin flip.)

- Someone you get along with.

Agents work for you, and they shouldn't forget it. They are legally and ethically obligated to get the highest possible price for you, on the most favorable terms. But some agents get so palsy-walsy with certain buyers that they seem to forget to whom they owe their loyalty.

You can help ensure an agent's loyalty by being courteous and affable. Be dubious of hiring any agent, no matter how splendid his or her reputation, if there isn't good chemistry between you.

- Someone knowledgeable.

You want an agent who knows your community and can tell the buyers about your local school system, religious institutions, shopping malls, and public transportation. You also want an agent who can direct buyers toward ready sources of money. If an agent knows next to nothing about mortgages backed by the Federal Housing Administration or the Veterans Administration, you may miss out on some potential buyers.

- Someone painstaking.

  The agent will, for example, thoroughly check out the credentials of the buyers, to make sure that they can afford to buy your house and can obtain a mortgage. One of the most famous real estate agents in the country was sued recently for not checking into buyers who had almost no chance of getting the mortgage they were seeking.

  Agents will also prod you about any potential problems you may have overlooked, such as a boundary dispute with a neighbor (in any event, this and similar matters should be reviewed with your lawyer).

## QUESTIONS TO ASK

- How long have you been selling real estate? (Be wary: One agent tells inexperienced agents that, if they started in December and it's now January, they should say, "I'm in my second year.")
- Are you a Realtor or Realtor Associate? What other designations do you have?
- What price range would you put on my house? Why?
- How long has it been taking houses like mine to sell?
- What would you recommend that I do to make my house more presentable? Is there anything wrong with my house that I should correct?
- How often will your firm advertise my house? What else will you do to sell my house? Will you have regular open houses? Will you contact the personnel departments of large companies in the area? Will you send literature to all my neighbors?
- Which lenders do you work with on financing?
- What kind of fact sheet will you create for my house? Can you show me examples of other fact sheets you've prepared?
- Is your firm a member of the local multiple-listing system? Will my house go onto the MLS? When?
- Is it a good idea for me to offer a bonus to an agent who brings in a ready, willing, and able buyer—like $500 or $1,000, or an extra percentage of the commission? (See Chapter 8.)
- How many houses have you sold in the past year? Can you give me the names and phone numbers of the sellers?

If you're undecided between two brokers and two agents, throw in with the one who offers you the more favorable contract (brokerage agreement) terms. The brokerage agreement will be taken up next.

## CHAPTER SUMMARY

A good real estate agent is one of the most important assets you have in selling your house quickly and at the right price. To ensure that you get the best broker you can find, you must investigate, interview, and ask a lot of questions. The ideas in this chapter provide a guideline to help you in this all-important task.

# 7 THE BROKERAGE AGREEMENT

## WHAT IS A BROKERAGE AGREEMENT?

When you decide which broker to retain, the broker's agent will almost assuredly insist that you sign a form contract that the broker (or perhaps the franchise that the broker belongs to) uses. The broker wants to ensure that he or she will be paid a commission if your house is sold. Also, a form may have to be signed for the listing broker to get the property listed with a multiple-listing service.

## WHY IT'S SO IMPORTANT TO UNDERSTAND YOUR BROKERAGE AGREEMENT

As with most forms, nonlawyers are inclined to simply sign, assuming that preprinted forms are somehow fair, or standard. This may be true, but only coincidentally. Nothing printed should be assumed to be fair or standard. The only thing standard about a broker's printed form is that it is that broker's standard policy to give all his or her customers that contract. You should carefully read the contract and, preferably, have it reviewed by your lawyer. A 6 percent commission on a $200,000 house is $12,000. That's a lot of money! It's worth a few minutes of time.

Significant changes are unlikely to be necessary, and your broker probably wouldn't agree to them anyway. However, there are a number of important legal matters that you should understand, and there are points you may want to add in your own interest. Remember that the brokerage agreement was written by brokers primarily to protect brokers. While it incorporates certain legal disclosure requirements, it wasn't written primarily to protect you.

The following sections highlight some of the issues that should be considered and reviewed with your lawyer before signing the brokerage agreement.

## ADDING PROTECTION THROUGH A LETTER AGREEMENT

Most good brokers are going to be reluctant to sign anything that differs from their standard agreement. "Everyone else signs it, why shouldn't you?" they may say. While you should make sure the brokerage agreement you sign protects your interests, you don't want to alienate the broker, and you don't want to hire the only broker willing to sign the agreement you want.

Approach the whole process in a positive way. You know the broker is the most important person in the sales process. You simply want to protect yourself because of the large amounts involved. An honest broker shouldn't object to reasonable requests you make. If charm and tact fail, blame it on your lawyer—most people will buy that as an excuse. Simply say that you're paying your lawyer a lot of money, and this is what your lawyer says you need. This should be your last resort, however, because you don't want the relationship to get formal or stiff. You just want fair and reasonable protection.

---

**TIP:** Get everything in writing! In many states, agreements with brokers must be in writing to be enforceable. So thank your broker for all the wonderful things he or she said, but then get it in writing (and that means signed by the broker).

Because the brokerage agreement will generally be a printed form, the easiest approach is sign the form, but add to the bottom (above the signature lines) the following phrase: "See attached letter agreement." (Be sure the broker signing the form initials this change.) Then simply have a short letter typed that includes in straightforward language any of the changes or additions suggested in this chapter. This can be far easier and far less threatening than rewriting the broker's standard form (which is likely to be an impossible battle to win).

A simple, clear letter, if properly done, should more than protect your rights. Always have the letter agreement reviewed by your attorney before signing it yourself and submitting it to the broker's agent.

---

---

**TIP:** You may have to sign a form agreement to get your property listed in the multiple-listing services. Using a separate letter agreement is probably the best approach because it will result in the least number of changes to the multiple-listing agreement and facilitate getting your house listed.

---

---

**TIP:** The first provision in your letter agreement must make it clear that the letter agreement is modifying the brokerage agreement to which it is attached. Your lawyer will include language similar to the following:

"This letter agreement is attached to and made part of a [insert exact title on the top of the brokerage agreement] between Sam and Susan Seller, and Barbara Broker, dated [insert date of brokerage agreement]. If any provision of this letter agreement conflicts with any provision of the brokerage agreement, the provisions of this letter agreement shall control."

This last sentence makes it clear that the changes made in the letter agreement are what control.

---

## TYPES OF LISTINGS

There are a number of different listings available, which call for different brokerage agreements. You should understand exactly what type of arrangement you're getting into. How do you know? The title to the agreement alone will usually indicate the type of arrangement. However, to be safe, read through the entire contract and make sure you understand exactly what rights you're giving the broker. Better still, have your lawyer read the agreement as well.

The most common listing arrangement is called an "exclusive right to sell," which means that if anyone buys your house during the period the brokerage agreement is in force, you must pay the commission to the broker. It doesn't matter who obtained the purchaser.

It may not seem fair that if your cousin brings over a friend who becomes the buyer, you still have to pay a commission to the broker. But if an agent is actively showing your house, it can be very difficult, if not impossible, to determine where the buyer came from. Your cousin may have seen an advertisement the broker paid for. Should the broker get the commission or not? To avoid these questions, along with the potential for lawsuits, agents generally prefer an exclusive listing. Going to court to decide who was responsible for introducing the buyer to you is expensive and time consuming. If the matter drags on long enough, the legal fees could exceed the commission that was in question.

If you have other leads, you could pursue your contacts before signing up with a broker.

---

**TIP:** Most sellers speak with neighbors and family about their selling their houses before going to a broker. Make a list of the names and addresses of all these prospects and attach it to the brokerage agreement. Be sure to add a sentence in the brokerage agreement stating that this list of people is excluded.

---

Alternatively, you could use an "exclusive-agency" arrangement where you must pay the agent if the agent sells the house. If you sell the house to a buyer who came to you directly and not through the broker, then you won't owe a commission.

Brokers have established shared listing arrangements (called Multiple Listing Services), according to which all participating brokers share listing information on houses offered for sale. Typically, the broker getting your listing and the broker selling your house will share the brokerage commission. If your broker got your listing and sold your house, he or she would earn the entire commission.

---

**TIP:** Make certain that your listing broker agrees to list your house with the multiple-listing services and to share any commission with another broker who sells the property. The brokerage agreement should contain a clause stating that "Broker agrees to list the house with the [insert name of multiple listing service] and to pay the selling or subagent [insert customary percentage] of the commission earned."

---

Another type of broker arrangement is a "nonexclusive relationship" which is sometimes called an open-listing arrangement. With this approach you can use any number of brokers and only pay the broker that finds the buyer. This is not a very practical choice. Brokers are not likely to be comfortable with such a "free-for-all" environment. You want an agent to work hard to sell your house, especially in a buyer's market, so seriously consider using the exclusive-right-to-sell arrangement instead.

A final alternative is an exclusive agency, which is an arrangement by which you agree to deal solely with one broker. That broker, however, will earn a commission only if he or she finds an acceptable purchaser.

## WHAT ARE YOUR TERMS FOR SELLING (OR RENTING)?

In the typical brokerage agreement, you will agree to pay the broker a commission if you sell, rent, or exchange your house. It's only fair that the broker be protected, but the agreement should also protect you by specifying the minimum price and terms you're willing to accept. If a second mortgage is acceptable (see Chapter 19), the agreement should state the maximum amount or percentage of the sales price you're willing to finance and at what interest rate. If you want a cash closing, the agreement should say that instead. If you'll need a certain amount of time after the contract is signed to move (say, 90 days to pack), the agreement could include this as well. What is the minimum amount of deposit (earnest money) you will accept? What happens to the deposit if the deal falls through?

---

**EXAMPLE:** The buyer puts down a $1,000 earnest money deposit. If there is a problem with the house, the buyer is entitled to get the deposit back. But occasionally buyers simply walk away from their deposits. The brokerage agreement must specify what should happen with this money. Should the broker get any of it? If the deal fell through because the buyer changed his or her mind, or simply found a better deal, you should be given the entire deposit because the broker didn't bring you a buyer who was ready, willing, and able to close on your house. Also, if the brokerage agreement specifies that the broker is entitled to a commission only when the title to the house closes or the deed is delivered, then the broker would not be entitled to anything when a potential buyer walks away from the deposit. However, it's still best to state in the agreement that the broker will promptly turn the money over to you.

---

Are you willing to rent the house? You may not want to rent, but if the market is particularly bad for sellers, that may be the only option. Do you want to pay the broker the same percentage commission on a rental lease as for selling? What if you sign a one-year lease? What if you sign a two-year lease? Also, when should the broker be paid this commission?

---

**EXAMPLE:** A typical form brokerage agreement might provide that the broker is entitled to 7 percent of the total rent payable under the lease when the first month's rent check is paid. If the house is rented on a one-year contract for $1,200 per month, you'd owe the broker $1,008. However, if the lease is signed for two years, you'd owe $2,016 even though you received only $1,200 from the tenant! You might want to specify that you don't have to pay more than 100 percent of the monthly rentals actually received at any one time. Alternatively, you could stretch the payments out into four equal monthly installments, or make some other reasonable arrangement.

---

You should also consider what will happen if the tenant defaults or moves out. If the tenant signed a two-year lease, paid one month's rent, and moved out, should you get anything back from the broker?

While this sounds like a lot to think about when signing a simple brokerage agreement, if you don't do it *before* you sign, you won't have another chance.


## WHAT IS THE BROKER GOING TO DO FOR YOU?


No lawyer would write a contract for you that gave you as little protection as most brokerage agreements. Think about it. You're committing to a broker's fee of many thousands of dollars, and most brokerage agreements say almost nothing about what the broker is going to do to try to earn this commission. The most you'll usually see is a sentence stating that, as consideration for your agreeing to pay the commission, the broker will agree to list the house and help you find a seller.

The majority of brokers and their agents are honest and will work hard to sell your house, because that's how they earn their living. However, there are brokers who will secure a listing on your house and not do much to make a sale. The problem is that if you've signed an exclusive agreement with such a broker for six months, there's really nothing you can do to get out of it. You can't cancel the contract on the basis that the broker hasn't done anything, because the contract doesn't require the broker to do anything! So now you're stuck with a do-nothing agency until the agreement expires.

If you've ever signed an employment agreement, you know that your employer required a fairly comprehensive explanation of your responsibilities. On a $225,000 house, a 6 percent commission is $13,500. For $13,500, can't your broker at least put into the contract the minimum efforts the real estate agency will make?

**TIP:** Don't rely on contract language that says your agent will "actively sell" your house because nobody knows what "actively sell" means. Instead, rely on a specific, concrete list, such as the one shown in the Case Study below.

**CASE STUDY:** Blue Realty, with offices located in Riverdale and Oak Ridge, New Jersey, offers a written "Service Warranty" stating what it will do for sellers. You can use it as a model of what your agent should do for you. Blue Realty will provide the following:

- Weekly advertising until your house is sold.
- Distribution within 24 hours of the listing information to brokers participating in the multiple-listing service (about 1,800 agents).
- Distribution within 48 hours to agents participating in another multiple-listing service.
- Immediate installation of a For Sale sign in front of the house and free replacement if the sign is ever damaged or stolen.
- An open house within seven days for all Blue Realty and other real estate agents.
- Inclusion in the Blue Realty listing of homes which is distributed to companies participating in Blue Realty relocation contracts, as well as to various real estate agents and potential home buyers.
- Presentation of your home "with the highest degree" of professional standards.
- The installation of a lockbox within 24 hours.
- A fact sheet, to be displayed in your home within seven days.
- Upon your signing up for Blue Realty's Buyer's Protection Plan, the printing and placement of brochures in your home within seven days explaining the program to potential buyers.
- The presentation to you of every offer received as soon as possible, and generally within 24 hours.
- Assistance with the delivery of any documents along with expeditious processing.
- Notification of any inspections that are necessary.

There are a few conditions attached. You must list your home with Blue Realty for at least six months and pay the usual commission for the area

where Blue Realty operates—6 percent. You also can't price your house
for sale at more than 10 percent above its fair-market value.

---

Other points you might want to have the broker agree to, in writing,
include the following:

- The broker should represent that it will use its best efforts to
  sell your house and that there are no obligations, commitments,
  or impediments that could hamper the broker's ability to properly
  render its services.
- The broker should represent that all persons working with the
  broker, and the broker, if required to be licensed, are properly
  licensed.
- The broker will provide you with a biweekly or monthly activity
  report of all steps taken, all prospects shown through your
  house, all appointments made, etc.
- The broker will conduct a minimum number of open houses,
  where an agent is present throughout the advertised hours.
- The broker or agent will make a floor plan of your house (if
  you don't have one). This can be an indispensable sales tool.

Having the duties spelled out is a great step toward protecting your
interests. But it's still not enough. What happens if the broker doesn't
live up to his or her end of the bargain?

You should have the right to cancel the exclusive listing agreement
and go to another agency. But suppose the broker didn't know that
the sign in front of your house was stolen? The fair way to handle
the situation is for you to be required to tell the agent (in writing)
what hasn't been done. The agency should have some reasonable
time to do what it had promised to do. If the broker doesn't respond,
then you should have the right to cancel the listing agreement. You
should have no further rights against the broker. No brokers would
agree to any arrangement that would expose them to a lawsuit. Nor
should they.

---

**TIP:** Consult with your lawyer concerning the appropriate language for
the letter agreement. The terms must be fair and reasonable. Remember,
your objective is to get the broker to do the things necessary to sell your
house, not to antagonize or sue the broker.

---

**EXAMPLE:** The following sample language indicates some of the terms your lawyer might want to consider:

"If the broker doesn't perform as promised in this letter agreement, the seller can give the broker written notice of the specific step that the broker has failed to perform. Within seven (7) business days of the broker's receiving the notice, the broker has the right to perform. If the broker does not do so, the seller's sole remedy shall be to cancel the listing agreement. Any notice shall be sent by certified mail with return receipt requested, Express mail, or personal delivery. The seven (7) day period begins with the next business day after the day on which the broker has received the notice."

One final caution is in order. Even if a broker does everything agreed to, and more, there is no guarantee of a buyer, or even that anyone will come to look at your house. Don't expect any guarantee of that sort, and if a broker offers one, be very skeptical.

## IS YOUR BROKER APPRAISING YOUR PROPERTY?

Many real estate brokers offer to appraise your property to help you decide on the best sales price. Before you accept this offer, find out if you're expected to pay for the appraisal. Some brokers will offer you free appraisals as an incentive to list with them. Others will charge. Appraising is a professional service, and if it's done properly, it takes time and effort. If the broker providing the appraisal is also the listing broker, the brokerage agreement should state, if it applies, that the appraisal is a free service for you. If the contract doesn't say this, have your lawyer add a simple sentence to the form: "ABC Brokers, Inc., will provide a professional, written appraisal of the fair market value of the house at no cost to the Seller."

There is no reason why any agent who says that he or she will provide a free appraisal should not put it in writing. And be certain you receive a written copy of the appraisal.

**TIP:** If the broker charges more than a nominal amount for the appraisal, investigate the cost of hiring a professional appraiser who carries one of the recognized industry appraisal credentials of SEA or MAI.

## CREATIVE APPROACHES TO COMMISSIONS

Commission rates are generally established by local custom. Although it is illegal for brokers to set commissions at any specific rate, most brokers will charge the going rate for the area you're in and the type of property involved. This doesn't mean you must pay the broker this rate. Brokerage agreements are contracts and *every* term can be negotiated.

The problem you will find is that many, if not most, brokers are unwilling to vary much from the going rates. The only way you'll know is to ask and to shop. Just remember, whatever you agree to in the contract is what you'll have to pay.

One of the drawbacks in paying the full commission is the potential situation that the house is finally sold for considerably less than the broker's appraisal.

---

**EXAMPLE:** Sell It Quick Brokers, Inc., appraises your house at no charge. They set the value at $220,000. You're pleased with the way they handled the appraisal and with all the promotional work they promised, so you sign an agreement giving them the exclusive right to sell your house for a six-month period, at a 6 percent commission. Three months later, after getting a number of offers around $170,000, you finally agree to sell the house for $173,000. Is it fair that Sell It Quick Brokers, Inc., should get its full 6 percent commission? They've sold the house for about 25 percent less than they said it should be sold for! Sure the broker will be getting a smaller commission, but you're getting a lot less than expected.

---

If the real estate agency is the one giving you the appraisal, it should be able to sell your house for something close to the appraisal amount. Because no appraisal can be exact, you can't expect the broker to get the precise figure. In many markets, coming as close as 10 to 15 percent is more than reasonable. But in the above example, the large difference suggests that the agency sold you on an inflated appraisal. Unless something substantial happened in the economy or local market to cause such a drop, the broker really couldn't have done an acceptable appraisal job.

If the market is tight and you really want to sell, try offering an incentive commission package. It's an unusual approach, but it's hard to see why a good broker would turn down a potentially lucrative offer of a bonus commission. When the market is slow, this extra step, beyond the others suggested thus far, just might be the key to distinguishing your house from the dozens of others for sale in your neighborhood.

Here's how it's might be done: If the house is sold within 60 days, for at least 95 percent of the broker's appraisal price, you agree to give the broker a higher commission, say, 7 percent instead of the usual 6 percent. If the house is sold for more than the appraised value, you'll give a bonus of 20 percent of the difference.

---

**EXAMPLE:** A house is appraised for $150,000 and sells for $163,000. You will be giving the broker $2,600 [20% × ($163,000 − $150,000)].

---

An alternative plan is to limit the bonus commission to the selling agent. The agent who listed your house might not be as aggressive as agents from other firms, and it's the selling you want to inspire. So instead of simply offering a 7 percent commission in a 6 percent area, offer a 1 percent bonus to the selling agent.

You can try for a scaled commission to cover both the upside and the downside possibilities, so that if the house sells for less than 80 percent of the appraised value, the broker gets only a 5 percent commission.

Brokers are in business to make commissions. In the above approach, you've given the broker a number of incentives both to push your house and to avoid inflating its value. When you combine the carrot and the stick you're much more likely to get a favorable response. Again, the key point is that everything in the brokerage agreement is legally negotiable. Whether or not the terms can be *practically* negotiated will depend on the brokers you interview.

## HOW LONG SHOULD THE LISTING AGREEMENT RUN?

The first point is to make sure the agreement contains both the date you sign and the date the agreement expires. The best approach is to state a specific day, such as June 13, 1990, for an expiration date, rather than simply saying, "six months" from the signing date.

The tougher problem is what the termination date should be. There are two sides to the issue. You want to give a good broker a period long enough to serve as incentive to give a 100 percent effort in selling your house. On the other hand, if you don't know the broker, you want a fairly short agreement period in case you want to switch to someone else. Some experts suggest a listing of three months or less, as appropriate to both objectives.

The truth is, the activity in a given time period will be affected by how the local housing market is doing, the time of the year, characteristics of the house itself, and other factors. Discuss the issue openly with the agent and express your concern about being locked in, in case things don't work out. Say that you're also sensitive to the agent's need to have a long enough listing period to warrant investing time and money in selling your house.

---

**TIP:** Remind your broker that if he or she does a reasonable job, you can always renew the listing for an additional period.

---

---

**TIP:** One partial solution to the problem is to use a letter agreement specifying the minimum steps the agent will take to sell your house. If the agent will list the steps it guarantees it will take, and if you reserve the right to cancel the contract if the agent doesn't keep its end of the bargain, you've achieved much of the same protection which a shorter listing period would hopefully provide. It's a give and take. If the agent wants a longer listing, the agent should be willing to give you the right to cancel if the agent isn't actively selling your house. Don't expect the agent to agree to "actively sell" your house since nobody knows what "actively sell" means. Instead rely on a specific agreed-to list as in the example above.

---

What happens if one week after the listing agreement expires, a buyer introduced to you by the broker signs a contract to buy the house? Most likely, the broker will be entitled to a commission. Court cases in many states interpret this point. But rather than face the uncertainty, the brokerage agreement should include a cut-off date. For example, if within 60 days, there is no contract signed with anyone the broker introduced you to, then no commission should be due. Whatever length of time you choose, make sure the agreement is specific.

---

**TIP:** Read the contract carefully. Some brokers include time periods as long as one year. In such a case, insist on a shorter period. After all, once the broker stops showing the house, the impetus for the sale really comes from you.

---

## MORE WAYS TO GET OUT OF YOUR BROKERAGE AGREEMENT

Most brokerage agreements are written for the broker's benefit, not for the seller's benefit. They typically won't provide for any way out of the brokerage agreement. One important condition of release you should insist on was discussed above—namely, when the broker doesn't perform the minimum services that have been agreed to. But there are other important conditions you might want to include in the letter agreement as well.

What if you're moving only because your employer insisted on transferring you and then your employer changes his or her mind? You're stuck with your brokerage agreement.

---

**TIP:** Include a clause similar to this:

"Seller is selling the house because seller has received a transfer by seller's employer [name of employer] to [name of city where relocating]. Should seller's employer provide seller with written cancellation of the transfer, at no fault and due to no action of seller, then seller may cancel this brokerage agreement upon providing 24 hours written notice to the broker."

---

What happens if there is a serious and unexpected illness, accident, or even a death, that forces you to delay your plans to move? Death, injury, and illness are not events you could anticipate, and you should have the right to cancel the brokerage agreement in these cases with no further obligation.

## DO YOU ALWAYS HAVE TO PAY THE COMMISSION (OR OTHER COMPENSATION)?

There are cases in which payment of the commission might not be appropriate. But if the brokerage agreement doesn't clearly state when you can avoid paying, it's likely you'll have to pay.

You shouldn't have to pay a commission unless the house is sold. Bringing you a willing and able buyer is not enought for the broker to collect. You don't want to pay unless the contract is signed, the closing of title occurs, and you have your sales proceeds. Be absolutely certain that the brokerage agreement says this.

**TIP:** If the agreement isn't already clear on this point, have your lawyer add a provision, similar to the following:

"Notwithstanding anything in the brokerage agreement or this letter agreement to the contrary, the broker shall not be entitled to a commission, or any other form of compensation, unless and until a contract of sale is signed by both buyer and seller, and if, and when, the closing of title to the house occurs pursuant to the contract of sale, and the buyer performs all obligations with respect to the payment of the purchase price as contained in the contract of sale. The broker shall not be entitled to a commission or any other form of compensation if the seller for any reason does not sign a contract of sale, or for any reason either the seller or buyer default under the contract of sale, whether willfully or otherwise."

If the broker won't agree to this point, ask why.

---

**TIP:** Are you responsible for any of the expenses your broker incurs in selling (or trying to sell) your house? If you don't think you should be (and you shouldn't), the letter agreement should say: "The commission is the only payment the seller may have to make to the broker. The seller shall not be responsible for reimbursing broker for any costs."

---

Brokerage agreements might contain other forms of compensation for the broker. For example, if you discontinue the arrangement, the brokerage agreement may require you to make certain payments to the broker. If there is a provision for this, make sure that there are ample opportunities for you to cancel the agreement without your being unfairly burdened with a cancellation payment.

If, however, you are willing to agree to such a payment, make sure it's small and reasonable when compared with the real out-of-pocket costs the broker incurred. And make sure you have legal rights to cancel the contract in reasonable situations.

## INDEMNIFICATION AGAINST CLAIMS BY OTHER BROKERS

If you give a broker an exclusive right to sell your house, you don't want to hear from any other broker that you also owe him or her a commission as a result of the sale of your house. Because your exclusive broker will be responsible for the listing and will earn a fee no matter which broker ultimately finds the buyer for your house, the broker should be willing to indemnify you against any problems from other brokers. While this problem is unlikely to occur, there is no reason not to protect yourself.

---

**TIP:** Have your lawyer consider adding a provision similar to the following to the letter agreement:

"The broker agrees to indemnify and hold the seller harmless against any and all claims, liabilities or expenses arising out of any claim for a commission or other compensation that may be made by any other real estate broker, or any person acting as a real estate broker, with respect to the sale of the house."

---

## FULL DISCLOSURE

You want full disclosure by your broker to you as to the representation of any of the buyers considering your house. If you use the broker for recommendations on a title insurance company, home-inspection service, termite-inspection service, or other reference, the broker must disclose to you any fees or other arrangements it has with any such references. If the broker owns 50 percent of the title company, you're entitled to know this.

## ARBITRATION CLAUSES

What happens if you and the broker have a dispute about the brokerage agreement, whether the commission is due, whether the broker is performing properly or some other matter? Either party can sue, but as noted above, this tends to be very expensive and time consuming. One alternative is to provide for a dispute resolution mechanism in the brokerage agreement, such as arbitration. In arbitration you and the broker present your arguments to a third person whose decision will generally be binding. It is generally much cheaper and faster than commencing a lawsuit and going to court.

But arbitration can have a number of drawbacks. It can be very *arbitrary*, and you may not have any recourse to sue further. Arbitrators are often chosen for their expertise in a certain area. Would you want the question of whether your broker is entitled to a fee to be heard by a retired broker? While your lawyer is the best person to discuss whether you should agree to an arbitration clause, you must also be careful in taking his or her advice. Your lawyer may have a vested interest because of wanting to handle the lawsuit for you and, therefore, advise against arbitration. So listen to what the broker has to say, discuss it with your lawyer, and then make the best decision you can.


## CHAPTER SUMMARY

A brokerage agreement is one of the most important documents you will sign when you sell your house. To properly protect your rights, be certain to read the document carefully, discuss it with your lawyer, and request any changes which are necessary. Understand the legal consequences of the type of brokerage arrangement you choose. Be certain that the agreement specifies what steps the broker will take to sell your house, how much you will pay the broker, when the agreement will end, and the limited conditions under which you can terminate the agreement at an earlier date.

# 8 HOW TO HELP AND NOT HINDER YOUR AGENT

In a slow market, your real estate agent can be as important as the admitting officer at a hospital with only a few empty beds. Antagonize your agent, or just not be on great terms with him or her, and you may not have many serious buyers visiting your house. Come 5 P.M., when the buyers want to see just one more house and then call it quits, the agent will bring them to Mrs. Jones's place and not yours—because the agent and Mrs. Jones are on the best of terms.

In a brisk market, agents would worry that if your house listing expired before your house was sold, you would sign up with someone else in frustration. In a slow market, agents who lose listings will have plenty of other listings to pick up.

Agents do push certain houses regularly—the houses being sold by relocation services and the houses being sold by developers. The reason is that they can expect repeat business if they do a good job.

Agents also push the houses of certain individuals—if the home-owners are cooperative and courteous, and if their houses are reasonably priced and in excellent condition.

## BE COOPERATIVE

If you haven't been cooperative, agents may not bring around as many buyers. Agents want to sell as many houses as possible, as fast as possible. So your interests and theirs seem to be identical. But if you haven't followed their advice, they are going to be less enthusiastic about you and your sale.

For example, you may have ignored their advice to keep your pets outside when prospects come. The agent may not know whether a buyer loves pets or is allergic to them or afraid of them. But why take the chance of bringing the buyer to your place when there are a dozen others available—without cats, dogs, gerbils, and so forth?

Agents witness buy-and-sell transactions every day, so they do know something about selling real estate. You ignore their advice at your peril.

Not that a few agents aren't lazy, careless, and inefficient. If your agent hasn't brought over many buyers, can't show you advertisements for your house, hasn't kept you informed about the market, and hasn't showered you with good suggestions, consider not renewing your listing. Or consider firing the agent: As indicated in the previous chapter, if your agent hasn't been working diligently for you, you can extricate yourself from the contract (as long as you have protected yourself appropriately).

### EIGHT WAYS TO HELP THE AGENT AND YOUR OWN CAUSE

But let's assume that your agent has been doing a good job. How do you help and not hinder your agent?

1. Make your house available. Agents complain that sellers who insist that they want to sell fast often aren't available when buyers want to drop by. A transferee may be in the area for just a few days and have only two hours left to see your place. Sure, you have good excuses—you just returned home from work, you're tired, the house is a mess, neighbors are coming over for coffee. . . .

Just bear in mind that Billy Buyer isn't going to want your house if he doesn't see it. And Priscilla Prospect may be willing to wait a day before seeing your house, but, in the meantime, she may see another house similar to yours and fall in love with it and buy it. If she'd seen your house first, she may have fallen in love with it instead.

If your agent knows that he or she has only a 50 percent or 75 percent chance of getting your permission to bring a buyer over who is on a tight schedule, the agent is going to phone a client where the chances are closer to 100 percent.

Some homeowners refuse even to allow brokers to install a lockbox (a metal safe attached outside the house for holding keys, to which only agents have access), so that agents can enter the house with buyers when the homeowners are away. In a lively market, you may have the luxury of deciding that you don't want strangers trooping through your house while you're out. In a slow market, your house is competing against houses that do have lockboxes. Why handicap your house?

2.  Solicit the agent's advice. Many brokers are afraid to give frank advice because they've learned how sensitive homeowners can be. Your job is to persuade the agent to be as frank and open as possible—even to tell you such things as "your house looks tired," "the wallpaper is too old-fashioned," "the abstract paintings on the wall will scare away buyers," "that collection of unicorn figurines on the mantelpiece makes the house too unusual."

You can convey your tolerance of useful criticism by your own comments: "A neighbor told me that my furniture is so old and battered that I should remove it all and rent new furniture. I'm willing. What do you think—frankly?"

Or this: "We know that people who live in a house for years don't notice its defects anymore—like odors from pets. That's why we're eager to have you give us an objective view."

3.  Pay attention to the agent's advice. Maybe you don't have the extra money to rent new furniture, or you don't want to board the cat or dog you love. But listen to your agent carefully. Agents see a lot of houses. They can readily identify any reasons your house won't be among the winners in the house beauty contest.

Here's an analogy: Perhaps the single most critical public-health problem is that patients don't do what their physicians tell them to do. They don't stop smoking, don't watch their diets, don't exercise more, and don't take their prescribed medications. Why not? Sometimes it's sheer human cussedness. Yet there's evidence that patients who don't follow their physicians' advice don't live as long as patients who do.

Similarly, it stands to reason that sellers who don't follow their agents' advice don't sell their homes as quickly as sellers who do.

If an agent suggests that you repaint the living room, remove your collection of old magazines from the den, rid your house of animal odors, etc., either do it or have a good reason why not, and check that the agent agrees that it's a good reason.

And if agents tell you not to accompany them and the buyers as they romp around your house, or not to volunteer any information, do as they say—unless you have good reason. (A good reason is this: You overhear the agent tell the buyers that the fireplace is only a decorative fireplace when it's a working fireplace.)

4. Be courteous, both to the agent and the buyers. Buyers, especially, can be rude and insensitive. They may criticize your house to your face ("the wallpaper clashes with the carpet"), thinking that this is what they're supposed to do to get you to drop your price. Or they may be inconsiderate—flushing toilets, opening closets, and peeking under rugs without permission. One buyer, wanting to see whether an attic was insulated, even broke off a piece of the ceiling tile to peer inside!

Agents won't behave as boorishly as buyers, but some of them can be a pain in the neck, too—leaving water running and lights on when they leave, treating you as if you were tenants and not homeowners when they visit.

As much as possible, smile and be friendly. Pretend that you *are* tenants—that your self-esteem isn't on the line, that you won't be offended by any comments from the buyers that you overhear. Sure, the buyers' children can use the bathroom. In fact, you'll give them cookies and milk while their parents tour your house.

Imagine that the buyers and the agents are invited guests—and you want them to come back. After all, you do. Or imagine that they're your potential employers—and you dearly want the job they have available. Don't act like a servant, of course. But don't act like the king of the castle, either.

If the buyers seem interested—if they remain awhile and ask the agents lots of questions—be prepared to lead them all into the kitchen for a cup of coffee or tea.

5. Tell the agent everything. These days, almost everyone is suing almost everyone else. And that includes buyers suing sellers who didn't reveal house defects, such as a little water collecting on the basement floor after a heavy rain. If you mislead your agent, and your agent misleads the buyer, both of you can find yourselves in very deep water. See the suggestions in the sample House Sale Contract following Chapter 25.

6. Ask the agent to tell you everything. What did the buyers say? What didn't they like? What did they like? Did they think the price was too high? Is the market picking up? Are mortgage rates going down? Should you lower your asking price?

7. Keep in touch with you agent, in a positive way. Be in regular communication, but don't be a pest, a nag. Don't do to any agent what one seller did. Encountering the agent at a supermarket, she

loudly demanded to know why the agent was shopping and not busy trying to sell her house. If you had been that agent, would you have worked harder to sell that person's house?

Do call your agent every two weeks or so. Ask if more advertisements are scheduled to run. Ask when there will be another open house. Ask if there is anything additional you can do.

8. Convince the agent that you're reasonable. Let him or her know that you won't be insulted by any offer, although you may reject it.

Agent: "I'm embarrassed to have to tell you this, but I'm obligated to do so. One buyer offered only $75,000 for your house—$35,000 below your asking price."

You: "Well, it's much too low. But we'll come down from $105,000 to $103,000, considering how slow the market is."

Yes, there have been instances where buyers bid $75,000 for a $105,000 house—and, when persuaded they couldn't steal it, bought it for $102,000.

## CHAPTER SUMMARY

If you and your agent aren't on the best of terms, your agent may bring motivated buyers to other houses instead of yours. Cooperate with your agent. If your agent asks to show your house in the next 10 minutes, agree. If your agent doesn't want you around when the buyers come, leave. Agree to have a lockbox installed.

Solicit your agent's advice—and be prepared to take it, unless you have an excellent reason not to.

Be frank with you agent. If your agent discovers you misled him or her about the property taxes, or some other point, the agent is going to worry that other things you said may be false, too, and that you could both be sued.

Be courteous to buyers. Also, let your agent know that he or she can convey any offers, even if they're insultingly low. Keep in touch with your agent, asking what buyers thought of your house, how the market is doing, whether you should lower your price, when there will be another open house.

# 9 FIZZBOS—SHOULD YOU GO IT ALONE?

Fizzbos are people selling their houses by themselves. (The word comes from the initials of For Sale By Owner.) Should you try it? The answer is yes—if you have the time, if you have the confidence, and especially if you have some real estate experience (as almost everyone in the country thinks they do). If you've ever been a salesperson, or worked in a bank, you'll have a leg up.

First we'll discuss arguments against trying to sell your house by yourself, then we'll cover the arguments in favor.

## THE CASE *AGAINST* GOING FIZZBO

1.  There are six negative points: You probably won't have access to your local multiple-listing service. The MLS allows all the brokerage firms in an area to try to sell the same houses. That means any house at all, if it's in the MLS, will have hundreds of agents trying to sell it—and those hundreds of agents will have hundreds upon hundreds of potential buyers. This can be a substantial drawback for a fizzbo, particularly in a slow market. On the other hand, some buyers prefer not to deal with agents and will concentrate on houses for sale by owner.

2.  You may waste a lot of your time dealing with buyers who aren't really buyers. They can't afford your house, and no mortgage lender would go near them. So you yourself will have to do what agents should do: "qualify" buyers (make sure that they can obtain a mortgage and can afford the monthly principal-interest-tax-insurance payments).

3. You will have to take measures to protect yourself against criminals—people claiming to be buyers who may try to burglarize

your house. Buyers sent over by a broker have been already been screened to a certain extent, and are usually accompanied by an agent. Agents see a lot more buyers than you will and will usually have a much better ability to screen out unwanted buyers.

4. You'll have to spend some of your own money—for fact sheets, for advertising, for fliers.

5. You should have some knowledge of real estate—what forms to use, what to say and what not to say, how to help your buyers obtain a mortgage. If the negotiations get a bit thick—if the buyers want you to give them a mortgage, or they want you to accept an automobile or other property they own as part of a down payment—you will, in all likelihood, need outside help.

6. Sharks target fizzbos. These crooks figure that fizzbos are desperate (they couldn't sell their houses through a broker, or couldn't afford a broker), and they're babes in the woods. In many cases, they're right.

Sharks may try, for example, to rent your house with an option to buy, then ensconce themselves with no intention of either buying the house or paying rent.

Or they will try to buy your house for a pittance. Shark A may visit your $100,000 house one day, and offer $60,000. You'll slam the door. Shark B, the confederate of Shark A, comes by the next day, with a $70,000 offer. Shocked and frightened by two such low offers, you might seriously consider the second.

## THE CASE *FOR* GOING FIZZBO

There's only one good argument for going it alone: You can save a lot of money. But this single argument can have more weight than all the arguments against it, if you can make it happen. If you're selling a $100,000 house, you can save $6,000 or $7,000. Sell a $300,000 house, and you save $18,000 to $21,000.

Granted, you may spend $500 to $1,000 on fact sheets and advertising, and a few hundred on an appraisal. Granted, you will invest some of your own time—maybe a lot. Plan on at least 40 or more hours. Granted, you may have to pay your lawyer more because of the extra assistance he or she provides. It's still a well-paying job. Sell your own home in 40 hours, saving $6,000, and you'll be making $150 an hour. That's the equivalent of $312,000 a year.

Brokers, after all, have to pay for their offices; agents have car expenses. The broker and his or her agents only share in any commissions they receive. So, by selling your house yourself, you won't have their overhead—and you won't have anyone to share your bounty with, unless it's the buyer.

And that's another advantage. If you do share savings with a buyer, you should be able to sell your house faster. If you're selling your house for $100,000 (and saving a $6,000 commission), you can comfortably accept an offer of $97,000.

Besides, fizzbos we've interviewed tell us that they enjoyed the process, and that success buoyed their self-esteem for months, if not years.

Our conclusion is, if you're really fizzbo material, go the fizzbo route for a while. Try it for 30 days or so—four weekends. When a house is fresh on the market is the very best time to make a sale. If, after 30 days, you're discouraged, and the market seems very slow, consider listing it with a top-notch agent.

## HOW TO START

To begin with, hire a lawyer. A lawyer can give you the advice that you would normally get from an agent—such as who traditionally pays for closing costs in your area, and what amount of earnest money you should ask a buyer for. Either ask your lawyer for a contract, or pick one up from a large stationery store in your area (but don't sign it or use it without having a lawyer review it).

You might even ask your lawyer to qualify the buyer—to check that the buyer can afford your house. No doubt your lawyer, if he or she is experienced in real estate, can also direct the buyer toward the best mortgage. A good lawyer can also help protect you against sharks. Refer any buyer who makes any unusual offer to your lawyer. Unfortunately, a fizzbo using a lawyer for these extra services should expect to pay more than that lawyer's usual fee for a house sale.

Don't allow drop-ins. When you put a bright, easily readable sign on your law, "FOR SALE BY OWNER," with your phone number, add: "By appointment only." And mean it.

If someone knocks on your door, says he or she is from out of town and has to catch a plane in a few hours, and asks for 10 minutes to inspect your house, be prepared to say no. Or, if you're tempted, tell the person to come back in five minutes—to give you time to alert a neighbor about what's happening. (The neighbor should phone you a few minutes after the visitor returns.) And when the visitor does return, tell him or her you're expecting neighbors over in a few minutes.

If someone phones for an appointment, and you'll be alone in the house when the person comes, first get the caller's name, place of employment, and home and business telephone numbers. That way, you can check his or her credentials beforehand by calling and speaking with him or her again. And, again, alert a neighbor about what's happening.

Make sure that any valuables you own—jewelry, valuable art, furs—are in your safe-deposit box, or a relative's home, not in your house.


## ADDITIONAL ADVICE

- If you don't want to pay for an appraisal, invite three or more agents to your house to estimate its market value. Then take an average of those estimates.

   Be candid with the agents. Tell them you plan to try to sell the house yourself for a while, but if you don't succeed, you'll be looking for a good agent—one who not only puts a reasonable and not exorbitant price on your house, but who has useful advice about how you can turn your house into a creampuff.

- If an agent drops by and says he or she has interested buyers, and will bring the couple in if you list your house with him or her, offer to compromise.

   Say you'll agree to sell the house to the agent's customer if it's at the full asking price, and if the agent will accept only a 3 percent commission. After all, the agent won't have to split the commission with another agent. Put it in writing, and have the agent list the names of the interested buyers on the document and have your lawyer review it.

- Ask friends or neighbors in to give you frank appraisals of your house. What's right with it, what's wrong with it? If they were visiting your house as buyers, what would they think?

- Keep a log of your visitors' names and telephone numbers. Phone them later for their comments. When you hold an open house, have people there to help you and don't let anyone enter without signing.

- Buy a telephone-answering machine, so that you can get names and phone numbers of prospects even when no one is at home.

- So that you don't hang around the house waiting for no-shows, plead with any callers to phone you if they can't make it.

- Schedule visits 45 minutes apart. Usually a house tour takes a half-hour.
- Exile your pets, or keep them in a spare room when buyers come.
- Vary your ads—don't run the same ad all the time. Push one theme in one, another in a second. (If people spot the same ad week after week, they'll jump to the conclusion that your house is hard to sell.)

See other chapters for advice on dealing with buyers, bargaining, writing ads, marketing your house, and so forth.

## THE MIDDLE WAY

You don't have just an either/or choice about going it alone or hiring a high-priced broker.

There are in-between agencies—discounters—that help you sell your house yourself. You pay them less, and they do less for you. For sellers who are intimidated by the thought of selling their houses, these agencies may be the solution. Just make sure that the agency you use has been successful. Ask for names of local people who have been clients and call them.

Among the discounters are the following:

**Help-U-Sell:** Founded in California in 1976, the company expanded in 1986 after being purchased by Mutual Benefit Life Insurance Company. It's headquartered in Salt Lake City and has over 500 offices in the United States and Canada. Fees vary, depending on the median price of houses in the area and the cost of doing business there. The national average for fees is $2,950. If a house is unusually expensive for the area, there may be an extra charge. The fee is payable only if the house is sold—at the closing.

A house is advertised every week. An adviser is available to help with the paperwork, but the sellers themselves show houses to buyers. The homeowner can have the house listed in the MLS but will then have to pay any selling agent a fee.

**Seller's Choice:** Based in Denver, this company has just begun opening up offices in other states. Typically the company charges $249 up-front to list a house in its publication. It also provides advice, a sign, advertising, and contracts. For an extra $100, the company will list the house with the local MLS. Again, the seller will owe a commission to the selling agent.

**WHY USA:** A small firm in Scottsdale, Arizona, that's beginning to spread, its name stands for We Help You. The franchises charge $990, half of which—$495—must be paid when the seller signs up. That pays for six months of marketing, an appraisal, newspaper ads, and a listing in the company's magazine. If the sellers agree to go with the MLS, again they will owe a fee to a selling agent.

## HOMEOWNERS WHO SHOULD CONSIDER IT

- You have time—during the evening, during weekends—to show the house.
- Your house is reasonably priced and in excellent condition—the kind of house that sells in a weekend, whatever the market.
- You have sales experience.
- You have a knowledgeable real estate lawyer, who will answer any of your questions.
- You have patience.
- You have self-confidence.

## HOMEOWNERS WHO PROBABLY SHOULDN'T

- You're selling an inexpensive house, and the potential buyers probably have no real estate experience. They need counseling about financing, mortgages, house types, and so forth.
- You don't have time.
- You don't have the confidence.
- You're worried about your safety.

## CHAPTER SUMMARY

There are some good arguments for trying to sell your house yourself, and good arguments against it. The best argument in favor: You can save a lot of money. But if you don't have the time, the patience, the self-confidence, or adequate relevant experience, you might consider a compromise: hiring an agency that helps you sell your own house, for a reduced fee. Or you can go the conventional route—not a bad choice in a slow market.

# 10 HAVING YOUR OWN HOUSE INSPECTED

## THE SELLERS ARE PAYING

Normally, the buyer pays to have house inspected—meaning, checked for its structural soundness (roof, floors, walls) and the working condition of its operating systems (furnace, water supply, electricity). But a good case can be made for the you, the seller, to pay for the inspection, even before an interested buyer strolls along.

More and more sellers, in fact, are paying for their house inspections before or just after putting their houses on the market. Here are the reasons:

1. A last-minute house inspection, ordered by the buyer, may uncover problems that delay or cancel the closing. The house inspector may report that the roof needs replacing, or the two bathrooms on the first floor are so close together that the floor is tipping, or that the furnace is at the end of its useful life. The buyer may want out—even if the seller offers to make all the necessary repairs. Buyers may not want, for example, a house with a basement so wet that it needs a sump pump. But if the sellers know beforehand about any problems, they can attend to them—or inform buyers when they come to look at the house—and not have the closing delayed or called off.

If an inspection reveals major, costly problems, rather than taking on the expense before selling, the sellers can offer to reduce their price to compensate for them. (See Chapter 11.)

2. The buyer can be reassured about the soundness of the house. At some point in the negotiations, you can simply say, "I had the entire house inspected a few months ago, and everything passed—

except for a leaky faucet upstairs, which I had fixed. Would you like to see the inspection report? I can also show you the plumber's bill for repairing the faucet."

3. In a buyer's market, when buyers have many choices, little things can mean a lot. Having written evidence that a house is in good shape, and saving a few hundred on a house inspection, may tip a buyer in your direction.

If buyers are interested in your house but skeptical of the inspection you ordered, encourage them to have their own inspection. But make sure that they don't insert in the sales contract a clause that is so vague that they can bow out on a whim—if the inspection report isn't "satisfactory," for example. (For an example of an inspection clause in the sales contract, see Chapter 25, For Your Notebook.)

## FINDING A HOUSE INSPECTOR

Ideally, your house inspector will be an engineer. But in some areas house engineers are hard to find. You may have to make do with an architect, a builder, or someone else with solid experience.

For names of inspectors in your area, get in touch with the American Society of Home Inspectors, 3299 K Street, N.W., Washington, D.C. Phone: (202) 842-3096.

The American Society of Home Inspectors was formed in 1976 as a nonprofit organization to develop formal inspection guidelines, to establish a professional code of ethics, and to give consumers an assurance of quality and professionalism. Today ASHI, whose membership extends across the United States, is recognized nationwide as the leading authority in the home-inspection field among inspectors and homeowners alike.

An inspection will cost $150 and up, depending on the size of the house and the area of the country. Some inspectors check for termites and for radon; some don't. Some will report on asbestos problems, others won't.

## WHAT STEPS DOES A HOME INSPECTION INCLUDE?

A thorough home inspection includes an examination of the entire house, from top to bottom. This should include an examination of the heating system, the central air-conditioning system (when temperature permits), the interior plumbing and electrical systems, the roof and visible insulation, walls, ceilings, floors, windows and doors, the foundation, basement, and visible structure.

## WHAT TYPE OF REPORT WILL A HOME INSPECTOR PROVIDE?

A professional home inspection is simply an examination of the current condition of the house inspected. It is not an appraisal. It is not an analysis as to whether the house conforms to the Municipal Code. A home inspector, therefore, will not pass or fail a house, but will simply describe the condition of the house and state which items need immediate repair or replacement (or will need it shortly).

## ASBESTOS

Asbestos is a mineral fiber, and breathing it can cause respiratory disease and cancer. Some home buyers are so afraid of asbestos that they won't even enter a house where there's any asbestos inside. Typically these are young couples with children. Older people tend to feel that they have been living with such hazards all their lives, so why worry?

---

**CASE STUDY:** A couple in Jasper, Florida, were having their house renovated when the workers sawed into asbestos wallboard, releasing the fibers all over the house. The couple were forced to abandon their house. They collected only one-third of its value from their insurance company and put the house up for sale. They have received one offer: $5,000. Eradicating all the asbestos from the house would have cost an estimated $24,000.

---

Usually fears about asbestos are overblown, as may be the case with fears over radon. In small amounts, asbestos shouldn't be worrisome. Because automobile brake linings contain asbestos, our streets have small amounts of asbestos fibers floating in the air, especially near crowded intersections. Be careful, however, since you really need a professional to determine what is, and what is not, an acceptable level.

With regard to asbestos in the house—in wrappers covering pipes, in floor tiles, in acoustical ceilings, and so forth—the general rule is, if it ain't broke, don't fix it (so long as it is safely enclosed).

Most asbestos in a house is in the heating system and furnace area. Check the wrapping around steam or hot-water pipes for nicks and cuts. The mushroom-shaped insulation around the furnace, which may also contain asbestos, could be damaged.

Confirming that any material actually contains asbestos can be difficult. Look for a label or phone the manufacturer. Otherwise, you will need a laboratory test of samples taken in two areas of the material. The price may be $25 to $35. Don't take the samples yourself. Call a professional asbestos removal company that has good references.

These are the situations requiring caution or attention:

- The material that apparently contains asbestos seems to be damaged. Call an expert. The expert may advise you to dampen the area with spray to keep fibers out of the air until further action can be taken.
- Your house is being renovated. If remodelers don't take proper precautions, they could saw into vinyl-asbestos tile or bump against asbestos-covered pipes. Knowledgeable workers will generally lay new asbestos-free tile over tile that contains asbestos.
- You're buying housing materials. Some products containing asbestos remain on the shelves of stores, so read labels and ask.

Inspectors who check for asbestos may charge $40 to $80 an hour. The cost of removing asbestos depends on how much there is and how accessible it is, but expect to pay over $1,000—sometimes way over.

---

**CAUTION:** Be sure that any asbestos-removing service you hire isn't a fly-by-night outfit—that it has proper credentials and a permanent office. You can find asbestos-abatement firms in the Yellow Pages. Better yet, get names from your state health and environmental agencies.

---

It's probably wiser to take care of any asbestos problems now, rather than waiting until an interested buyer inquires or hires an inspector of his or her own, or is simply scared off. Some buyers will walk through a house, see the asbestos wrappings over the pipes or around the furnace—and quietly decide to buy another house that has no asbestos at all. And they won't say a word to you about the reason that was, to them, the clincher.


## RADON

An odorless, colorless gas, radon is formed from the decay of uranium. People exposed to high indoor concentrations over long periods of time have a greater than normal risk of developing lung cancer.

Radon can permeate soil, and the gas can enter buildings through openings in the foundation, through cracks in concrete floors and walls, and through floor drains, sump pumps, and hollow-block walls. It can also be drawn into a house where there is low air pressure, which may be caused by kitchen or attic exhaust fans, a warm indoor temperature, furnaces, clothes dryers, or other appliances that use indoor air. In a house with a private well, radon can enter through faucets, shower heads, and dishwashers and clothes washers.

Concentrations of radon in a building can vary tremendously from day to day and from season to season. Yet you won't notice. The gas does not irritate eyes, skin, or nose, and it has no immediate effect on breathing. Radon enters the body only through the lungs, and it can take 5 to 50 years before a health problem develops.

Radon levels are generally highest in the basement or ground level of a house. Measuring the levels over different seasons, and in different areas of a home, can you give a good idea of what the average levels in that home are. Two of the most common devices to detect radon are the charcoal canister and the alpha-track detector. For the canister, you need a test period of three to seven days; for the alpha-track detector, one to three months. Nowadays, you can buy radon detectors cheaply in most drug or hardware stores.

A typical American house has about one picocurie of radon gas per liter (pCi/L) and about 0.005 working levels (WL) of radon decay products. If the average annual radon concentrations in your home exceed 4 pCi/L or 0.02 WL, you should call an expert and consider taking steps to reduce the levels. If the concentrations are greater than about 200 pCi/L or about 1 WL in a living area, you have an extremely serious problem.

If the test does show a high level of radon, get in touch with your state's department of environmental protection, which may conduct further tests, free of charge to you.

The amount of danger that radon presents depends on

- the average concentration of radon in the building,
- the number of years a person has lived in the building, and
- the amount of time the person spends at home each day.

To combat a radon problem, several steps can be taken aimed at (1) preventing radon from entering your house, and (2) getting rid of radon that is already there.

These steps may include sealing cracks and openings, covering exposed earth, and improving natural indoor ventilation.

Here are some other methods:

- Forced ventilation. Fans and such exchange the radon-contaminated air with outdoor air.
- Heat-recovery ventilation. A heat exchanger uses the hot or cold air being ventilated to heat or cool the radon-free outdoor air that comes in.
- Block-wall ventilation. A solid horizontal duct is sealed in place over the horizontal wall-floor joints around the sides of the entire basement. The radon-contaminated air is then mechanically vented to the outside.
- Pressurization. The basement is sealed off from the rest of the house, and air from the upper floors is delivered to the basement, increasing the gas pressure there.
- Sub-slab suction. Pipes are installed vertically into the foundation, to draw the radon-contaminated air from below the building to the outside.

Real estate contracts now commonly contain contingency clauses with regard to radon, stipulating that the seller will reduce the radon concentration to an acceptable level before the closing, or calling for a certain amount of money to be set aside. In some states, certain banks offer home-improvement loans, from $1,000 to $15,000, to remedy radon problems, at a low interest rate such as perhaps 7 percent.

Correcting a radon problem may cost from a few hundred to two thousand dollars. As with asbestos, a homeowner is usually better off confronting a radon problem sooner rather than later.

## CHAPTER SUMMARY

Wise homeowners will pay to have their houses inspected before buyers come. That way, they can head off problems that otherwise could arise to spoil a nearly closed deal. Asbestos and radon may pose special problems, and homeowners are advised to deal with them as early as possible.

# 11 MAKING REPAIRS TO TURN YOUR HOUSE INTO A CREAMPUFF

## WHAT IS A CREAMPUFF?

A creampuff is a well priced, clean, spiffy, beautifully maintained house in a fine area. Every buyer's dream house is a creampuff. And so is every agent's dream house—because creampuffs sell fast.

After a day or many days of driving around with agents from one overpriced, nondescript house to another, when buyers are feeling jaded and disillusioned, a creampuff makes an entrance the way Michelle Pfeiffer would in a high-school musical. But a creampuff doesn't bring the house down; it takes a house off the market.

To sell your house quickly, try to turn it into a creampuff. As one knowledgeable real estate authority bluntly put it, "People will *kill* for creampuffs."

Other chapters discuss how to set a good price on a house, and how to gussy it up through decorating. Here, we'll talk about making sure it's in top-notch working order.

## WHY HOUSES HAVE GONE TO POT

If you haven't been maintaining your house properly, welcome to the club. House inspectors report that, all across America, our castles are becoming more and more like shacks. The two chief reasons are

1. Both members of the family are working (that's how they were able to buy a house in the first place), and when they come home

at night, they are too tired, or too busy with children or with office work they've taken home, to inspect their houses properly and take remedial steps.

One house inspector says the typical homeowner these days wouldn't notice a roof leak until the water had penetrated the floor of the attic into the bedroom areas. It may be better for parents spend quality time with their children than to spend it fussing over the house, but at least once every month they should give their house the once-over, looking for water spots, corrosion, rust, discoloration, anything out of the ordinary.

2. A good repairperson is hard to find. These days, repairpeople prefer big, expensive jobs to small, inexpensive ones, such as fixing faucet leaks, aligning doors, etc. They may give you an estimate and then never contact you again. Have you ever tried to get a house painter to paint only the side of your house that is exposed to the sun and is peeling?

---

**TIP:** To find a good repairperson, ask friends and neighbors for recommendations. When you hire the repairperson, mention the names of the people who recommended him or her. Someone with a good reputation will want to keep that reputation untarnished and do a good job for you. Test your repairperson, painter, or wallpaperer on a few small jobs first. Some painters, for example, are accustomed to painting inexpensive houses, and may not scrape off old, peeling paint first. Make sure that the repairperson does the kind of job suitable for your house.

---

## WHAT'S WRONG WITH HOUSES FOR SALE

HouseMaster of America, in Bound Brook, New Jersey, the largest home-inspection service in the country, reports on the frequency of common flaws in resale houses according to their ages. Its findings are summarized in the following table.

### Frequency of Problems by Age of House

| Problem | 1–12 years | 13–29 years | 30+ years |
|---|---|---|---|
| Water leaks in basement | 15.4% | 25.5% | 32.8% |
| Electrical (need to upgrade service, need new outlets) | 7.3 | 12.3 | 18.9 |
| Plumbing (shower pan, water heater) | 6.7 | 20.1 | 25.1 |
| Heating | 8.0 | 23.6 | 31.0 |
| Cooling | 6.8 | 13.2 | 11.3 |
| Needs roof or wall insulation | 3.2 | 18.7 | 34.1 |
| Foundation | 5.1 | 4.2 | 8.0 |
| Roofing | 3.9 | 20.0 | 27.0 |
| Mixed plumbing (replace pipes) | 0.0 | 5.2 | 44.2 |

Here's how long you can expect the various systems in a house to last, and what they cost to replace, according to a national survey by HouseMaster of America:

### Life Span and Replacement Costs of House Parts

| System | Number of Years | Average Cost to Replace |
|---|---|---|
| Roof: | | |
|   Wood shingles | 15–25 | $2,000–3,000 |
|   Asphalt shingles | 15–20 | 1,500–2,200 |
|   Cedar shakes | 20–40 | 3,000–5,000 |
|   Gutters/downspouts | 20–30 | 600–900 |
| Heating systems: | | |
|   Hot air furnace | 15–20 | 1,500–1,800 |
|   Hot water boiler | 20–25 | 2,000–2,500 |
|   Water heater | 7–12 | 350–500 |
|   Compressor | 6–10 | 800–1,000 |
|   Compressor/condenser | 10–20 | 1,500–2,000 |
| Other: | | |
|   Kitchen appliances | 8–15 | 500–1,000 |

Finally, from HouseMaster of America, here are the "Most Annoying" problems in houses for sale, based on more than 100,000 inspections:

- Loose toilet bowls
- A continually running toilet

- Poorly calibrated thermostats
- Water in the basement or lower level of a house
- Low water pressure
- Roof leaks—discovering where they start
- Discovering cause of stains on ceilings below bathrooms
- Inadequate electrical power
- Insufficient electrical wall outlets
- Windows that don't open and close properly
- Doors that can't close easily because of warping
- Kitchen appliances that don't work properly
- Repeated clogging of gutters
- Squeaky or bouncy floors and stairs
- Carpenter ants

## TROUBLESHOOTING ADVICE

Here's a troubleshooting guide from HouseMaster of America, with repair or replacement costs, of what to look for when you inspect your house for problems and flaws (and what buyers will look for):

**Structural:** Look for horizontal and vertical cracks in foundation walls, cracks in house slabs, missing supports, bowing walls. It can cost from $25 to patch a crack, $3,000 or more to resupport a wall.

**Roofing:** Faulty flashing is a common cause of leaks. Look for excessive roof wear, missing or broken shingles or slates. A bow in the roof may indicate a framing flaw, especially if there are more than two layers of roofing. To seal flashing can cost about $50. Expect to pay $3,500 for a new wood-shingle roof, or $1,500 to $2,200 for asphalt roofing. Also check gutters and downspouts. Malfunctioning gutters and stopped-up downspouts can cause water damage inside the house.

**Heating and Cooling:** Check operation and cooling/heating effect, room by room. A new water boiler can cost $2,000 to $2,500; a new warm-air furnace, $1,500 to $1,800; a new air-conditioning compressor, $800 to $1,000.

**Plumbing:** Look for older galvanized/brass pipes (usually dull silver-bronze in color), poor water pressure, and sluggish drains. They can signal the need for a major replumbing job. Stains or leaks in ceilings below bathrooms can mean a bad shower pan, or the need for retiling, new fixtures, or regrouting. Replumbing an entire house can cost thousands. A new shower pan costs $900 to $1,600.

**Electrical Service:** You should have 220-volt service and at least 100 amps, with a disconnect switch at the panel box. Circuits should be wired with copper—aluminum can be hazardous. Upgrading an electrical panel costs $600 to $1,000. Rewiring an entire house can cost thousands.

**Siding:** Look for signs of bowing, slipping, cracking, and poor installation or materials (swelling, rot, delamination, contact with soil). Re-siding an entire house can cost $8,000 to $20,000, depending on the house's size and materials used.

Other miscellaneous problems to look for:

- The flame in a hot-air furnace, and in your gas range, should be blue. If it's yellow, call in a repairperson.
- The pressure gauge next to a hot-water boiler shouldn't register over 20 pounds per square inch.
- The sight glass in a steam furnace should be half to three-quarters full, and the water should be clear.
- The pipes in a house should be free from discoloration or rust. You may have a special problem if the pipes are made of different metals—copper here, brass there, that may interact chemically.
- The shingles on the roof should be flat, not curling up. There should be no cracked or missing shingles.
- The rubber gaskets on your kitchen appliances should be tight, so that a refrigerator remains cold, and water doesn't escape from dishwashers and washing machines.
- Squeaky or bouncy floors and stairs
- Carpenter ants

## THE CASE AGAINST MAKING MAJOR IMPROVEMENTS

It can be a bad mistake to pay for expensive improvements before putting your house on the market. Only if your house has a deficiency that could prevent its being sold should you go the home-improvement route (for example, your kitchen is badly outdated, or your house is in the price range where buyers would normally expect a working fireplace). Home improvements almost never pay for themselves, and here are some of the reasons:

1. The buyer may not want your improvement, such as a swimming pool, or even a third bedroom. If only one person is buying, or a couple, or one adult with a child, the buyer might be especially

interested in a two-bedroom house that's being sold for significantly less than a three-bedroom.

2. It's more expensive to add something to a house than it would have cost to put it there in the beginning. When a three-bedroom house is constructed, for example, the third bedroom doesn't cost as much as adding a third bedroom to a two-bedroom house. To build an addition, you have to tear down walls, protect the rest of the house from damage, cart away debris—all extra expenses. If you add a third bedroom, and boost your sales price to cover the cost, your house will be significantly pricier than other houses originally constructed with three bedrooms.

3. A house originally built with three bedrooms isn't structurally or aesthetically the same as a house built with two bedrooms to which a third has been added on. The first house will be better proportioned, probably with more spacious rooms (it was constructed with a larger family in mind) and perhaps have more bathrooms.

---

**CAUTION:** Brokers may tell you that your house won't sell unless you have another bathroom installed, or that your house will command a far higher price if it has a new deck. While these brokers may be absolutely right, or honestly wrong, a few brokers who give this kind of advice will also recommend a contractor—and get a kickback from that contractor.

---

### What Typical Improvements Cost and Their Recovery Value

| Project | Average Cost | Resale Value |
| --- | --- | --- |
| Full bath | $9,130 | 95% |
| Fireplace | 3,513 | 95 |
| Minor kitchen | 7,266 | 78 |
| Major kitchen | 20,527 | 70 |
| Remodel bathroom | 6,370 | 68 |
| Skylight | 3,335 | 68 |
| New siding | 6,538 | 68 |
| Insulation | 1,535 | 64 |
| Room addition | 29,786 | 62 |
| Reroofing | 3,964 | 61 |
| Wood deck | 5,531 | 59 |
| Greenhouse | 15,290 | 55 |
| New windows, doors | 10,556 | 55 |
| Swimming pool | 20,692 | 38 |

Sources: National Association of the Remodeling Industry, Remodeling magazine, Qualified Remodeler magazine.

## CHAPTER SUMMARY

House buyers will kill for a creampuff—which means, among other things, a house in move-in condition. Besides making your house spic and span, be sure that everything is in working order, inside and outside. Hire a repairperson if you don't have the time, or expertise, to do it yourself. And learn how long the various house parts last—so you know which parts of your house are near the end of their life span.

But be dubious about springing for major improvements. Rarely do they pay for themselves. Only if an improvement will take care of a major deficiency—an outdated kitchen, for example—should you seriously consider it.

# Part Three

# PROMOTING YOUR HOUSE

# 12 THE FACT SHEET AS A SELLING TOOL

## A RÉSUMÉ FOR YOUR HOUSE

A few years ago, many real estate agents had never even heard of fact sheets. Now fact sheets are everywhere. Estimates are that two out of every three agents prepare fact sheets for houses they list.

A fact sheet is sort of a résumé for a house. It lists all of the basics: acreage, sizes of rooms, taxes, utility costs, amenities. But it also describes everything unusually desirable, from a working fireplace to the imported marble tile in the bathroom.

Naturally, expensive houses call for lavish fact sheets, inexpensive houses for modest fact sheets. For a $500,000 house, you would think of attaching a color photograph to your fact sheet; for a $75,000 house, a photocopy of a Polaroid should do. By the same token, a mansion may call for several pages, a modest abode for one page.

Place your stack of fact sheets next to your front door. You'll pass them out to all visitors, including real estate agents from firms other than the one you are listed with (assuming you're not selling your house by yourself). They are especially useful for open houses: Even if a visitor doesn't find your house suitable, he or she may pass along your fact sheet to someone else.

Blanket the local area with your fact sheets. Put them on supermarket bulletin boards; mail them to your neighbors; pass them around where you work. (See Chapter 14.)

## WHY FACT SHEETS HELP

Oddly enough, some agents don't use fact sheets. It's an extra expense, after all, that they must pick up. And they may be prejudiced against fact sheets because they associate them with open houses—and many agents, for good reason, are antagonistic toward open houses. (Buyers may drive from one open house to another, and, because they haven't narrowed down their choices to what they want and what they can afford, they waste everyone's time, including their own.)

Yet these days fact sheets are indispensable. Here are three reasons:

1.  They etch your house into the memory of buyers. Today, with so many houses available, buyers may inspect 20 or 25 houses instead of the usual 5 or 10. All those houses can wind up becoming just a blur in their minds. As one broker has said, a confused buyer may put Mrs. Jones's living room into Mr. Brown's house. If they are transferees, they may be in town house-hunting for only a few days and can't even go back for a second look.

But a fact sheet can bring your house back into focus. The photograph (or drawing) will remind buyers of your house's appearance, and all the other special features will be right there in the text.

Distinguishing your house from the rest of the pack, remember, is one of your chief goals. When consumers have a cornucopia of choices, little things mean a lot. House A ($100,000) may have four bedrooms, three baths, modern appliances, a swimming pool, and high taxes, and be close to a school with only a so-so reputation; House B ($90,000) may have three bedrooms, two baths, older appliances, and low taxes, and be in the district of another so-so school; House C ($85,000) may have two bedrooms, two baths, new appliances, no fireplace, and low taxes, and be in the district of the best school.

When choices are difficult, buyers tend to pick for emotional or trivial reasons, such as a house's having an automatic garage-door opener, or built-in bookcases, or a marginally lower sales price. Your fact sheet marshals together all your selling points—the reasons your house should be chosen over houses that are keen competitors.

2.  Fact sheets answer most of a buyer's questions. What are the yearly heating costs? What goes with the house, and what stays? How old are the appliances? How large are the closets?

Suppose the buyers are trying to decide between your house, for which they have a fact sheet, and another one, which doesn't have a fact sheet. They know that your closets are sizable, that your taxes are low, that your heating bills are low, but that your house doesn't have a working fireplace. They know that a competing house also has big closets and low taxes, along with a working fireplace. But they can't remember whether its heating bills were high, whether the appliances were new, or how many bathrooms it had. They will, more than likely, choose to bid on the house they know more about.

3. Fact sheets mean that owners have no good reason to accompany buyers on house tours. Many agents hate to have the owners trail along when they show a buyer a house. It's not just that the owners may say the wrong thing (for example, that the neighborhood is filled with little children, when the buyers have no children and want a quiet neighborhood). It's not just that the owners may scowl if the buyers open closets, flush toilets, or peek under rugs.

It's also because, with the owners around, buyers aren't free to make frank comments, such as, "That wallpaper is a scream." (An agent could then respond, "Wouldn't the room look so much better with tasteful wallpaper?") And, with the owners right there, the buyers may be reluctant to beat a hasty retreat if they quickly decide a house isn't right for them.

If the buyers have a fact sheet to study, an agent can tell the sellers, "Don't bother coming with us—everything is in the fact sheet."

## HOW TO WRITE A FACT SHEET

Visit several local brokerage offices, and pick up a sampling of fact sheets that may be available. Then, whether or not you are using a broker, you'll know what the competition is up to.

If you're using a broker, the two of you will collaborate on a fact sheet. If your agent protests against an expensive fact sheet (on heavy paper, with a color photo), and you think it's a good idea, offer to pay the extra cost yourself. Some agents circulate wretchedly unimpressive fact sheets—with photocopies of Polaroids, typewritten text, and minimal details. If that's what your agent has in mind, object. You want a fact sheet that is both impressive and suitable to your house's price range.

The actual fact sheets presented at the end of this chapter are good models to follow. But bear in mind these pointers:

- Don't overdo it.
  Don't mention the brand of paint used in the living room. Don't include any information that should be obvious—that the noisy old washing machine in the basement goes with the house, for example. Try to keep the fact sheet short and concise,

at the same time that you include every important detail that might sell your house.

- Be imaginative.

  If your house doesn't photograph well, consider using a sketch—made by an artist friend, ideally. If your house is hard to find, provide directions—through the more impressive streets in the area. If you have the blueprint for the house, provide the house's layout.

- Tour your house to remind yourself of its virtues.

  Mention the newness of appliances, and if you had a new roof installed, give its age. Provide brand names if they're impressive (Andersen windows, Kohler plumbing fixtures). Consider including whatever is desirable that goes with the house—like the fireplace equipment or the living-room chandelier. If you're offering a deal on the buyer's mortgage, say so.

- Don't confine the fact sheet to the house itself.

  Mention the school district the house is in. Tell how close public transportation is, or highways. If your house might attract people from outside the community, describe the area's advantages. ("A well-to-do, safe, quiet suburb of Middletown, where 95 percent of high school students go on to college. Supermarket in walking distance.")

- Give the price—if it's low.

  But if your price isn't clearly a bargain, think twice about giving the figure. You soon may have to cross out that price and put a new one in. And some buyers may be startled if they see a huge price drop—from $200,000 to $150,000, for example. You can just write in the current price on top.

- Organize your fact sheet.

  Describe the residence floor by floor, or area by area. That way, buyers can easily double-check an item (is there a bath connected to the master bedroom?) and won't see just a jumble of information.

  You might start out with a short, general description of the house; then provide the nuts and bolts (house style, acreage, taxes, heating costs, etc.); then give room-by-room details, starting with the main floor. You might conclude with "Other highlights," where you mention points of pride that you weren't able to specify anywhere else, such as that the place was once featured in *House Beautiful*.

- Don't make any mistakes.

  For example, don't say that your basement is dry if you haven't lived there during a heavy rainstorm. When in doubt, leave it out. If there's a serious mistake, a buyer who's dissatisfied might have cause to go to court later on. So double-check everything for accuracy.


## CHAPTER SUMMARY

Because buyers see so many different houses these days, fact sheets have become almost indispensable. They remind buyers of your house's appearance and desirable special features, answer buyers' questions, and eliminate the need for you to be present when the house is shown. They are a house's résumé, and sellers should hand them out like campaign literature.

Fact sheets should match the house for sale. The more luxurious the house, the more lavish the fact sheet. For any fact sheet, a photograph or a drawing is appropriate; a one-page fact sheet will usually do, unless the house price is stratospheric.

A fact sheet that contains any errors—such as last year's instead of this year's tax bill—could spell trouble later on.

# FOR YOUR NOTEBOOK

## SAMPLE FACT SHEETS

# Sale by Owner
## Applewood West ~ Maple Grove School

° Five bedroom
° Two car garage
° 1/3 acre
° Mature shade trees
° Hutchinson home
° Excellent neighborhood
° Quiet street

1234 Home Street
Hometown, USA

Call John and Jane Doe
555-5555

° Brand new carpet
° Brand new remodeled bathrooms
° Fresh paint inside and out
° Engineered foundation
° Next to Denver West
° Quick access to I-70, 6th Avenue, C470
° 43 minutes to Loveland Ski Basin
° More than 50 trees and shrubs
° Spacious lawn
° Jogging distance to South Table Mountain Open Space
° Jogging distance to Clear Creek Open Space

PRICE:
$93,500.00

| | |
|---|---|
| **Main Floor:** 1218 sq. ft. | 3 Bedroom (13 x 10 master), 2 Baths, Living Room (17 x 14), Dining Room (13 x 9), Kitchen (13 x 9), Laundry Room, Fireplace |
| **Basement:** 1218 sq. ft. | FINISHED: 2 Bedroom, ½ Bath, Family Room (23 x 13), Bar, Fireplace<br>UNFINISHED: Work Room, Store Room |
| **Assumable Loan:** | 15 year loan, 11 years remaining, $80,000 balance, FHA 9.5%, qualify: yes |
| **Water & Sewer:** | Public |
| **Included:** | Dishwasher, Range, Refrigerator, Drapes |
| **Taxes:** | $1,068.10 per year |
| **Age:** | 1961 |
| **Zoning:** | Residential |

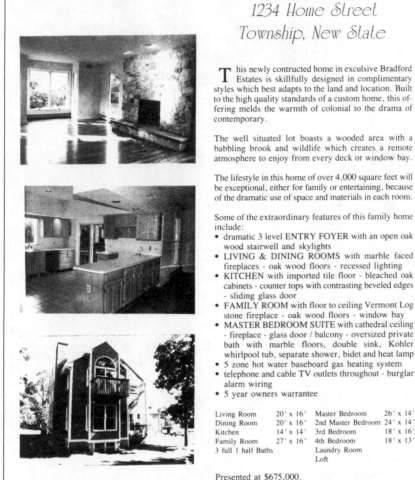

## 1234 Home Street
## Township, New State

T his newly contructed home in exculsive Bradford Estates is skillfully designed in complimentary styles which best adapts to the land and location. Built to the high quality standards of a custom home, this offering melds the warmth of colonial to the drama of contemporary.

The well situated lot boasts a wooded area with a babbling brook and wildlife which creates a remote atmosphere to enjoy from every deck or window bay.

The lifestyle in this home of over 4,000 square feet will be exceptional, either for family or entertaining, because of the dramatic use of space and materials in each room.

Some of the extraordinary features of this family home include:
- dramatic 3 level ENTRY FOYER with an open oak wood stairwell and skylights
- LIVING & DINING ROOMS with marble faced fireplaces - oak wood floors - recessed lighting
- KITCHEN with imported tile floor - bleached oak cabinets - counter tops with contrasting beveled edges - sliding glass door
- FAMILY ROOM with floor to ceiling Vermont Log stone fireplace - oak wood floors - window bay
- MASTER BEDROOM SUITE with cathedral ceiling - fireplace - glass door / balcony - oversized private bath with marble floors, double sink, Kohler whirlpool tub, separate shower, bidet and heat lamp
- 5 zone hot water baseboard gas heating system
- telephone and cable TV outlets throughout - burglar alarm wiring
- 5 year owners warrantee

| Living Room | 20' x 16' | Master Bedroom | 26' x 14' |
| Dining Room | 20' x 16' | 2nd Master Bedroom | 24' x 14' |
| Kitchen | 14' x 14' | 3rd Bedroom | 18' x 16' |
| Family Room | 27' x 16' | 4th Bedroom | 18' x 13' |
| 3 full 1 half Baths | | Laundry Room | |
| | | Loft | |

Presented at $675,000.

**ELEANOR LOEW**
CONVENT STATION/MORRIS TOWNSHIP OFFICE
218 MADISON AVENUE
MORRISTOWN, N.J. 07960
(off.) (201) 539-3435

SCHLOTT
REALTORS®
*The Extra-Effort People*

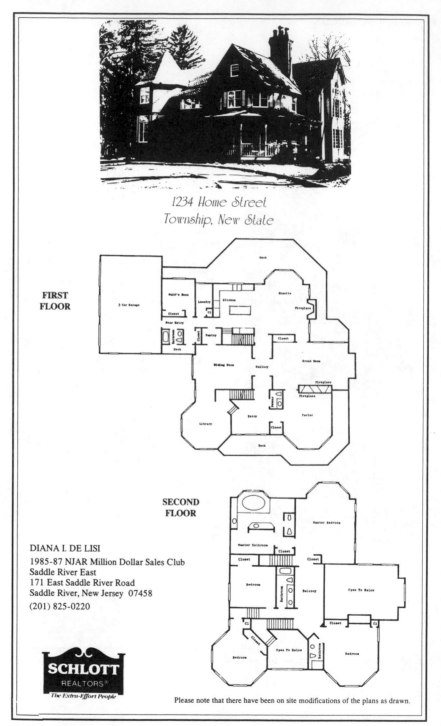

1234 Home Street
Township, New State

**FIRST FLOOR**

**SECOND FLOOR**

DIANA I. DE LISI

1985-87 NJAR Million Dollar Sales Club
Saddle River East
171 East Saddle River Road
Saddle River, New Jersey 07458

(201) 825-0220

**SCHLOTT**
REALTORS®
*The Extra-Effort People*

Please note that there have been on site modifications of the plans as drawn.

© Schlott Realtors. Reproduced by permission.

# 1234 Home Street
# Township, New State

Departing from the usual, this 6000 square foot VICTORIAL REVIVAL home is the ultimate blending of two eras. Combining the best of Victoriana with the finest of current luxury design and construction. Victorian features such as spindled wrap around front porch with sunbursts, stained glass windows, widow's peak, half round shakes, detailed roof design, and ornated brick flues with clay pots are featured.

## First Floor

**ENTRANCE HALL:** 15'6" X 13'
Two story space, marble floor, double leaded entry doors with leaded glass side and overhead panels

**GUEST POWDER ROOM:**
Well located, marble floor, luxury appointments

**FRONT PARLOUR:** 19'4" X 17' 1"
Entry alcove of marble and dimensional wood, bow shaped front wall, mantled fireplace, deep wood moldings and baseboard, 9' ceiling, six 6' windows, double walnut outlined diagonal select oak floor

**GREAT HALL:** 28' X 16'
Two story space featuring floor to ceiling dimensional wood fireplace with mantle, magnificent arched 2 story window wall, alcoved oak wet bar, 2 sets of double door to rear deck, one set double doors to front wrap around porch, open balcony

**FORMAL DINING ROOM:** 19'3" X 16'3"
Dimensional wood wainscot, deep moldings and baseboard, ceiling rosette for chandelier, 9' ceiling, double walnut outlined select oak floor, butler's pantry for dishes and silver with granite corian countertop, oak cabinetry

**LIBRARY:** 17' octagon
Triple banded wedge shape select oak floor, 11' ceiling, eight 6'3" windows with stained glass transoms, beveled glass french doors. Magnificent all wood room, strongly reminiscent of the elegance of a by-gone-era even to the concave ceiling rosette for a chandelier.

**KITCHEN:** 35' overall length separated into:
WORK AREA: 17' X 14' Custom oak cabinetry, featuring glass lights on many upper cabinets, corian center island with Thermador hoodless range, Double Thermador ovens, Sub-Zero refrigerator and freezer, recessed lighting, 9' ceiling, back staircase to bedroom level

DINING/SITTING AREA: 22'3" X 18'8"
Impressive floor to ceiling fieldstone fireplace with hearth, select oak floor throughout, picturesque window view of heavily treed rear property, transom rear door to wrap around deck

**FAMILY POWDER ROOM:**

**REAR HALLWAY:** Double family closets, door to rear deck

**MAID'S ROOM/BEDROOM:** 12' X 11'5"
Hardwood floor, double closet and PRIVATE BATH with shower over the tub

**LAUNDRY ROOM:** 8'7" X 5'6"

**ENTRY TO THREE CAR GARAGE WITH ELECTRIC DOOR OPENERS**

## Second Floor

**HALLWAY:** 20' X 9'6" Open to GREAT HALL, double closets, recessed lights

**MASTER BEDROOM:** 25' X 16'8" Wonderful tray ceiling sitting area, select oak floor, wonderful windows, magnificent wood trim

**MASTER BATH SUITE:** Beige travertine marble floor, tub platform and steam shower, Koehler jacuzzi, separate entry water closet and bidet, palladium window + double side windows, intricate vaulted ceiling, extensive wood trim

**BEDROOM:** 20' X 16'8" with PRIVATE BATH with stall shower

**BEDROOM:** 14'3" X 12'6"

**BEDROOM:** 17' octagon with wonderful tree-top views

**BATH:** Double vanity, water closet and tub are behind separate door

**ADDITIONAL AMENITIES:** 6 zone heating, 3 zone air, burglar alarm, 300 amp. underground service, BUDD CENTRAL vacuum, belgium block curbed circular drive, sprinkler system

Subject to errors and omissions                    All room sizes are approximate

# 13 WRITING BRISK, VIVID ADVERTISEMENTS

## WHY ADVERTISE YOURSELF?

Your broker advertises your house, and you're paying the broker. So why should you spend more money doing your own advertising? To boost your chances of selling the place, that's why—to increase the odds that buyers will want to inspect your house rather than the competition's.

If your house is advertised only as much as all other houses in the area, it may not stand out. But if you occasionally buy an ad on your own, some buyers will mention your house in particular to the broker: They'll notice it because it's had more exposure in the newspaper. (Of course, if you're selling on your own, you'll expect to write, and pay for, your own ads.)

## WHOSE PHONE NUMBER?

In the ad, you can list either your own phone number or your broker's number. Arguments for listing your own number are (1) you'll get feedback on how well your ad is drawing; (2) you'll get phone calls from buyers who think you're selling by yourself, and who may jump to the conclusion that your price, without a broker's commission, will be especially reasonable; and (3) unlike a broker, if you get the phone calls, you won't try to talk the callers into looking at another house if your own doesn't seem to be exactly what they want.

But tell the callers that you're using a broker, and that the broker's agent will make the arrangements for them to view the house. You'll owe the broker a commission in any case, so have the agent do the work of making sure the buyers can afford your house, along with escorting them through your house. As a compromise, run your phone number, then the number of your broker.

If you do run ads with your own phone number, make sure you have an answering machine, so you won't miss inquiries when you're out of the house. Better yet, try to be home on the day your ad appears.

## WHERE, HOW MUCH, AND WHEN TO ADVERTISE

Don't go wild. Set a total budget—something like 0.25 percent of the asking price ($250 for a $100,000 house)—and stick to it. You might, for example, advertise only on days when your own broker isn't.

Follow the crowd. If houses in your area are mostly advertised in The Record of Hackensack, New Jersey, that's where you should advertise—because that's where most buyers will look.

The same goes for days of the week. Fridays, Saturdays, and Sundays are the days when most housing ads appear, and generally that's when you should advertise. You may also get a discount for advertising on all three days. Check with your local papers.

You might also consider going against the trend once in a while. Advertise in a small weekly newspaper occasionally, or in a big newspaper that's not the biggest in your area, just to try to reach all possible buyers.

If you're using an agent, ask his or her advice about when and where to advertise.

## WHAT SHOULD THE AD SAY?

Naturally, the higher your house is priced, the larger the ad you should write, and vice versa. When in doubt, go for an extra line or two. You can say much more in an eight-line ad than a five-line ad—and you'll cream the competition that's buying five-line ads.

Run larger ads when your house first goes on the market, because the pool of potential buyers should be greatest then. Also buy larger ads during the high season in your area—typically spring and early summer.

Change your ad. Don't run the same one all the time, or buyers will become wary—and weary. They'll be tired of seeing your ad, and they may conclude that, if no one else seems to want your house, why should they want it? Besides, with different ads, you can focus on different selling points. One ad might say how close the house is to public transportation; another might emphasize that you'll help buyers with a mortgage; a third could push the house's suitability for a single parent and child.

Before you start, check the other ads—especially those from big brokerage firms, which should have the most expertise in writing them. Another reason is that buyers in different areas of the country are interested in different things. In many areas, for example, buyers are eager to know a house's square footage; in other areas, you never see that figure in an ad. Also, the words used in ads may have different meanings in different parts of the country.

Circle ads that appeal to you, and try to decide what's attractive about them. Chances are that the ads will use lively, colorful language—words like "roomy," "sparkling," "sunny," "immaculate," "elegant." They'll have pleasant surprises in them—"3 fireplaces," "Olympic pool," "3-car garage." They'll be fairly comprehensive, describing not only the house but the grounds.

If you're using an agent, ask him or her to help you write the ad, or critique it for you. See if your newspaper has a free leaflet on how to write house-for-sale ads.

---

**CAUTION:** Beware of certain words that have acquired special associations. "Cozy" indicates small, for example. A "starter home" is also small, with no more than two bedrooms. A "great room" is a combination living room and dining room.

---

Be specific, not vague. Instead of "large yard," say "full acre"; instead of "bright," mention "skylights" or "floor/ceiling windows"; instead of "your dream house becomes reality," use "garage, EIK, frplc, 4 bdrms."

Ads usually begin with the name of the community and then provide the basics: the house type (colonial, bi-level, Cape Cod, whatever), number of bedrooms, whether there's an eat-in-kitchen (EIK), a separate dining room, a fireplace. Naturally, they include the price and one or more telephone numbers, and, if you're sure about it, whether you can help with financing.

When you write the ad, have your fact sheet in front of you, to help you recall all of your house's key selling points. If yours is a small, inexpensive house, you can play up whatever apartment dwellers would love—even an attached garage, or a family room. Higher-priced houses should mention important extras—like a sauna, exercise room, greenhouse, three-car garage.

The headline should, ideally, be arresting. "JUST LISTED" is powerful. So is "PRICE REDUCED." "FOR SALE BY OWNER" will attract bargain-hunters, along with buyers who don't like dealing with agents. Don't be timid about swiping someone else's clever headline. But don't be timid about creating your own, such as, "WE HATE TO LEAVE THIS CREAMPUFF," or "$100,000—AND WORTH MUCH MORE."

Keep in mind that you want your ad not only to attract the largest number of buyers but also to ward off buyers who wouldn't be interested. If your house has only two bedrooms, say so. Otherwise, you may get a host of callers who want three or more bedrooms. On the other hand, don't write "Needs work" or "Handyman's special" or "Needs TLC" unless the place is on the verge of being condemned. The low price will indicate that the house needs work.

Don't try to tell everything about a house in an ad—that could be expensive. State the most important features, and for the rest, "Many extras" should do.

The conventional wisdom is that you shouldn't say "Asking $100,000," which indicates that you'll lower the price drastically. Or even "$100,000 firm," because some buyers might believe it— even if you'll gladly accept $98,000.

Don't use the word "desperate" unless you're looking for bargain-hunters. Buying a house should be a happy occasion, and buyers may be turned off by a sad situation.


## SOME SAMPLE ADS

Here is an assortment of ads that ran recently in various newspapers (except the last, which appeared in a magazine), plus our critiques:

    **Ad #1:**            THE BEST BUY EVER!
*We would stop reading right there.*

    **Ad #2:**        A MODERN COUNTRY SQUIRE
would delight in this Charming 1840s Colonial on shy 5 acres in Alpine area. Lgr bright rms, 5 fpls, 4 bdrms, 2½ baths, wonderful country kitch/keeping room, 2 car gar, inground Pool! Tennis Court! Modernized Guest Cottage! Live surrounded by echoes of a gentler time!                                    $750,000
*Too many Capital Letters and too many exclamation points! But effective.*

**Ad #3:**          $250,000 COLONIAL.

Ultimate commuter's home, walk to RR, ultra mint decor, new EIK, deck. Lge LR & DR, 2 bdrms, 1½ baths.

*Says a lot in four lines.*

**Ad #4:**          INCOMPARABLE!

Distinctive, spacious & immaculate! Very pvt setting, short walk to schls, shops & RR. 10 stunning rms w/huge deck & flagstn terr. Must see!                                                                $875,000

*Doesn't sound "incomparable." And "Distinctive, spacious & immaculate" are three vague words in a row.*

**Ad #4:**          $2,500,000 THE ULTIMATE . . .

in custom living, Spectacular estate w/dramatic Contemp interior. Fpls in Lr & fam rm, gourmet EIK, mstr suite w/2 dres'g rms & Jacuzzi bth. 2 lanscpd acres w/tennis ct.          HTD POOL/SPA!

*Sounds at least "comparable" to the previous ad.*

**Ad #5:**          ARCHITECTURAL DIGEST Contemp

on 2 acres in Middletown, 12 large rms, spectacular kitchen w/ greenhouse. master suite. Loft, rec rm w/dance floor, 50 × 46 heated pool w/Jacuzzi, waterfall. Very special          $1,699,000

*It's hard to go wrong writing about such a house. But what about fireplaces?*

**Ad #6:**          ELEGANT CONTEMPORARY

Dramatic foyer, soaring skylit ceils, center-aisle gourmet kitch, lavish master suite, stone fireplace & all amenities + heated IGP. 1 acre
                                                                     $395,000

*Compared to the previous two, sounds like a bargain.*

**Ad #7:**          PASSAIC PARK AREA

Charming fieldstone Colonial nestled on 175 ft. deep prop. w/brick walkways & patio. Mod. int. blends w/Old World Charm of fieldstone frplc. Kitch w/ceramic tile, 3BRs + 2nd flr solarium. Beautifully maintained & appealing. By Owner.          $229,500

*A little too much purple prose, but distinctive. (The ad appeared a few years ago, hence the low price.)*

**Ad #8:**          SUN VALLEY

A mansion on a mountain, this 36-room house stands on an equal number of acres, with 360-degree views of the desert and valleys. With 14 bedrooms and 15 baths, the 31,000-square-foot house glories in such luxuries as inlaid walnut walls and doors, terrazzo flooring, and eight marble fireplaces imported from Portugal and Italy. There are decks on all three levels, and its spaces include a study and a library, as well as a formal dining room. To delight the winter sports lover, there's an indoor ice-skating rink. There is also an Olympic-sized swimming pool . . .                                                    $11,000,000

*When you're selling a house for $11 million, you don't stoop to abbreviations.*


## CHAPTER SUMMARY

Raise your chances of selling your house quickly by running your own ads, incorporating advice from your agent. Change your ads, so they emphasize different features for different buyers, and so readers don't get tired of seeing the same ad.

Use your fact sheet to remind yourself of your house's key features. Be specific, not vague. Use vivid language. When in doubt, go for extra lines. Filter out buyers who wouldn't be interested by being frank; don't skip over the fact that a house has only two bedrooms, for example.

# 14 SPREADING THE WORD

## GET THE WORD OUT

Two couples were playing tennis one sunny day. One of the men happened to say that he and his wife were looking for a house to buy. "Oh, there's a house for sale near us," said the other man's wife. After the game, they all drove off to see it. The first couple bought the house on the spot.

Yes, that's how houses get sold sometimes—through word of mouth.

It's not enough to put a reasonable price tag on your house and make sure everything is clean and ship-shape. To sell your house, you must get the word out. And in a market like today's, relying on your real estate broker and the newspaper ads may not be enough.

Newspaper ads will reach people committed, or almost committed, to buying a house. But what about people who are just toying with the idea—renters or mover-uppers? People who check the advertisements only occasionally? They could use a reminder.

You've already created one of the best promotional tools there is—the fact sheet; now all you have to do is get it around. Spreading the good word to a larger percentage of buyers may give your house an extra edge.

## THE GOOD NEIGHBOR POLICY

Don't be shy about letting people know that your house is for sale. It's nothing to be ashamed of. If you were selling your car, would you feel embarrassed asking everyone in your neighborhood, office, or club whether they wanted to buy a car?

Tell people you bump into in your neighborhood and put fact sheets in the doorways of everyone living within a few blocks of your house (if it's not a violation of local ordinances). Neighbors are good carriers of this kind of word. First of all, they know the area—and like it. So they'll not only tell people who are looking for a house about yours; they'll also sing the praises of the area. Neighbors also may have relatives or close friends, perhaps grown children, who want to move nearby and be close to them.

Expand neighborhood to mean community, and tell anyone who is widely acquainted in your area. You might drop these people a letter, enclosing a fact sheet, and write, "Would you pass the enclosed along to anyone you know who is house hunting?"

Among the people to write to: .

- Your physician and your dentist. They may have as patients couples with expanding families who may be looking for a house.
- Your clergy or rabbi. A smart home buyer moving to an unfamiliar area will telephone local clergy or rabbis for advice—on which neighborhood to move to, which schools have the best reputations.
- Your lawyer.
- Your tax adviser.
- Your banker.
- Your librarian.
- Anyone you know in local politics. Politicians are careful to introduce themselves to newcomers in the area, who may be looking for a house.

### WHERE TO HUNT FOR DUCKS

Next, go duck hunting where the ducks are. Who wants to buy a house most? People who live in apartments, or in small condominiums or cooperatives. If they have children in school in the neighborhood, or they just like the community, they'll want a house there. So drive around the area. Look for rental units, and put your fact sheets in the lobby areas or on the windshield wipers of cars parked in their lots. (Check with the management office first. You don't want problems.)

Many an apartment dweller will tell you, "I don't know the first thing about buying a house. How much money do I need? How do I get a mortgage?" With a fact sheet and a phone number, these babes in the woods will finally find a place to get help: from an eager home seller.

Where else can you find ducks? At companies that have lots of employees. Their personnel directors will be helping new arrivals get settled, which includes helping them find houses. Phone such companies, talk to their personnel directors, and ask if they would like copies of your fact sheet. Follow the same procedure with any schools in your area—colleges, universities, business schools, medical schools. Post fact sheets on their bulletin boards, too.

Put fact sheets on any other bulletin boards that seem appropriate—at your church or synagogue, at your country club, at your office or the offices of friends.

What other bases should you cover? Get out your personal phone book and spend an evening calling people you know—everyone from your former college roommate to your Aunt Millie.

"I'm selling my house," you might say. "Got any suggestions?" Murmur expressions of heartfelt gratitude when they advise you to bake cookies before buyers arrive. What you hope they'll say is, "Hey, I know a family that's moving to your area. I'll tell them about your place." Have some fact sheets in the mail to them the next day.

## THE CASE FOR HARD WORK

All this effort may seem like overkill—unnecessary. Putting fact sheets into the hands of strangers . . . calling personnel departments . . . contacting your entire universe of friends and acquaintances: Will it really do any good?

True, all your efforts may produce just three extra prospects who inspect your house. But if other house sellers have 50 buyers look through their houses, and you have 53, your chances of selling your house are 6 percent better than theirs. And maybe more, because those three buyers are less likely to be sellers-in-disguise, doing comparison shopping.

Selling a house in a slow market is a competition. Almost anything you can do to boost the odds in your favor, if only slightly, is probably worth the effort.

### CHAPTER SUMMARY

You can boost your chances of selling your house quickly, for a good price, if you spread the word that your house is for sale—to neighbors, to professional people in your area, to big companies or schools nearby, to apartment dwellers and other renters, to your entire circle of friends and acquaintances. Make liberal use of your fact sheets in this promotional campaign.

# 15 FIFTEEN DECORATING TIPS TO MAKE YOUR HOUSE MOVE

## MAKE IT CLEAN ENOUGH FOR FELIX UNGER

We needn't tell you to get your house squeaky clean. Hire a house-cleaner for five straight days if you have to, at least before the very first buyers arrive; go over every room, inch by inch, making a list of tasks to do. Make sure there are no leaky faucets, no corroded mailbox, no animal odors, no peeling paint, no loose wallpaper, no water marks on the basement walls. Even your house number should be new and bright.

You yourself may be an Oscar Madison, tolerant of a little mess and dirt, but the buyer who's most interested in your house may be a perfectionist like Felix Unger.

As indicated above (see Chapter 11), everything should be in apple-pie working order. You don't want buyers to go through your property and be thinking of edging the lawn, fixing cracked windows, oiling windows and doors, patching plaster cracks, sanding floors, and such. The buyer should view your house and be thinking: "Creampuff."

## LEAVE ROOM FOR BUYERS TO PROJECT

Beyond cleanliness and efficiency is decor. If selling your house is like a contest for the prettiest girl in the class, the winner will probably be the young lady who's dressed to the nines.

You may be familiar with the old advice: Make everything bland. Beige and off-white. Nothing should make the buyers feel territorial anxiety. Anything distinctively yours, such as your collection of Hummels or old magazines, has to be put in a drawer or somewhere out of sight lest the buyers feel that this property will never belong to *them*. As Bruce A. Percelay, who has pioneered in this area, has noted, "If the house is dominated by strong personal statements, the buyer is less likely to feel comfortable, and therefore less able to visualize the property as his or her own."

For the most part, it's true. The contest really *isn't* about choosing the prettiest girl in the class. As the economist John Maynard Keynes put it, the contest is over deciding whom *everyone else* will choose as the prettiest girl in the class. (Keynes was talking about how to choose stocks, and actually he went further: To win, you must decide who everyone else will think everyone else will think is the prettiest girl in the class. And on and on.)

The winner of the prettiest-girl-in-the-class contest won't be dressed funny, or even very distinctively. If she were, she would turn off a few voters—just enough to lose.

But there's a major exception. If your house is drab, predictable, tired, and dull, don't paint it off-white or beige. Liven it up a bit, even with distinctive wallpaper and paint. Not wild, but tasteful. The music critic Ernest Newman once dismissed the opera singer Nellie Melba with the words, "Her voice is uninterestingly perfect and perfectly uninteresting." If your house is just plain dull, you'll have to liven it up—even with some fancy wallpaper and paint colors—and forget about the advice that blandness is next to God-liness.

---

**CAUTION:** Just don't go too far—distinctiveness and good taste, not wild and way out. Nellie Melba, after all, despite her uninterestingly perfect voice, was one of the most popular opera singers who ever lived.

---

Here are 15 ideas you may not have thought of to brighten up a house that needs a little pizzaz. You can start anywhere you want, but we will start with the outside and then go inside.

Outside:

1. You never get a second chance, as the saying goes, to make a first impression. So give your house "curb appeal." Paint the front door—yes, again—and add a brass kickplate; install a fancy brass

knocker; put in a new bell attached to a glitzy set of chimes. Repaint your fence and oil your squeaky gate. Install a smashing new mailbox and outside light fixture. Spend a few hundred for a decorative and not just functional storm door. Buy a fancy new doormat.

2. You don't own the fire hydrant in front of your house, but if it's in dreadful shape, get permission from your fire department to paint it.

3. Instead of having the entire house repainted—if it's too costly, or not all that shabby—have just the shutters repainted.

4. Install window boxes with bright flowers. And make sure the windows themselves are perfectly clean. From inside, they may seem clean; visitors, looking from the outside, may not think so. And there's a big difference between perfectly clean and almost clean.

5. Reseal your driveway, even if it's not early fall, when you usually do it. If your car is a jalopy, park it down the street.

Inside:

6. Remember the old saying, "Buyers have no imagination." So *show* them how they could use your house. If your kitchen has room for a dining nook, but you don't use it that way, install a table and chairs in the corner. If your basement has room for exercise or other equipment, think of borrowing or renting a table-tennis table to put there.

If your attic has room for visitors to sleep, set up a cot there, along with an area where children could play on rainy or cold days. If your dining room is enormous, consider putting a desk in a corner. In the basement or garage, if you don't already have them there, set up a table and tools for a work area.

7. Most buyers want space. They're moving up from a smaller house, or getting out of a cramped apartment. So . . . give them space, or at least the impression of it. Rearrange your furniture to create more room. Ruthlessly clear out your attic, garage, basement, and other storage areas to show visitors that there is room where they themselves could stash things.

---

**TIP:** Hold a garage sale to remove extraneous furniture (most of us have much too much). Get rid of extra pots, pans, and plates from your kitchen; dispose of clothing you'll never wear again; put your summer, or winter, clothing in the attic—don't keep it in the guest closet.

---

Put storage boxes under your bed, and fill them with half the clothing in your closets; this will make the closets look bigger. Buy big, colorful plastic boxes to contain the overflow in your basement or attic.

---

**TIP:** Well-placed mirrors can help give the illusion of space, especially if they're opposite a window.

---

8.  What else do most buyers want? A sense that they're moving up in the world. Give them little luxuries. Spend a few hundred dollars in a fancy store to add classy touches to your house—brass or porcelain switchplates, the latest in hall-light fixtures, fashionable new knobs or hardware for the kitchen, a new fireplace screen, knock-'em-dead towel racks, oak toilet seats, light dimmers, ceiling fans, and so forth. If you have a friend known for his or her good taste, ask for suggestions.

9.  Deal with defects. You have a long, dark hallway? Put colorful pictures on the wall (*not* pictures of your relatives), and install new lighting. Is a room dark? Add a touch of glass—a decorative, framed mirror that captures whatever light is available. If outside shrubbery is blocking the light, trim the foliage back. Is a room small? Light colors, mirrors, and removing some of the furniture may help.

10.  Use flowers and plants—especially in rooms that need brightening. In fall and winter, use dried flowers. In spring and summer, if your yard is just a lawn, plant flowers and shrubs from your local nursery.

Don't go overboard and turn your house into a virtual nursery or florist shop, distracting buyers from the house itself. But colorful flowers can accent a portion of a room. If you want to direct attention to a built-in bookcase, for example, put a vase of fresh, cut flowers there, or even a small potted plant.

11.  If your furniture is old and beat-up, get rid of it—even if you only put it in the attic. While it's usually true that a lived-in house appeals to buyers more, there's a limit: when your furniture looks as if it came from the Salvation Army. See Chapter 18 for information on renting furniture.

12.  Ideally, every room in your house will have a highlight. If a room has none at all, consider a chandlier or track lights, an area rug, unusual curtains, a mirror—*something* to impress the visitor.

13. Brighten up your bathroom with a new shower curtain and new towels—and maybe even a phone. As mentioned, little luxuries like telephones in bathrooms (or an automatic garage-door opener) can make buyers feel they're really moving up in the world.

14. Make everything seem brighter. Put in brighter lightbulbs or new fluorescent tubes. Install new lights where they're needed, such as in garages. Open drapes and curtains before visitors come, or make sure your drapes and curtains aren't so heavy that they block off the light.

15. Appeal to the buyers' children. Put a swing on a tree in your backyard; if you have a playground set, check it over for safety and let buyers' children use it; if your children have a train set in the den, show your buyers' children how it works.

## CHAPTER SUMMARY

Your house should be squeaky clean, and everything should be in tip-top working order.

The general rule is: Appeal to the lowest common denominator. Your house shouldn't be so distinctive, or unusual, that it loses a few votes. Your hobbies or special interests shouldn't be so prominently on view that buyers cannot imagine your house ever becoming *their* house. But if your house has no sex appeal at all—it's dull and tired-looking—experiment with tasteful, somewhat unusual decorations, like fancy wallpaper.

Some general rules about decorating: Show buyers how they could use your rooms for various purposes; give buyers the feeling that your house has plenty of space; buy a few hundred dollars worth of little luxuries; try to mitigate defects—put track lighting in dark rooms, for example; and use flowers and plants to liven up the place.

# 16 SHOWING YOUR HOUSE

If you're dealing with a broker, you will rarely be called upon to show your house to prospective buyers yourself. In fact, most agents prefer that you leave everything to them. One good reason is that owners tend to make buyers uncomfortable.

But if you're selling your house yourself (see cautions about this in Chapter 9), without a broker, or if your agent is tied up and can't make an appointment, you'll be on your own, and you want to make a good impression.

Don't be a Uriah Heep, virtually begging buyers to make an offer, any offer. Does the prettiest girl in the class say yes if you telephone her at the last moment for a date? Not if she knows she's the prettiest girl in the class and doesn't have a complex.

On the other hand, don't be cool to the point of hostility. Don't treat any particular buyer shabbily just because the other people who came through your house were supercilious, critical, frosty, or whatever.

## LAST-MINUTE TOUCHES

Apply the traditional home remedies when buyers are coming. Open the windows to air the house out. Or, if you must, bake cookies or put a drop of vanilla onto a light bulb. (It's a well-known strategy by now, but it may at least bolster your confidence.) Check that all rooms are neat. Consider making a fire in winter, turning on the air conditioners (if they're quiet) on a warm day.

Put brighter bulbs in all your sockets. If a room is dark, open the blinds or draw the curtains before visitors come. Put your cats and dogs into a spare room. Store half your children's toys in the attic.

### BEFORE THE GRAND TOUR

The first step is to discuss strategies with your broker. Consider the following while deciding how the house should be shown.

Start showing off your house even before the buyers arrive. When they call and ask for directions, give them the scenic route—not a major highway. Have them get a good impression of where you live by driving past the best houses in the area, the most impressive public buildings and stores.

If you're showing your house yourself, your first step is to get acquainted with the buyers. Are they familiar with the area? Do they have a house now? Do they have children? Do they both work? Where do they work? What are their hobbies? Do they like to garden, or work with wood, or see plays? Are they handy with tools? By knowing something about the buyers, you'll know what to emphasize as you escort them through the premises. If they have young children, you can assume that they'll be interested in the school district your house is in, and the local school's reputation. If they like to garden, you might play up how much acreage you have. If they both commute, you would talk about public transportation. If they're from out of town, you should talk about the benefits of your house's location.

Ascertain whether the buyers have seen the fact sheet on your house. If they haven't, wait until after your tour to give them one. Reading and seeing are different, and one reinforces the other. And you don't want to wait five minutes while the buyers read the sheet.

### THE GRAND TOUR

Smart house shoppers may want to see the basement first. The basement alone may persuade them not to buy the house—because it's damp or smelly, or the furnace and hot-water heater are old, or they can see deteriorating asbestos wrapping on the pipes. Some homeowners neglect their basements, which is why their houses remain on the market while others get sold. A clean, dry, brightly lit basement with a modern furnace, plus plenty of storage room, can help enormously in selling a house.

Unless the buyers specify one, any convenient route will do. You might start with the first floor, so the buyers can exit without doing any stair-climbing if they're not interested.

Spend more time in impressive rooms than in humdrum rooms. One way to do this is to bring buyers all the way into the impressive rooms but stand in the doorway of dull rooms and just let them peer in. You'll know which rooms are to be shown off: You have something to say about them, or something to demonstrate in them.

If your grounds are impressive—there are lots of trees and gardens—take the buyers outside for a stroll. If your lot is the size of a postage stamp, let them have a brief look.

Don't talk too much, just to fill up pauses. If you catch yourself saying, "This is the living room," you're talking too much. But be sure to point out anything appealing that buyers might miss:

"You can see the lake, over there on the left."

"That's an electrostatic precipitator, to help keep the air clean."

"The fireplace works—here's the damper. And there's a clean-out pit in the bottom."

"The doorways are metal—they wear better than wood."

"We had extra outlets built into the den because of all the electronic equipment."

If the buyers are young and apparently unsophisticated, you might explain more than you would otherwise (novice home buyers can jump to ridiculous conclusions). You might tell them:

"We have double-insulated glass windows—we don't need storm windows."

"The attic is cold because we keep the vent open—to get rid of moisture from the rest of the house."

"The pipe opening in the basement floor is in case there's a flood from the washing machine—you can get rid of the water easily."

Take cues from your buyers. Does your pace seem too slow, too fast, for them? Do they just glance—or do they walk around and study?

One way to sound them out is to ask, after you've completed much of the tour, "Would you like to see the attic now, or the basement?" Ask it with a pleasant smile—don't give them the impression that you're really saying, "How about leaving already? I'm tired." But if they indicate they would rather not go upstairs or downstairs, let them leave—with a pleasant smile, a cheerful goodbye, and the offer of a fact sheet. (The fact sheet may persuade them to return—or they may turn it over to a friend who's also house shopping.) Occasionally the buyer you think is least promising submits a bid, so always end on a positive note.

Try to point out at least one highlight of every room you enter, even if it's "We just had this room painted." Better yet, show them how large the closets are, mention the model of the kitchen range, direct their attention to the fancy chandelier, or indicate how large a room is: "We've had a party for fifty people in this room."

Be active. Turn on lights, turn off lights, run water, open and close closets, open and close the refrigerator door, press buttons. You're not just showing that everything works; you're also trying to get and keep the buyer's attention.

## MAKING SMALL TALK

The tour is over. The buyers either are bored, interested, or you just don't know. Now is the time to hand over your fact sheet. But before you do, read it over quickly to see if there's anything you forgot to mention.

If the buyers read it over on the spot, you might say, "If you have any questions, I'll try to answer them." (See the next chapter on encouraging an offer.)

If the buyers prepare to leave, ask them if they'll sign your book of visitors' names. You might want to phone them later, to ask them what they really thought—and what you can do to improve your house's appeal. And you may want to call them later on if you've decided to lower your house price.

## OPEN HOUSES—ARE THEY IMPORTANT?

Many old-fashioned agents loathe open houses. Many buyers drive around town visiting any place with a sign—whether they want a colonial or a contemporary, whether they can afford the houses they visit or not. They wind up confused—and don't buy anything. In fact, many agents swear that open houses never result in house sales.

But they do, of course. And whether or not an open house will be the way you sell your house, it *could* be, so you'll have to join the flow. If certain buyers travel from open house to open house, you don't want your house remaining behind, like Cinderella.

There are two types of open houses: those for real estate agents and those for buyers.

**The open house for agents:** This is the time everyone selling real estate takes a gander at your house. You want as many agents as possible to drop by. Every agent may represent a score or more of possible buyers. So, let out all the stops. If your own agent suggests that you serve hot hors d'oeuvres and champagne, go along.

Ideally, the agents will be impressed not only with the cleanliness and sparkle of your house, with the fresh paint and attractive decoration, but with the reasonable price. You want to leave agents with one idea: Your house is a creampuff and will sell fast. So, if they want to earn half the commission, they should bring their most eager, most motivated buyers around as quickly as possible.

Make sure every agent who visits your house gets a few copies of your fact sheet.

**The open house for buyers:** With these, you need not have caviar and toast points. You can just serve coffee, tea, and cookies.

Open houses are usually scheduled for weekend mornings or afternoons. You or your broker should advertise in the papers; put up signs around town, too, checking with your police department first. If you can't hang signs on telephone poles or trees, drive your car to a well-traveled spot and post them on your car. Also ask friends for the use of their cars as temporary billboards.

Two mistakes to avoid in holding open houses:

1. Don't risk having hardly anyone show up. A buyer attending an open house, with no one else in attendance, might conclude that the house was not exactly the belle of the ball. So, invite friends, relatives, and neighbors to come over. Tell them to bring their friends. A bustling crowd at an open house makes buyers feel that a house may be special.

Just don't get so carried away by the crowd of guests that interested buyers can't get near you to ask question.

2. Try not to run an open house by yourself. If your agent is running the open house, let the agent manage the event and do whatever he or she tells you. If you're showing it on your own, you need at least one helper there to entertain visitors while you escort small groups around the house. If you try to do everything yourself, and too many people come at once, you'll have an impatient crowd in the living room while you're showing the basement to buyers who may just be lookie-lookies.

If you have no choice but to hold an open house by yourself, arrange with a neighbor to phone every 20 minutes—to make sure there are no problems.

## CHAPTER SUMMARY

Before you escort buyers through your house find out a little about them, so you know what will appeal to them—and what might not.

Don't point out the obvious; point out features they might miss. Try to say something interesting and informative about every single room. If they make a critical comment about anything, and it's fixable, your best reply is: Make me a reasonable offer, and I'll pay for having that problem taken care of. Try to obtain the buyers' names and phone numbers, and phone them afterwards to see if they will give you their frank evaluation of your house over the phone.

Open houses are unavoidable. You and your agent should make sure that visitors don't come to a house where gloom reigns because there are no other visitors. At the other end of the spectrum, recognize the problems you may face if you get a big crowd. The best solution, if you don't have an agent, is to have an associate helping you.

# 17 WHAT TO SAY TO BUYERS, RIGHT UP TO THE OFFER

## WHEN *NOT* TO TALK TO BUYERS, AND WHY

By and large, if you have a broker, you should say nothing to prospective buyers of your home. Let your real estate agent do all the talking. Here are the reasons:

1. You may say the wrong thing. The buyers may have told the agent that they're looking for a quiet neighborhood, with no children to run across their lawns or wake them up early in the morning or use the side of their house as a backboard. You may innocently tell the buyers, "This is a neighborhood full of friendly, welcoming children, and the elementary school is half a block away."

2. The buyers may say the wrong thing. They may unthinkingly murmur, "The wallpaper is a fright, and those photographs! I never saw such silly-looking people in my whole life." Better that the agent should respond to such remarks than you.

3. You may get carried away and exaggerate about your house—for example, say that the basement never leaks a drop, or that the house is "new" (meaning it was built 20 years ago), or that radon isn't a problem (without your having had the house checked). If the buyers wind up purchasing your house, you might wind up in court later on. Smart agents would be careful, and, if they say that the basement is dry, they would have a ready reply if the buyers ask, "Will you put that in writing?" (A ready reply: "The house inspector is the expert. If he or she reports that the basement isn't dry, the sellers say they will make amends.")

4. You may not pick up hints. The buyers might ask, "Would you take $ _____ for this house?" or "Do the appliances go with

the house?" Such statements are loud and clear signs that the buyers are serious. A smart agent would start nudging such buyers along—telling them that the price is slightly negotiable, and asking them what they can afford to pay. And, whether or not the appliances go with the house, certain other very desirable items do. A good agent would recognize that there's been a strong tug on his or her fishing line—and start reeling in.

5. Many buyers are uncomfortable dealing directly with sellers. Or, to put it another way, they're comfortable with the agent. On a tour of the house, if the seller isn't present, the buyers can openly discuss the house features with the agent and with each other. Buyers are also more comfortable negotiating through the agent. They can ask the agent, "How much will they come down?" Or: "If we offer $20,000 less than the offering price, will they get mad?"

---

**NOTE:** Most agents are supposed to be on the side of the sellers, and they may even be liable if they reveal that a seller's price is negotiable. But many of them sympathize with buyers, and will help them bargain.

---

If a buyer told a seller, whose asking price was $150,000, "We can afford $120,000," a deal might be off. If the buyer deals with an agent, the agent can tell them, "The sellers are angry—they just lowered their price by $15,000, and they're in no hurry to sell—so don't tick them off with a very low bid."

Not that the sellers should never say a peep. They should answer questions asked directly by the buyer or the agent. They should volunteer information that's important: If the buyer asks what the yearly taxes are, and the agent gives last year's numbers, the seller should provide up-to-date information.

If the agent has a fact sheet, there's usually no reason for the seller to deal directly with the buyer. The buyers will know almost everything the seller wants them to know. A capable agent will be the perfect intermediary.

## WHEN AND HOW TO TALK TO BUYERS

But sometimes the buyer and the seller must deal directly with each other. Perhaps the homeowner is selling the house without a broker. Or the buyers are last-minute drop-ins, and the agent is delayed or can't make it.

To begin with, sellers should not convey an air of desperation—even if their house has been on the market for two years without a nibble. An anxious, nervous seller may scare away buyers.

Sellers should try to be relaxed and confident, as if their house had just gone on the market and these were the first visitors. They should tell themselves that others didn't buy because the house was too expensive for them, or not ritzy enough; that the market has been reviving, and buyers will begin flocking around—whatever will boost their confidence.

On the other hand, don't get annoyed at pushy, rude buyers—the type who make snide comments ("Cripes, I'm getting tired of visiting houses where you can smell the cookies in the oven"), or who—without permission—open closets, run water, lift up rugs, and generally act as if they are examining a lawn mower at K-Mart rather than trespassing on a homeowner's privacy. With so much competition now, just putting down buyers who are a little rough around the edges, or giving them a cross look, is risky. Suppose they would have bought?

In dealing with buyers, don't lie—but don't necessarily tell the entire truth. If the buyers ask, "Why are you moving?" naturally, you wouldn't reply, "The house is too cold in winter and too hot in summer." In fact, you might not even want to say, "We've bought a house on the (East)(West) Coast," because the buyers might start driving a really hard bargain, knowing you're eager to move. Innocuous answers include: "The house is (too big, too small) for our family now." "We want to be closer to the (job, and to relatives)." "We want to move to a warmer climate."

Certainly don't disguise any defects the house has—whether it's a leaky roof, radon, asbestos, or high taxes. If you think that "Let the buyer beware" is still the law, be careful. If you don't level with the buyers about any defects, especially defects that they can't readily notice, such as radon (latent rather than patent), you can get into a peck of trouble.

In dealing with buyers, in fact, sellers should behave like the ideal salesperson.


## THE IDEAL SALESPERSON

When you show your house, you're a salesperson. Think of the ideal salesperson: someone pleasant and helpful. Not someone nervous, who hovers over you, who yaps away like a lunatic, who eyes you as if you're a notorious shoplifter just itching to sneak something into your pocket when nobody's watching.

Here's what you want for service when you go into a store: You browse around by yourself for a while, and then, just when you start feeling the need for help, a smiling salesperson comes up and says, "May I help you?" The salesperson gives you clear and concise answers to your questions. He or she volunteers important information—the suit you want doesn't come in navy blue, or you can get a discount by buying a particular brand of VCR.

If you mention that the VCR you're looking at is flawed because it doesn't automatically record 30 different programs, the salesperson may say, "You'll pay $2,000 extra for such a VCR. Would you want to spring for that much?" Or: "That's a limitation of this model, but it's very inexpensive, and it has a one-year warranty." Not: "What kind of nut would want to record 30 different programs?"

## BE POSITIVE

Keep in mind the example of the ideal salesperson when you talk to buyers. If the buyers aren't right for your house, you'll want to spare them as well as yourself wasted time. If they have objections, courteously counter them by mentioning advantages. Do they complain that there are no walk-in closets, or that there are too few bathrooms? Do they say the third bedroom is tiny? Do they point out that the plaster on the living room ceiling is cracked?

You can say, "That's true. We wish we had had bigger closets, and that's one reason we've priced the house so reasonably. Especially considering how large the master bedroom is." Or: "It's true the third bedroom is small, but it's for a baby." Or: "Plaster always gets small cracks."

If they say, "The taxes are high," you can say, "That's why we have such a fine school system—our teachers are well paid." (Just don't be clever, the way some sellers try to be: The buyers say, "There's no living room." The seller says, "One less room for you to clean.")

Gently remind buyers not only about the house's good points, but also the community's: "The supermarket's only two blocks away, and the elementary school's also within walking distance. There's a bus to downtown on the corner. This is a very convenient location."

If they point out true flaws or limitations of the house, say you can remedy them—if you get an offer. Here are a few possible exchanges:

Buyer: "The kitchen could use more cabinets."

You: "Another cabinet could be installed right over here, and if I had a good offer, I'd have the cabinet installed myself."

Buyer: "The wallpaper in the living room doesn't go with my rugs."

You: "For the right offer, I'd pay for new wallpaper."

Buyer: "The hot-water heater seems old."

You: "I've been thinking of having a new one put in. If someone wanted to buy the house, I'd take care of it before the sale."

If the response to that is, "Would you put it in writing?" your answer should be: "Of course. . . . Would you want to put a deposit on the house now?"


## ENCOURAGING AN OFFER

Be prepared at any time to start negotiating seriously. Be prepared both to receive an offer and, if your prospective buyers are hanging back, to encourage them. Remember our ideal salesperson? In a case when buyers are hesitating, but seem very interested in a product, the salesperson who is alert may volunteer, "Should I write up the order?"

House buyers tend to be nervous. They're investing tremendous amount of their worldly wealth—now and for years to come—and they're afraid of making the wrong decision. Wouldn't you be? Weren't you nervous when you bought the house you're selling now?

To help the situation along, try something like, "Do you like the house? Do you think it would suit your needs? As I've said, we have good schools, public transportation nearby, convenient shopping. It's a wonderful community. And you'll love the two ovens in the kitchen if you're really into cooking."

"Yes, it seems just right for us," they may respond. Or: "Nice house." Or: "We'd like to think about it." Or: "We think we may need a (bigger) (smaller) (less expensive) house." (Be as sweet as sugar to those people. They may be back.)

If the response is positive ("Nice house" will do), then you can ask the direct question: "Would you like to put down a deposit?"

**CAUTION:** Don't try to manipulate the buyers. Most buyers are fairly sophisticated—familiar with the old tricks sellers use—and they may be turned off.

**TIP:** It's better to ask, "Would you like to put down a deposit? than "Would you like to make an offer?" The latter is inviting the prospects to knock some money off your asking price.

At this point, you may want to add, "Should I leave you alone for a few minutes to discuss it? I can make some phone calls." You can also talk more about the house, reviewing what's on your fact sheet, while they use the time to think. Ask them if they would like a cup of coffee or tea. Ask them what they're looking for in a house.

Don't ask "Would you like to put down a deposit?" indiscriminately. You may frighten away some buyers by appearing overeager. But often there's a pregnant pause in the conversation. Husband is waiting for wife to say something; wife is waiting for husband; both may be waiting for the agent or seller to say something. That's the perfect time to put in, "Would you like to put down a deposit?"

Now you're at the point of negotiation. If the next question is, "Would you consider taking back a mortgage?" you should proceed to Chapter 19. If the offer is enough lower than your asking price for you to make a counteroffer, proceed to Chapter 23.

### ENDNOTE: OFFERING TAX TIPS AS A MARKETING TOOL

Why would you, the seller of a home, be concerned about the tax consequences of a sale to a prospective buyer? Generally you're not. But in a slow housing market, or any market for that matter, if you can suggest to a buyer that he or she can save money taking your house, why not? The objective isn't to make you a tax adviser but simply to add a few more ideas to your house-selling arsenal.

Buyers can disclose a lot of information about their financial conditions, housing wants and needs, and so forth. Stay alert for clues as to how the following suggestions may be used. If conversation permits, you might be able to suggest one or more of the following at the appropriate times:

**Does It Really Pay to Own a House?** It would seem that a serious home prospector would have already reached a decision that home ownership is preferable to renting. Unfortunately, there has been so much press given to the slow appreciation of house values, or even the decline in some areas, that your buyers may be having second thoughts even while they're peeking in your closets. Here are a few points to throw at a prospect who is still waffling:

- For many taxpayers, their home is their best tax shelter.
  The tax deductions for home-mortgage interest and property taxes can still generate an excellent benefit, although, admittedly, it isn't as excellent as it was before the 1986 Tax Act.
- Homeowners can deduct interest on home-equity loans of up to $100,000, which can still be a significant tax savings.

---

**EXAMPLE:** Ron Renter takes out a $100,000 loan to put his children through college and to pay for certain personal expenses. The interest rate on a loan unsecured by real estate is 14 percent. Ron's out-of-pocket cost is $14,000. Hilda Homeowner takes out a $100,000 home-equity loan for similar purposes. Hilda, because she can use her home as collateral for the loan, obtains a 13 percent rate. Her cost is $13,000 per year. But Hilda is able to deduct the $13,000 interest payments on her federal and state tax returns. Her marginal tax bracket is 30 percent, so her tax benefit is $3,900 [$13,000 × 30%]. Thus, Hilda's out of pocket cost is only $9,100 [$13,000 − $3,900].

---

Therefore, even if houses don't appreciate in value, because of tax benefits and building equity through mortgage principal payments depending on the assumptions, the homeowner may still be better off then the renter, who receives no benefit.

- Historically, real estate has appreciated considerably; just because appreciation may not be as dramatic as in recent years is no reason to discount the investment value of home ownership.
- A home shouldn't be viewed as merely an investment. It's a lifestyle decision. It's a decision to send your children to a specific school system and to have them grow up playing in a particular neighborhood. To look at a home as a mere investment is quite a mistake.

**Home-Office Deductions:** Your house may have an office area; one more bedroom than other homes the buyer is considering; a separate entrance to the basement, where an office could readily be constructed; or some other characteristic well suited to separating a particular room or area for exclusive business use. This can be a selling point in terms of tax savings and not only in terms of the advantages of your layout or space.

If your prospective buyer works at home or runs a business out of the house, he or she may be eligible for a home-office deduction. A home-office deduction can generate substantial tax benefits for depreciation, utilities, and a host of other costs. To qualify, the buyer must use a particular area or room both regularly and *exclusively* as a home office.

**Moving-Expense Deduction:** To qualify for a moving-expense deduction, the home the buyer purchases must meet a distance test. The distance (measured by the most commonly traveled route, not as the crow flies) between the location of the buyer's new job and the buyer's old home must be at least 35 miles more than the distance from the location of the buyer's old job to the buyer's old home. If your house fits the bill and other houses or neighborhoods the buyer is considering don't, drop a hint.

In conclusion, tax planning may not be your thing, but keep the above pointers in mind. Anything that can reasonably help you interest a buyer is worth considering.


## CHAPTER SUMMARY

If you have a broker, you'll probably want to let your agent do all the talking with buyers. If you're selling on your own, or a situation arises when the agent can't be there, talk to buyers like the ideal salesperson: Be courteous, calm, open, and honest. Don't lie to them, and don't tell them anything that could get you into trouble later.

In dealing with objections, be positive. Counter with other advantages of your house, or reasons why these negative points can be seen in a different light. If buyers point out actual flaws, offer to remedy them. Be ready for serious negotiation at any time, and if the buyers seem interested but hesitant, encourage them to make an offer: Leave the room to make a phone call, so they can talk alone; offer coffee or tea. At the right time, ask, "Would you like to put down a deposit?"

Besides mentioning all the selling points you have listed in your fact sheet, including the benefits of living in your community, you can offer tax tips for buyers to take up with their accountants that may save them money. You can tell them why it really pays to own a house, the possibilities of writing off a home office, and about the deduction for moving expenses.

# 18 WHAT TO DO ABOUT A PROBLEM HOUSE

## THREE PROBLEM SITUATIONS

A problem house is one that

- you must sell quickly, perhaps because you can't continue making the mortgage and tax payments, or because you're moving across the country;
- you haven't been able to sell, while similar houses have sold;
- has a significant defect.

In all cases, lowering the price is probably the single best remedy. You can do it indirectly—either by offering to give a sum of money to reduce the buyer's mortgage, or by paying some or all of the closing costs. A benefit of lowering the price indirectly is that buyers may think they're getting a $120,000 house (your asking price), when the house would have cost less if you had lowered it directly. A drawback is that you'll still have to pay the broker a commission based on your selling price. But the difference won't be enormous: A 7 percent commission on a $200,000 house is only $700 more than on a $190,000 house.

You might embark upon a price-reduction program: Every month that the house doesn't sell, you can lower the price by 1 percent. A house that was offered originally for $100,000 would drop to $99,000, then to $98,000, then to $97,000, and so forth.

Now let's deal with specific remedies for the three situations mentioned above:

1. *You simply must sell quickly.* Auctioning your house is quick—but it may be painful. If you agree to do it, try to set a

minimum price you'll accept. If yours is a house valued at $200,000, you don't want it to go for $150,000—unless you're truly desperate. Selling "absolute," as it's called, will draw more buyers, but selling absolute is a course for only the most desperate sellers.

---

**TIP:** For a free directory of auctioneers, write to the Certified Auctioners Institute, 880 Ballentine, Overland Park, Kansas 66214. Auctioneers often receive 4 percent to 10 percent commissions.

---

One national brokerage firm, ERA, advertises that if it doesn't sell your house, it will buy it. It may buy it—but possibly at a low price. If you have a good house and can't wait—say, you're living in Oshkosh and your old house is in Ho-Ho-Kus—you might check to see what kind of deal ERA and others will offer you. Some brokers may pay as little as 80 percent or 75 percent of your house's fair-market value.

Some builders of new houses offer to buy your house if you buy one of theirs. They're doing it, of course, because their own houses aren't selling, and they feel confident that they can sell your house even though you can't. Why? Because they'll sell it cheap, and make their money on selling you a house that has a big margin of profit built in. If you must get out, and you've moved heaven and earth to sell your own house, without success, inquire. Check local newspaper ads, or telephone developers in places where you want to move.

2. *You haven't been able to sell your house.* Consider changing real estate brokers. Your current agent may talk a good game, but perhaps he or she hasn't been advertising enough, or pushing your house hard enough.

An agent, if he or she tries hard, can do a lot to sell any particular house. Many buyers are young, inexperienced, and nervous, and will listen to the agent's advice. An agent eager to sell a particular house can praise it to the skies to buyers. He or she can even say— the ultimate compliment—"If I didn't love my current home, I'd be real interested in this one." Or, more manipulatively, the agent can take buyers to all the worst and most overpriced houses in town before showing them yours.

How can you get an agent to push your house hard?

First, by indicating that, when your listing agreement expires, you'll consider changing brokers if the house doesn't sell during the period of the listing. Remind your agent a few weeks before the listing is set to run out that the agreement period is almost over, and that you're unhappy your house hasn't sold yet.

Next, call in agents for other brokerage firms, and ask them what they would do differently to sell your house, or what advice they would give you on how to speed up your house's sale. Consider listing with the one who has a realistic strategy and practical advice.

---

**TIP:** Are you worried about hurting the feelings of your current agent by switching brokers? Write him or her a letter like the one below, courtesy of Boston lawyer Charles E. Westcott:

*Dear John/Joan:*

*The purpose of this letter is to advise you that I have decided to retain a new broker. Effective the first of the month, So-and-So Realty will represent me. I would appreciate it if you would cooperate with So-and-So Realty toward an orderly transfer of my records.*

*I appreciate your efforts on my behalf, and if you are agreeable, I may call upon you for special needs in the future. But I feel that my new firm may be more capable of serving my current needs.*

*If you wish to discuss any aspect of the basis for this decision, I would be pleased to talk with you personally.*

*Sincerely,*
*Sally Seller*

---

Second, offer a bonus to the selling agent (the agent for any brokerage firm in the multiple-listing service that brings in a ready, willing, and able buyer). The bonus might be $500, or $5,000, or a new car, or an extra 1 percent of the selling price. (See Chapter 7.) If you run a travel agency, you might come up with a flight to somewhere at a low cost. If you own a furniture place, you might offer a free bedroom set—up to $3,000 in value, say.

Is it ethical for agents to accept such bonuses? It's not prohibited, although some agents report that they won't accept them. Do bonuses work? Of course. If you're an agent, and there are a half-dozen similar houses but one comes with a new car for the selling agent, which one would you push?

The best evidence that bonuses work is that many agents selling their own houses offer bonuses to the agent who brings in a ready, willing, and able buyer.

**TIP:** If your house is empty of furniture because you moved out, and it looks barren, or if no one is taking care of the place—sweeping, cleaning, maintaining the lawn—be aware that two companies provide furniture and house sitters, *free of charge to the home seller.* The sitters pay the cost of utilities, and maintain the place. The companies are Showhomes of America, (214) 243-1900, and Caretakers of America, (303) 832-5553, both of which have offices scattered throughout the country.

Showhomes provides a home manager to maintain your property, inside and out. The home manager is a subcontractor, not a renter, and is ready to move out within five days of your giving notice. Home managers are insured.

Managers provide their own furniture, which Showhomes matches with your house. Says Showhomes, "They are people that are relocating, young couples saving for the purchase of their own homes, graduate students; they are executives, engineers, teachers, and professional people from all types of careers. . . ."

The home manager will pay all utility bills, and maintain the property. Showhomes makes money by charging the managers a fee.

So far, 2,500 houses have participated in the Showcase program. Eight new market areas are slated to open up soon, including areas in New Jersey, Arizona, and Massachusetts.

Here are areas that currently have Showhomes offices:

 Dallas/Fort Worth: 214-243-1900

 San Antonio: 512-344-9501

 Austin: 512-328-9488

 Houston: 713-333-5732

 Oklahoma City: 405-340-3794

 Tulsa: 918-627-5125

 Denver/Colorado Springs: 303-740-6656

 Atlanta: 404-392-3410

 Connecticut: 203-221-0228

The other outfit, Caretakers of America, has a similar program. Its properties are showable from 8 A.M. to 9 P.M., seven days a week. Caretakers will relocate on 10 days' notice. As with Showhomes, the caretakers are subcontractors, not tenants, and as with Showhomes, they pay a fee to live in properties. They do all minor maintenance and pay utilities.

Caretakers, which began in Colorado, has expanded into nine other states and 18 cities, including Utah, Arizona, New Mexico, Texas, Oklahoma, Kansas, Missouri, Florida. It plans to expand into Connecticut, New Jersey, and Pennsylvania.

---

3. *Your house has an obvious flaw or defect.* Start running your own ads: Don't just wait for your agent to run them. Do this especially

during the liveliest selling season, typically spring and early summer. (See Chapter 13.)

Or take your house off the market for a month or two. In that time, a new cohort of buyers should replace most of the old cohort. Consider lowering your price a bit, and changing any ads you've been running. A newly offered house is almost as good as a house fresh on the market. Have your agent call all the buyers who looked at your house before, if you know they haven't bought yet, and tell them about the price reduction.

Consider offering buyers more incentives. Throw in more appliances, along with the lawn furniture, or offer to pay more of the closing costs (but don't pay the buyer's points since the buyer will lose a valuable tax deduction). Or offer to take back a mortgage (after checking with your lawyer first).

Call in neighbors and friends and ask them frankly: What's wrong with my house? Why isn't it selling? What advice would you give me? Ask smart people you know—lawyers, bankers, insurance agents, stockbrokers (you'll also be reminding them that your house is for sale). Run the information and advice you receive past your real estate agent.

Is the advice to fix the defect? And is the cost a major stumbling block? One homeowner had paved over his backyard, overlooking a brook, with blacktop. Whatever his reason, he didn't sell his house until he had the blacktop removed and new sod put in. Sure, he was embarrassed to have to own up to his foolishness. But he was leaving the area, so what did he care what his neighbors thought of him?

If you need money to remedy a flaw or defect—an outdated kitchen, perhaps, or inadequate wiring—consider a home-equity loan. Or see if any local banks offer government-assistance home-improvement loans.


## CHAPTER SUMMARY


Among the ways to move a hard-to-sell house, or one you must sell quickly, are the following: Lower your price, perhaps by 1 percent or more for every month it remains on the market. List your house with a broker that may offer to buy the house if it doesn't sell. Check whether any builders of new houses will take over your house if you buy one of theirs. Consider having an auctioneer sell your house. If your house is now empty, hire a housesitter.

Consider changing real estate brokers. Whether you change or not, offer a selling agent an extra incentive, like a new car or just cash.

If your house has a special problem, confront it. Ask people you respect why they think your house isn't selling, and what you can do about it. Get a home-improvement loan to fix up your outdated kitchen, wiring, or whatever.

# Part Four

# FINANCING STRATEGIES TO PROMOTE A SALE

# 19 SELLER FINANCING: YOU ALWAYS WANTED TO BE A BANKER

## WHAT IS SELLER FINANCING?

Seller financing is when you help finance the purchase of your house. You do this by letting the buyers owe you money instead of paying the full price of the house at the closing. Obviously, if you need the cash, say to buy your new house, this might be more difficult. A partial solution is to keep your loan small.

In the traditional house-purchase transaction the buyer uses savings to pay for about 20 percent of the purchase price. The remaining 80 percent is usually obtained from a bank as a loan. This loan is secured by a mortgage. The seller receives cash for the house at the closing—part from the buyer and the rest from the bank.

When wouldn't you do it? In some instances, you may agree to serve as a bank for the buyer, instead of, or in addition to, the regular bank. From a legal perspective there are two basic ways that a seller can lend the buyer money, or give the buyer credit: (1) by taking back a mortgage from the buyer, and (2) by conveying the property on the installment method.

1. When a seller (mortgagee) accepts a mortgage from the buyer (mortgagor), it is called a purchase-money mortgage (PMM). This is the equivalent of the seller's lending the buyer an amount of money equal to the mortgage.

In other words, the seller accepts the buyer's "paper" (the mortgage), signed by the buyer at the closing, instead of cash. The seller may provide all of the financing or only some, and the borrower will get the rest of the financing from a bank or other lender.

2. In the second approach, the installment method (also known as a land contract), the buyer typically gives the seller a downpayment and makes payments for the balance over a number of years.

The difference from a mortgage is that, in an installment-sale contract, the buyer usually doesn't receive title to the property until all of the required payments are made. This approach is generally usable only when the seller provides all of the financing, because, without having title to the property, the buyer may not be able to obtain additional funds from another lender.

The purchase-money mortgage that the seller takes from the buyer can be arranged in almost any way you and the buyer agree. If you're planning to sell the mortgage, you should use standard mortgage documents and standard terms to make the mortgage readily salable. If you're planning to hold the mortgage, the major restrictions are open to negotiation. This is a reason seller financing can be used as an incentive for the buyer in promoting a sale.


## THE MARKETING VALUE OF SELLER FINANCING— ADVANTAGES TO THE BUYER

A buyer gains a number of advantages from seller financing. You should stress all of these when negotiating with any potential buyer:

- Speed.

Seller financing can be arranged as quickly as the buyer and seller can agree on the basic terms of the transaction and the lawyers can draft the loan documents. This can be far more rapid than bank financing, which typically (but not always) has long and formal review procedures from the initial loan application to the final disbursement of funds.

---

**TIP:** If you will not be buying another house, you won't qualify for the tax-free treatment available when a homeowner sells one home and replaces it within two years with a more expensive home. If you will face a tax on the gain from selling the home, it may be very advantageous to have that gain taxed in a specific year. The flexibility and speed of consummating a purchase-money mortgage may enable you to choose in which tax years to take the gain.

---

- Easier qualification.

Perhaps the buyer had a personal bankruptcy a few years ago, or had a prior house foreclosed upon. Traditional lenders may not be willing to extend a loan. However, if the buyer's bankruptcy was caused by a business failure that was not avoidable, you may be willing to consider the circumstances.

---

**CAUTION:** Seller financing can be a great sales tool, but if a bank won't lend to a buyer, you had better be extremely cautious. You must proceed very carefully when considering extending credit to a buyer. The risk of default can be a major problem. The buyer could fall months behind in tax and other payments. He or she could trash the house and then disappear without a trace. You might have to go through an involved foreclosure proceeding to get your house back, only to discover that after paying off all of the debts and making the necessary repairs, the house can't be sold for enough to cover the costs you've just incurred.

---

- Lower downpayment.

Accepting a lower downpayment than would be required by traditional lenders may provide the only way the buyer can buy your house.

---

**EXAMPLE:** Paul and Pauline Purchaser wish to buy a house from Heidi Homeowner. Heidi wants $89,000 for the house. The Purchasers called the local banks and savings and loan associations and found that the financing they want requires no less than 20 percent down.

Unfortunately, they can't afford to pay the $17,800 downpayment, the estimated $1,500 for moving expenses, and the $4,350 their lawyer says they'll need for closing costs. They really want the house, so they work out an arrangement with Heidi. Heidi will take back a $15,000 second mortgage. Since Heidi will be getting cash equal to the amount of the mortgage the Purchasers get from another lender, she is willing to delay her receipt of this additional amount in order to earn a good interest rate on it. This will give the Purchasers enough breathing room to make a 20 percent downpayment on a $75,000 loan from a local savings and loan association, while leaving them with enough money to to move, close, and have a bit of a cushion for a rainy day. Without the seller financing from Heidi, they could not have made the deal.

---

- Additional loan.

Many traditional lenders will extend a loan to a house buyer only up to a specific percentage of the appraised value of the house. Seller financing can fill this gap.

---

**EXAMPLE:** Bob and Betty Buyer are buying a home from Suzy Seller for $125,000. The Buyers have saved carefully for a number of years and now have $18,750 that they can use as a respectable 15 percent down-payment. They believe they've obtained a reasonable price, and the house meets their special needs. Betty is a free-lance writer and needs an extra room that could be converted to an office. Bob is an artist and needs a scenic place to paint. The backyard of the house abuts a small river, which Bob will use for much of his work.

The local bank recently changed its loan policy and will now finance a house purchase up to only 80 percent of appraised value. The appraiser hired by the bank values the home at only $112,000; apparently he doesn't have the artistic appreciation of Bob and Betty. Based on this value, the bank will lend the Buyers only $89,600. The Buyers are thus coming up short of the purchase price for their dream house.

They need an additional $16,650 [$125,000 purchase price − ($18,750 downpayment + $89,600 bank financing)]. If Suzy will take a $16,650 second mortgage, they can close the deal.

---

**CAUTION:** Think very carefully about the fact that your financing is only a second mortgage and that the bank comes first when it comes to repayment. During a time when home prices regularly increase, the risk might not be that severe; if the home is worth more than the mortgages, there will be sufficient equity both to pay off the bank's first mortgage and leave enough for you. However, in many parts of the country home prices have been rather flat; in some parts of the country they have actually declined. In these situations, extending a second mortgage becomes very risky because the house value may not be sufficient collateral to protect you if the buyer defaults.

---

**TIP:** If you must extend seller financing when the housing market looks soft, take extra steps to protect your interests. Have the buyer get one or more persons to personally guarantee repayment of the mortgage loan. See the sample guaranty form and comments in the "For Your Notebook" section of this chapter. Also, if you're concerned about declining housing values, insist on a larger downpayment. A no- or low-downpayment loan to a buyer can be particularly risky in a falling house-price environment.

---

- In case of high interest rates.

When bank and mortgage interest rates get very high, as they did in the early 1980s, seller financing can be a critically important component of the purchase price for a home.

## WHAT ARE THE ADVANTAGES TO THE SELLER?

Although some sellers think that taking back a purchase-money mortgage is a step of desperation to sell a house in a slow market, this is far from the only benefit or use of seller financing:

- High return.

Taking back a purchase-money mortgage on the sale of a house may offer less risk and more reward than many of the alternative investments open to a seller. The interest rate on a purchase-money mortgage is likely to be higher than what the seller could earn on money market funds or CDs. The risk, however, must be considered carefully.

- You know the security.

An argument can be made that taking back a purchase-money mortgage from the buyer of their house is a lower-risk investment than many of the other types of investments that typical house sellers have available. This is because you know the house and thus know the security for the loan. Also, you have met and had an opportunity to interview the borrower and, thus, are in a position to assess the risks. If the borrower defaults you get back the same house.

This argument, however, must be tempered by reality. First, depending on the size of the purchase-money mortgage you are taking back, you are placing a large portion of your net worth in a single asset—the second mortgage. Admittedly, you had a major portion of your assets in your home before, but this doesn't change the fact that a new investment decision is being made to concentrate assets in the purchase-money mortgage. You are unlikely to have any formal background as loan officers, so it is questionable whether you really know how to evaluate the buyer's qualities as a borrower. Perhaps one of the biggest risks is that the buyer of the house will not maintain it, or worse yet damage or destroy it. There is no assurance that if house prices fall, the buyer will not walk away. If you move to another state and the buyer defaults, you will be forced to handle the problems at a distance. Finally, foreclosing on a house on which you hold a purchase money mortgage is not always the best deal. As a result of these concerns, you may prefer buyers who have some reasonable net worth (say, a closely held business) that will give some assurance that the buyer's personal guarantee on the purchase money mortgage has value.

- A sale is made.

If the housing market is soft, it may be that providing financing to the borrower is the best, or perhaps the only, way to consummate a sale on a house *at a price that you will accept.* Providing favorable financing is a way for sellers to entice buyers to meet their prices.

- It's not forever.

If you should need cash and cannot wait for the purchase-money mortgage to be paid off, it's often possible to sell the PMM to a private investor and obtain cash immediately. This process is called "discounting," because the mortgage buyer typically pays the seller less than the face value of the mortgage. This reduction, or discount, reflects the investor's concerns about risk as well as the legal and other expenses associated with the transaction.

There are also some tax advantages of helping finance the sale of your house. These are explained in the next chapter.

---

**EXAMPLE:** Suzy Seller took a purchase-money mortgage from Bob and Betty Buyer for $16,650, as in the above example. Suzy thought the interest rate on the mortgage would provide her with a good investment. Suzy, always on the lookout for a good real estate buy, found a great house for sale by an estate at a very low price. She needed cash to close the deal so she placed an advertisement in the real estate section of the local paper for the $16,650 purchase money mortgage. She sold it to an investor for $14,500, which she used as the downpayment on the estate property.

---

**TIPS:** Suzy should make sure that her attorney properly records (files) the mortgage she receives from the Buyers with the appropriate county's recording office (or other appropriate government agency) to ensure that her lien on the property is publicly known. This will help Suzy foreclose on the property if the Buyers don't pay, and collect the money due her before other creditors of the Buyers get paid (except for the bank holding a first mortgage, which will have priority over Suzy).

If Suzy thinks she may try to sell the mortgage to an investor, she should consult an attorney or banker before consummating the loan to make sure that she uses the appropriate forms and has the necessary terms to facilitate such a later sale.

## SOME TERMS AND EXAMPLES

Some basic mortgage terms you should know if you're going to be the banker are the following:

"Amortization" is the process of paying off the principal amount of a debt. Amortization occurs when your payments are greater than the interest you owe.

**EXAMPLE:** Bill Borrower owes Linda Lender $1,000. He agreed to pay Linda interest at a rate of 10 percent and therefore owes Linda interest of $100. If Bill pays Linda anything above $100, the excess portion will amortize (reduce) the principal due.

The "term" is the period (usually 25 or 30 years for a first mortgage and perhaps 3 to 5 years for a second mortgage) over which the mortgage is amortized. At the end of this period the mortgage "matures" (comes due), and the remaining principal and any interest due must be paid.

Often mortgages are structured to mature before they are paid up. This is called a "balloon." For example, a mortgage could have a 30-year amortization period (i.e., if you made payments for 30 years you would repay all the principal and interest) but may balloon in five years. This means that most of the principal would still be due, because in the early years most of the payments go toward interest rather than principal.

**EXAMPLE:** Barbara Buyer is purchasing a condominium from Howard Homeowner for $178,000. She has no substantial salary history—she's been working as a secretary to put herself through law school—and little money for a downpayment. She can't qualify for a conventional loan to buy Howard's condominium, but Howard is confident she will get a top-paying job and do well.

Howard can earn only about 8 percent on his money in a money-market fund. But Barbara is willing to pay 14 percent interest on a three-year purchase-money mortgage if she can have the condominium for only $2,500 down. After three years, she will refinance the condominium and repay Howard.

Barbara's monthly payments will be substantial. Assuming Howard and she agree to a 30-year amortization schedule and a three-year balloon, her payments will be approximately $2,055 per month. After the three years, when the mortgage matures, Barbara will owe Howard about $175,000.

---

The sellers/lenders and buyers/borrowers should understand the consequences of the transaction they are undertaking. If the buyers "default" (they don't repay the loan as required), the sellers can "foreclose" on the house. This process sets a limit on the borrowers' right to pay the amounts due on the mortgage and keep the house. The court can cut off these rights and have the property sold at an auction to repay the sellers/lenders their loan, with any remaining money going to the buyers/borrowers. The process is generally carried out by a sheriff, who sells the property at public auction.

## THE DOCUMENTS YOU WILL NEED TO PROTECT YOURSELF

Seller financing, purchase-money mortgage, taking back paper—whatever you call it—can be a great approach to moving your house in a tough market. But you better take every step possible to protect yourself. Legal protection comes by having well-drafted documents that provide the rights you need to collect the money due you, and most importantly, to recover your interests if the buyer/borrower fails to make payments, damages the property, or tries to sell the property.

Although your lawyer will undoubtedly prepare the necessary forms for you, you will be able to use your lawyer more effectively (and cost effectively) if you understand the basic documents that are involved. More importantly, if the two lawyers (yours and the buyer's) have differences, your understanding of what the documents mean, and of what protection you really need, will make it easier to work with your lawyer to close the deal. Make sure you have a lawyer who is familiar with real estate transactions and who is willing to explain the terms and procedures, if you have questions beyond what is explained here.

Your legal protection can involve a number of different forms, including:

1. *Note:* The note is a legal document in which the buyer acknowledges owing you money, agrees to the terms of the loan (interest rate, maturity date, etc.), and, most importantly, promises personally to repay the amount due. (This is why it is sometimes called a "promissory note.")

Thus, if the buyer defaults the house cannot be sold for enough money to repay the loan (either because of declining prices or damage done by the buyer), you can sue the buyer personally for any amount still due you. In some cases, the note and mortgage will be combined into a single document called a "Note and Mortgage."

2. *Mortgage:* The mortgage is the document in which the buyer/borrower agrees to make your house serve as collateral for the loan. If the buyer doesn't repay the amount due, you can foreclose on the house and sell it to repay the amount still owing to you. In most cases, you as the seller will loan the buyer only part of the purchase price. The buyer will make some downpayment and the balance of the purchase price will typically be provided by a commercial lender (bank, savings and loan, etc.). Your loan (purchase-money mortgage) will probably be a second mortgage, coming behind the bank's first mortgage. (Although a second mortgage to the buyer by an unrelated lender is sometimes also called a purchase-money mortgage, the emphasis in the forms and comments below are for the situation when the seller is the provider of the second-mortgage financing.)

Because this claim is a lien against real estate, it can and should be recorded in the public records so that anyone seeking to purchase the property, or investigating the possibility of making another loan against the property, will see the seller/lender's mortgage. This is critically important for the seller/lender's protection, because any mortgages or other liens recorded in the public records at a later date will generally be paid after the seller's mortgage if there is a foreclosure. The seller/lender's mortgage is said to have "priority" over the liens recorded later.

3. *Deed of Trust:* Generally, mortgage documents are used in the eastern portion of the country, and deeds of trust in some western states. The purpose of the documents is similar, and your lawyer can advise your whether to use one or the other.

4. *Guaranty:* If the buyer/borrower doesn't repay the loan, if the house isn't of sufficient value when sold to repay what you're due, and if the buyer personally doesn't have enough assets or can't be found (i.e., he or she skipped town), what can you do? Not much, unless you have an agreement by another person to pay the balance. This is called a "guaranty." Examples of the note, mortgage, and guaranty are shown below (see "For Your Notebook").

---

**CAUTION:** As with all legal documents, consult a competent lawyer to protect your interests. The documents and comments offered in the "For Your Notebook" section are for guidance only. Local laws differ from state to state, the procedures differ, and each house sale can have its own nuances. For example, if the buyer is a corporation (perhaps buying your house to use in its business, or for use by one of its executives), there are a number of other documents you should obtain and a number of additional preliminary investigative steps you should take. The only way to be certain you've adequately protected your interests is to retain the services of a competent real estate lawyer.

---

**TIP:** Your lawyer will most likely prepare many of the documents for your transaction using standard preprinted forms. Remember, just because it's printed doesn't mean it can't be changed. Just be certain that when the forms are signed, you and the buyer(s) (all of them must be included) initial in the margin next to all of the changes.

---

The most common type of seller financing, as noted in the introduction to this chapter, is for the seller to take back paper—in which case, the process for a seller/lender to get the house back historically has been somewhat simpler. However, in most cases a legal process which is similar to foreclosure must be used where a lender seeks to take property held under a deed of trust or a mortgage. A practical difference will be that you use a mortgage agreement in mortgage states and a deed of trust agreement in states that use the deed of trust approach. Your lawyer will help you with any distinctions that you must know.

## WRAPAROUND MORTGAGES

Although more complicated arrangements, such as wraparound mortgages, are common in larger commercial real estate transactions, they are not frequently used in residential real estate transactions. A wraparound mortgage is most readily understood from a simple example.

---

**EXAMPLE:** Sam Seller sells his house to Betty Buyer for $90,000. Sam has an existing mortgage with a balance of $60,000 with interest at 8 percent. Betty puts $5,000 down and gives Sam a mortgage for the remaining $85,000 at the prevailing interest rate of, say, 11 percent. Sam receives monthly payments from Betty and then uses a portion of the money to make the monthly payments on his underlying $60,000 mortgage. In addition to making 11 percent interest on the $25,000 Sam is effectively lending to Betty to buy his house, Sam is also making the interest spread (11 percent to 8 percent) on the underlying mortgage of $60,000. The new $85,000 mortgage to Betty is said to "wrap around" the old mortgage— hence the name "wraparound mortgage." This interest spread is the reason most residential mortgages can't be assumed—the banks and savings and loans want to earn the additional interest by requiring a new loan.

---

## ENDNOTE: CAN THE BUYER ASSUME YOUR MORTGAGE?

It doesn't happen often, but don't assume that your mortgage cannot be assumed—taken over by a buyer. It's definitely worth checking into as an incentive for buyers, especially if your mortgage is insured by the Federal Housing Administration or guaranteed by the Veterans Administration. If your mortgage *is* assumable, you should play this fact up in newspaper ads, on your fact sheet, and in talking to buyers directly.

The advantage to buyers of taking over your mortgage is that they can reduce their closing costs, particularly the cost of "points"— special charges that a lender may assess when granting a mortgage. A point is 1 percent of the loan; on an $80,000 mortgage, three points would amount to $2,400. (Usually, lenders charge one to three points on a mortgage.)

It's true that if your mortgage is old and you've paid most of it off, the buyers probably cannot take it over without getting a second mortgage to pay you the balance they owe you. It's also true that if your house has appreciated tremendously, the buyers will have to come up with a huge amount to make up the difference.

Further, most fixed-rate mortgages can no longer be assumed by buyers. Many lenders sell their mortgages to quasi-government agencies—Fannie Mae and Freddie Mac—and those two agencies want buyers to obtain new mortgages at, very likely, higher interest rates. They don't want to be stuck with old, 8.5 percent mortgages when current rates may be 10 percent.

But if the lender has kept the fixed-rate mortgage, rather than selling it, the lender may be amenable to your buyer's taking it over. Check with your mortgage holder.

Just make sure that, if a buyer assumes your mortgage, the lender will not hold you accountable if the buyer defaults. Your agreement with the lender should make the buyer totally responsible for the mortgage from the day the house changes hands.

It's more likely that buyers can assume an adjustable-rate mortgage (ARM), one in which the interest rate moves up or down in accordance with an economic indicator of interest rates, like one-year Treasuries. But the buyer will have to do some calculations. If your ARM has reached its ceilings on rate increases (typically two percentage points a year, six percentage points over the life of the loan), the buyer may be happy to take it over, knowing that the interest rate cannot rise much in the future.

On the other hand, by obtaining a new ARM, the buyer may get a special, low interest rate for a year or so. (New ARMs offer low introductory interest rates, to attract buyers.) So the buyer will have to weigh the pros against the cons.

The types of mortgages that may be relatively easy to assume are those backed by the FHA or the VA. But the FHA has a new rule: If the mortgage was taken out on or after Dec. 15, 1989, the new buyer must undergo a credit check, and the lender may charge up to $500.

As for the VA-guaranteed mortgages, a buyer can assume your mortgage even if he or she isn't a veteran. But as of March 1, 1988, a buyer cannot assume a VA-guaranteed mortgage without undergoing a credit check, either by the VA or by whatever lender holds the mortgage.

Another way a seller may benefit if a buyer assumes his or her mortgage is that the seller might avoid a prepayment penalty for paying off a mortgage early—if there was such a stipulation in the mortgage agreement.

## CHAPTER SUMMARY

Seller financing means helping buyers finance the purchase of your house by lending them part of the purchase price. The usual way of doing this is to take back a mortgage on the house (a second mortgage; the first mortgage is held by the bank). The advantages to the buyer, which make seller financing a good marketing tool, are speed, greater ease of qualification, and often a lower downpayment than the bank would require. The advantages to the seller are a higher return on his or her money than on many traditional investments, knowing the security for the loan, and getting the house sold, especially in a soft market.

There is considerable risk, though. Sellers need to protect themselves carefully. Consult a competent attorney who can not only draft and/or record the necessary legal documents (note, mortgage, guaranty), but who can explain your rights and obligations under these documents. Sellers should proceed with the utmost caution, getting additional guarantors from the buyer for the loan, and possibly a larger downpayment.

Also check to see if your mortgage can be assumed by the buyer. This is more likely with FHA- or VA-backed mortgages than with conventional mortgages.

# FOR YOUR NOTEBOOK

## SAMPLE PURCHASE-MONEY MORTGAGE AND OTHER DOCUMENTS

### SECURED PROMISSORY NOTE (WITH COMMENTS)

**FOR DISCUSSION WITH YOUR LAWYER ONLY—
DO NOT USE AS A CONTRACT**

$105,000            Centerville, Onestate
December 1, 1988

FOR VALUE RECEIVED, the undersigned jointly and severally promise to pay to the order of Sam Seller and Sue Seller or the holder hereof ("the Payee") at Centerville, Onestate, or at such other place as the Payee may, from time to time, designate in writing to the undersigned, without offset or defalcation or relief from appraisement or valuation laws, the principal sum of Twenty-Five Thousand Dollars ($25,000) in lawful money of the United States of America in equal monthly installments of Three Hundred Forty-One and 38/00s ($341.28) on January 1, 1991 and the first day of each month thereafter inclusive of interest at the rate of Eleven percent (11%) per year. The remaining principal balance and any unpaid interest shall be due and payable on November 30, 2000, unless accelerated to an earlier date in accordance with the terms of this Secure Promissory Note ("Note").

---

**COMMENT:** The provision requiring payment without offset is crucial. Without it, the buyer could claim that there are problems with the house you sold, for which you are at fault. While the matter is being resolved, the buyer may have the right to cease payments specified under the note, and offsetting the amounts due you under the note by what it is claimed you owe as a result of your breach of the sales contract.

The acceleration provision is critical to protect your interests. It enables you to sue for the entire note (i.e., all the money the buyer/borrower owes you) if there is a default on one month's payment. Without the protection of this provision, you could have to sue for each month's payments separately.

---

Payments made under this Note shall first be applied against payments of interest and then toward the reduction of principal.

---

**COMMENT:** This is identical to the provision discussed in the mortgage, below. You want payments applied to reduce past due interest, and only then to reduce principal.

---

A default shall occur in the event of: (i) the nonpayment of any sums due under this Note after a Ten (10) day grace period; (ii) the breach of any other covenant, warranty, or agreement in this Note or the Purchase Money Second Mortgage dated the same date as this Note ("Mortgage") after written notice and a Thirty (30) day grace period; or (iii) then at the option of the holder of this Note immediately and without notice upon the appointment of a Receiver or Trustee in bankruptcy or the filing of a petition in bankruptcy ("Default"). Upon the occurrence of a Default, the entire unpaid principal balance and interest due shall immediately become due and payable. Following any Default, interest shall accrue at the rate of Eighteen percent (18%) per year or the highest rate allowed by law.

---

**COMMENT:** It is important to spell out precisely when you can declare the loan (i.e., the note) to be in default. The buyer's lawyer will likely scrutinize this section carefully to make sure the buyer/borrower at least has the opportunity to have notice of what the problem is and a reasonable opportunity to correct ("cure") the problem. There is no reason not to give the buyer an opportunity to cure a problem before putting the loan in default. However, there should be a tight limit on how many times you should have to accept late payments and give the buyer a chance to make the payments. Also, in certain cases, such as when the buyer files for bankruptcy, you shouldn't have to wait at all. Discuss with your lawyer when you should have protection.

---

The undersigned does hereby pledge, transfer, and grant to Payee security for the payment of his obligations under this Note his entire right, title, and interest in ALL that tract or parcel of land and premises, situate, lying and being in the City of Centerville, in the County of Oakland, and State of Onestate. BEING known and designated as Lot No. 3 in Block No. 13 on a certain map entitled "Map of Elmora Manor, Centerville, Onestate, O.L.P. Jones, Surveyor, dated June 10, 1812" and filed in the Register's Office as Case #38-CH-4.

BEGINNING at a stake in the Northeasterly side of Main Street, at a point therein distant 50 feet Southeasterly from the intersection formed by the said Northeasterly side of Main Street and the Southeasterly side of Glenwood Road; thence running (1) North 36 degrees 01 minutes East, a distance of 100 feet to a stake for a corner; thence running (2) South 54 degrees 18 minutes East a distance of 48.02 feet to a point for another corner; thence running (3) South 35 degrees 42 minutes West a distance of 100 feet to a point in the aforesaid line of Main Street; thence running (4) North 54 degrees 18 minutes West a distance of 48.57 feet to the point or place of BEGINNING. BEING also known as 123 Main Street, Centerville, Onestate.

BEING known as Lot 3 in Block 13, Account No. 10-504B on the official tax map of the City of Centerville, Oakland County, Onestate (the "House).

Together with all the appurtenances attached thereto, all easements, rights of way, buildings, structures, improvements, and fixtures thereto described in the Mortgage.

All covenants, conditions, warranties, and agreements made by the undersigned in the Mortgage are hereby made part of this Note, and undersigned shall keep same as if each one were set forth herein.

The undersigned may prepay any portion of the principal amount due under this Note without penalty.

---

**COMMENT:** In some cases you may not want to let the borrower repay early because you will want to continue earning the high interest being paid. Discuss this with your lawyer before the agreements are sent to the buyer's lawyer.

---

Notwithstanding anything in this Note or the Mortgage to the contrary, the total interest payments and payments that could be characterized as interest, shall not exceed the amount allowed to be charged under the applicable usury laws. Any interest payments in excess of the amount permissible shall be refunded by first applying such excess against amounts due under this Note and refunding any excess remaining to the undersigned.

---

**COMMENT:** This section is an attempt to fix any problem that may arise concerning the state's usury laws. This point is discussed at length in the mortgage document below.

---

If the Payee shall institute any action to enforce collection of this Note, there shall become due and payable from the undersigned, in addition to the unpaid principal and interest, all costs and expenses of that action (including reasonable attorney's fees), and the Payee shall be entitled to judgment for all such additional amounts.

The undersigned (and any guarantors, endorsers, or sureties) irrevocably consent to the sole and exclusive jurisdiction of the Courts of the State of Onestate and of any Federal court located in Onestate in connection with any action or proceeding arising out of, or related to, this Note. In any such proceeding, the undersigned waives personal service of any summons, complaint, or other process and agrees that service thereof shall be deemed made when mailed by registered or certified mail with return receipt requested to the undersigned. Within Twenty (20) days after such service, the undersigned shall appear or answer the summons, complaint, or other process. If the undersigned shall fail to appear or answer within that Twenty (20) day period, the undersigned shall be deemed in default and judgment may be entered by the Payee against the undersigned for the amount demanded in the summons, complaint, or other process.

The undersigned (and any guarantors, endorsers, or sureties) waive presentment, demand for payment, notice of dishonor, and all other notices or demands in connection with the delivery, acceptance, performance, default, or endorsement of this Note.

The undersigned agree that they shall each be unconditionally liable on this Note without regard to the liability of any other party to this Note.

No delay or failure on the part of the Payee on this Note to exercise any power or right given hereunder shall operate as a waiver thereof, and no right or remedy of the Payee shall be deemed abridged or modified by any course of conduct. No waiver whatever shall be valid unless in a writing signed by the Payee.

---

**COMMENT:** If you decide to be a good sport and not throw the buyer into default because of one violation of the terms of the note, you don't want the buyer to be able to argue that you've waived your right to enforce that default provision at a later date if the buyer again violates the terms of the note.

---

This Note shall be governed by and construed in accordance with the State of Onestate applicable to agreements made and to be performed in Onestate.

This Note cannot be changed orally.

IN WITNESS WHEREOF, the undersigned jointly and severally intend to be legally bound by this Note and execute their signatures as of the date first above written.

Witness: _____      _____
              Paul Purchaser

Witness: _____      _____
              Pat Purchaser

              Address for Communication:
              123 Main Street
              Centerville, Onestate

STATE OF ONESTATE      )
                        :   ss.:
COUNTY OF OAKLAND     )

On this 1st day of December, 1990, before me personally came PAUL PURCHASER, to me known and known to me to be the individual described in and who execute the foregoing instrument, and he duly acknowledged to me that he executed the same.

_____
              Notary Public

STATE OF ONESTATE      )
                        :   ss.:
COUNTY OF OAKLAND     )

On this 1st day of December, 1990, before me personally came PAT PURCHASER, to me known and known to me to be the individual described in and who execute the foregoing instrument, and she duly acknowledged to me that she executed the same.

## PURCHASE-MONEY SECOND MORTGAGE (WITH COMMENTS)

**\*\*FOR DISCUSSION WITH YOUR LAWYER ONLY—
DO NOT USE AS A CONTRACT\*\***

This Mortgage, made on December 1, 1990, by Paul Purchaser and Pat Purchaser of 456 Redwood, Apt. 12E, Ridgewood, Onestate (the "Mortgagor"), and Sam and Sue Seller of 123 Main Street, Centerville, Onestate (the "Mortgagee").

## W I T N E S S E T H

A. Mortgage, Collateral.
    That Mortgagor, jointly and severally, for and in consideration of the sum of Twenty-Five Thousand Dollars ($25,000) applied toward the purchase price of the house described below as the property subject to this Second Mortgage, mortgages to Mortgagee all buildings and improvements thereon, erected, situated, lying, and being in the City of Centerville, County of Oakland, State of Onestate (the "Property").

---

**COMMENT:** It is important that the mortgage (and note) be signed by all the buyers, usually being the husband and wife, and that it be stated that both are jointly and severally bound. This gives you the right to sue both, or either borrower individually, for the entire balance due.

---

    The Property is more particularly described as follows:

    ALL that tract or parcel of land and premises, situate, lying and being in the City of Centerville, in the County of Oakland, and State of Onestate. BEING known and designated as Lot No. 3 in Block No. 13 on a certain map entitled "Map of Elmora Manor, Centerville, Onestate, O.L.P. Jones, Surveyor, dated June 10, 1812" and filed in the Register's Office as Case #38-CH-4.

    BEGINNING at a stake in the Northeasterly side of Main Street, at a point therein distant 50 feet Southeasterly from the intersection formed by the said Northeasterly said of Main Street and the Southeasterly side of Glenwood Road; thence running (1) North 36 degrees 01 minutes East, a distance of 100 feet to a stake for a corner; thence running (2) South 54 degrees 18 minutes East a distance of 48.02 feet to a point for another corner; thence running (3) South 35 degrees 42 minutes West a distance of 100 feet to a point in the aforesaid line of Main Street; thence running (4) North 54 degrees 18 minutes West a distance of 48.57 feet to the point or place of BEGINNING. BEING also known as 123 Main Street, Centerville, Onestate.

BEING known as Lot 3 in Block 13, Account No. 10-504B on the official tax map of the City of Centerville, Oakland County, Onestate (the "House).

---

**COMMENT:** The legal description of the property should be identical to the description contained in the sales contract. The description will generally be taken from the deed you received when you purchased the property. However, the survey should also be consulted. See the discussion in the sample sales contract contained in a later chapter.

---

Together with all the appurtenances attached thereto, all easements, rights of way, buildings, structures, improvements, and fixtures thereto.

---

**COMMENT:** It is important that the document make clear that the property serving as your collateral include not only the land, but all other property that is permanently attached to the land (other structures such as sheds, fixtures, personal property—i.e., movable items that have been permanently attached to the land). If the buyer defaults, you don't want an issue to arise as to which property you're entitled to claim.

---

B. Security Interest in Personal Property.

The Mortgagor grants to the Mortgagee a security interest in all personal property located on or at the house. The Mortgagor also authorizes the Mortgagee to file, with or without the Mortgagor's signature, one or more financing statements as allowed by law to perfect Mortgagee's interest in this Mortgage.

C. Note, Term, Principal, Interest.

This Mortgage is intended to secure the payment of a certain Secured Promissory Note made on the same date as this Mortgage (the "Note"), the terms of which are hereby incorporated by reference into this Mortgage, in which Mortgagor promises to pay to Mortgagee or to order, for value received, on or before November 30, 2000, the sum of Twenty-Five Thousand Dollars

($25,000), to be paid in equal monthly installments of Three Hundred Forty-One and 38/00 Dollars ($341.38) on January 1, 1991 and on the 1st day of each month following until the whole shall have been paid, inclusive of interest thereon at the rate of Eleven percent (11%) per year, the interest on each installment being payable when it becomes due, and, if not then paid, to bear interest at the same rate as the principal. Payments shall be applied to interest, then principal.

---

**COMMENT:** The payments under the mortgage are on a fully amortizing, self-liquidating basis. This means that over the 10-year life of the second mortgage, all of the interest and principal will be repaid in equal monthly payments. This is the safest method; you have your money outstanding for less time so it is at risk for a shorter period. Many purchase-money second mortgages are structured as shorter-term, say five-year, balloon mortgages calculated with perhaps a 25-year amortization period. Smaller payments would be made each month, and then, at the end of the five-year term of the loan, the buyer would still owe you a substantial portion of the original loan. Still other purchase-money second mortgages are interest-only payments so that the buyer will still owe you the entire principal at the end of the loan.

An important provision is that if the buyer doesn't make payments on time, interest will accrue (be charged on the unpaid interest). Further, the documents should provide that all payments are first applied to reduce outstanding interest owed to you, and only after all outstanding interest is paid should the principal be reduced by the buyer's payments.

It is critically important that the interest rate charged does not violate the usury laws of your state. Have your lawyer verify this. Usury laws set maximum amounts of interest that can be charged for certain types of transactions. If your interest rate is greater, you may not be entitled to the excess, and in some states, you could risk losing the right to collect any interest. Some usury laws may exclude purchase money mortgages because it would be easy for you to simply increase the purchase price in exchange for having to lower the interest rate charged. If the usury laws restrict your interest rate, discuss with your lawyer whether you can negotiate a somewhat higher sale (and mortgage) amount to compensate you.

---

The principal and interest are payable in lawful money of the United States of America.

D. Default.

In case of a default in the payment of the principal, or any installment thereof, or any interest, as provided in the Note, the entire principal and interest shall be due at the option of Mortgagee, their successors, or assigns, and suit may be immediately brought and a decree issued to sell the House, with all of the appurtenances, or any part thereof, in the manner prescribed by law. Out of the money arising from such sale, Mortgagee is to retain the principal and interest, although the time for payment of such principal sum may not have expired, together with the costs and charges of making such sale and of suit for foreclosure, including reasonable attorney's fees, and also the amounts, both principal and interest, of all such payments of liens or other encumbrances as may have been made by Mortgagee by reason of the permission hereinafter given, and the remainder, if any, shall be paid, on demand, to Mortgagor, his successors, or assigns.

---

**COMMENT:** The above section contains what is called an "acceleration clause." The easiest way to explain an acceleration clause is by an example of what happens when the mortgage doesn't contain one. If the buyer/borrower defaults on the mortgage payment due on March 1, you could sue for the amount that should have been paid to you, or $341.38. You can't sue for any more, because the buyer doesn't owe you anything more on March 1. In April, if the buyer misses the April 1 payment of $341.38, you can sue for that, too. It should be readily apparent that the right to sue one month at a time is rather impractical. Thus, the acceleration clause provides that all payments are immediately due should the buyer default on one payment due, which enables you to sue for the entire mortgage balance and foreclose on the house if necessary.

---

E.  Covenants, Representations, and Warranties of Mortgagor.
    Mortgagor, for themselves and their successors and assigns, do hereby covenant, represent, warrant, and agree:
    1.  Principal and Interest.
        To pay all the principal and interest and other sums of money payable by virtue of such Note and this Mortgage, or either, promptly on the days respectively they are due. Mortgagor shall not have any right to offset any claim for any matter arising out of a Sale Contract of even date, against any other payments due Mortgagee under this Mortgage.

---

**COMMENT:** The buyer may try to negotiate what is called a right of offset. In case you should violate some provision of the sales contract, the buyer will want the right to automatically reduce what must be paid to you under the mortgage (or deed of trust) and note. For example, if you represent in the sales contract that the roof is free of leaks (which most buyers will insist on), and the buyer finds a leak and spends $2,000 to replace the damaged portion of the roof, a $2,000 reduction would immediately be made to the amount due you under the mortgage. You should instruct your lawyer to vigorously oppose such a change because it puts the buyer, instead of you, in control of the situation. If the buyer can simply stop paying on the mortgage by virtue of having a right of offset, you're out the money until the roof issue is resolved. This shifts the balance of power in the negotiating process to the buyer. If the buyer is still paying what is due under the mortgage, you will have more clout in negotiating a settlement of the roof issue.

---

2. Taxes, Etc.

To pay all the taxes, assessments, levies, liabilities, obligations, and encumbrances of every nature on the House. If these are not promptly paid, Mortgagee may at any time pay them without waiving or affecting the option to foreclose or any right hereunder, and every payment so made shall bear interest from the date thereof at the rate of Fourteen percent (14%) per year, or the highest rate permitted by law, and shall be repaid with such interest by Mortgagor.

---

COMMENT: The phrase "or the highest rate permitted by law" would lower the 14 percent rate if the state's usury limit was lower. It is generally best to charge a greater interest rate when you have to advance monies for expenses the buyer/borrower hasn't paid. This should serve as an incentive for the buyer to pay what is required, and it should reward you for the extra efforts the buyer is forcing you to make.

---

3. Costs and Fees.

To pay all the costs, charges, and expenses, including attorney's fees, reasonably incurred or paid at any time by Mortgagee because of the failure of Mortgagor to perform and to comply with each stipulation, agreement, condition, and covenant of the Promissory Note and this Mortgage, or either, and every such payment shall bear interest from the date thereof at the rate of Thirteen percent (13%) per year, or the highest rate permitted by law.

4. <u>Insurance</u>.

To keep the House insured against loss by fire and other casualties, included in the standard form of house insurance policy with extended coverage insurance. At an amount of not less than One Hundred Forty Thousand dollars ($140,000) with a company whose rating is not less than "A" by Best's Insurance and which company is licensed to do business in the state in which the house is located. The policy or policies shall contain the standard clause used in the state in the name of the Mortgagee. In the event any sum of money becomes payable under such policy or policies, Mortgagee shall have the right to receive and apply the proceeds on account of the debt secured by this Mortgage, or to permit Mortgagor, his successors, or assigns, to receive and use it, or any part thereof, for other purposes, without waiving or impairing any lien or right under or by virtue of this Mortgage. In the event Mortgagor, his successors, or assigns do not so keep the building or buildings insured and furnish such policy or policies, as agreed, Mortgagee, his successors, or assigns may pay for such insurance or any part thereof, without waiving or affecting the option to foreclose or any right hereunder, and each and every such payment shall bear interest from the date thereof at the rate of Twelve percent (12%) per year and shall be repaid with such interest by Mortgagor, his successors, or assigns, to Mortgagee, his successors, or assigns. Mortgagee shall insure the house for any other reasonable risk requested by the Mortgagee within Thirty (30) days after Mortgagee receives notice from Mortgagor demanding such additional coverage.

---

**COMMENT:** You must make sure the house is adequately insured against fire or other loss, and that you're a named insured in the policy. You should also discuss with your lawyer whether flood, earthquake, or other insurance is available and appropriate to request. The minimum amount of insurance should be set high enough to repay the first mortgage and your mortgage.

---

5. <u>Repair and Maintain Property</u>.

Not to commit, permit, or suffer any waste, impairment, or deterioration of the premises or any part thereof.

6. <u>Perform Agreements.</u>

To perform and comply with, every stipulation, agreement, condition, and covenant in the Note and in this Mortgage.

7. <u>Receiver.</u>

In the event that at the beginning of or at any time pending any suit on this Mortgage, to foreclose it, to reform it, or to enforce payment of any claims hereunder, Mortgagee, his successors, or assigns, may apply to the court having jurisdiction of that suit for the appointment of a receiver that court may and should appoint a receiver of the House. That receiver should have all the functions and powers that a court may entrust to a receiver. That appointment may and should be made by the court as an admitted equity and a matter of absolute right of Mortgagee, his successors, or assigns, without reference to the adequacy or inadequacy of the value of the premises or to the solvency or insolvency of Mortgagor, his successors, or assigns, or of the defendants in that suit.

8. <u>Estoppel Certificate.</u>

Within Five (5) days of receiving a written request by Mortgagee, give the Mortgagee a signed statement stating the amount due under this Mortgage and the Promissory Note.

---

**COMMENT:** There may be times when you will need written confirmation from the buyer/borrower of the amount of the loan—for example, if you are trying to sell the mortgage to an investor. It's best to have this requirement in the mortgage so that the buyer will have to take the time to comply.

---

9. <u>Inspections.</u>

Permit Mortgagee, or any person reasonably authorized by Mortgagee, to enter and inspect the House at reasonable times.

---

**COMMENT:** You want the right to inspect the house periodically to make sure that no major damage has been done that could jeopardize your collateral. Also, if you try to sell the mortgage, the investor who buys it would probably want the right to inspect the house first. Don't expect the buyer to be cooperative; reserve the right in the mortgage. The buyer's lawyer will probably insist on limiting the number of inspections to one or two a year. A reasonable limit is not objectionable.

### 10. Title to House.

That Mortgagor is the lawful owner of the House, that it is free of all encumbrances and liens except as specifically set forth in this Mortgage, and that Mortgagor has good right and lawful authority to sell or mortgage the House and will defend the same against the lawful claims of any person.

### F. Assignment.

This Mortgage applies to, and inures to the benefit of, and binds the Mortgagee, the Mortgagor, their respective heirs, legatees, administrators, devises, executors, assigns and successors. Notwithstanding anything in this Mortgage to the contrary, this Mortgage shall become due and payable upon the sale, transfer, or assignment of the house by the Mortgagor.

---

**COMMENT:** You want to be sure that if the buyer dies, his estate remains liable for all the provisions in the mortgage. However, you probably don't want to let the buyer transfer or sell the house. The loan you made was to help the buyer buy your house, not to permit a favorable sale by the buyer to someone else. When the buyer sells the house, your purchase-money financing has served its intended purpose and you should be repaid. More importantly, you've made the decision to lend money to the buyer, not to the buyer's purchaser. You don't know the credit worthiness of the person buying the house from your buyer, so you shouldn't be obligated to lend to that person.

---

### G. Notice.

Any notice required to be given under this Mortgage, shall be a written notice, given by personal delivery, Federal Express, Express Mail, or certified mail with return receipt requested, postage and mailing costs prepaid, to the address of the parties listed above, unless notice of a different address is given as specified in this section ("Notice"). Notice by personal delivery shall be effective upon receipt, Notice by Federal Express or Express Mail shall be effective on the next business day following the day the Notice was sent, and Notice by certified mail shall be effective on the Fourth (4th) day following the day it was sent.

H. Waiver or Modification.

No modification or waiver of any right by the Mortgagee under this Mortgage shall be effective unless contained in a writing signed by the Mortgagee. Any waiver by the Mortgagee of any right or power under this Mortgage, shall not be deemed to constitute a waiver as to any future right or power. If the Mortgagee accepts any payment by the Mortgagor after the due date for the payment, or if the Mortgagee performs any act which is the obligation of the Mortgagor (including but not limited to the payment of insurance premiums, property taxes or the cost of repairs, on the house), the Mortgagee will not by such actions waive the right to declare the Mortgagor in default under this Mortgage.

I. Governing Law.

This Mortgage shall be construed in accordance with the laws of Onestate.

J. Miscellaneous Provisions.

The use of masculine, feminine, or neuter, singular or plural, shall, wherever the context so requires, include the masculine or feminine, or neuter, the singular or the plural. Captions and section headings are inserted for convenience only and shall not be used to limit or interpret any provision of this Mortgage.

---

**MISCELLANEOUS COMMENTS:** A number of other points should be reviewed with your lawyer when discussing the second mortgage, including the following:

1. Although you are agreeing that your mortgage is a second mortgage and is subordinate to the loan the buyer/borrower will make from a commercial lender, you don't want your mortgage to be made subordinate to any other mortgages that the buyer may later put on the property.

2. Taking back a mortgage from the buyer will permit you to report any gain for income tax purposes on the installment method (assuming you are not a dealer in real estate and the house is personal and not investment property). Discuss this with your accountant. (See Chapters 20 and 22.)

---

IN WITNESS WHEREOF, Mortgagor has executed this Mortgage the day and year first hereinbefore written.

_____
Paul Purchaser, Mortgagor

_____
Pat Purchaser, Mortgagor


STATE OF ONESTATE          )
                           :  ss.:
COUNTY OF OAKLAND          )

On this 1st day of December, 1990, before me personally came PAUL PURCHASER, to me known and known to me to be the individual described in and who execute the foregoing instrument, and he duly acknowledged to me that he executed the same.

_____
Notary Public

STATE OF ONESTATE          )
                           :  ss.:
COUNTY OF OAKLAND          )

On this 1st day of December, 1990, before me personally came PAT PURCHASER, to me known and known to me to be the individual described in and who execute the foregoing instrument, and she duly acknowledged to me that she executed the same.

_____
Notary Public


**COMMENT:** Documents generally must be notarized in order to be filed in the public records. Your lawyer should automatically take care of completing the necessary sections.

## GUARANTY AGREEMENT (WITH COMMENTS)

### **FOR DISCUSSION WITH YOUR LAWYER ONLY— DO NOT USE AS A CONTRACT**

THIS GUARANTY is made the 1st day of December by Gary Grandparent and Gertrude Grandparent, residing at 425 Rich Avenue, Hightown, Onestate (the "Guarantor") and Sam and Sue Seller of 123 Main Street, Centerville, Onestate (the "Lender").

---

**COMMENT:** If the buyer/borrower is young, not particularly well to do, or just not a great credit risk, insist on the buyer's finding someone with a better credit record to serve as a guarantor. If the buyer can't pay up, the guarantor may be able to.

---

## R E C I T A L S

WHEREAS, Paul Purchaser and Pat Purchaser of 456 Redwood, Apt. 12E, Ridgewood, Onestate (the "Mortgagor") has borrowed from the Lender a loan in the principal amount of Twenty-Five Thousand Dollars ($25,000.00) (the "Loan"), to be evidenced by Mortgagor's Promissory Note of the same date (the "Note") payable to Lender's order in such amount, with interest at the rate of Eleven percent (11%) per year, and a Mortgage of the same date (the "Mortgage") securing certain real property located at 123 Main Street, Centerville, Onestate (Lot 3 in Block 13, Account No. 10-504B on the official tax map of the City of Centerville, Oakland County, Onestate) (the "House").

WHEREAS, the Lender requires the unconditional personal guarantee of the Guarantor on the Note, and the Mortgage securing the Note, on the terms and conditions contained in this Guaranty, as consideration and inducement for extending the Loan to the Mortgagor.

NOW THEREFORE, the Guarantor hereby agrees as follows:

1. Unconditional Guarantee.
   a. Guarantor unconditionally guarantees to the Lender the payment of all principal and interest due under the Note and Mortgage on the due dates contained in the Note and Mortgage (with consideration to any grace periods permitted). Guarantor acknowledges that the due dates for these pay-

ments may be accelerated according to the terms of the Note and Mortgage and agrees to such accelerated due dates.

b. Guarantor guarantees the actual payment and not the mere collection of the amounts due under the Note and the Mortgage. The liability of the Guarantor under this Guaranty are primary, direct, and immediate and not conditional or contingent upon the Lender pursuing any remedies he may have against Mortgagor, or Mortgagor's successors and assigns, with respect to the Note, Mortgage, or law. Without limiting the generality of the foregoing, Lender shall not be required to make any demand on the Mortgagor, or otherwise pursue or exhaust its remedies against the Mortgagor, before, simultaneously with, or after enforcing its rights and remedies under this Guaranty against the Guarantor.

c. The genuineness, validity, or enforceability of the Note and Mortgage, or any other circumstance which might constitute a legal or equitable discharge of a guarantor, shall not affect the unconditional nature of this Guaranty.

---

**COMMENT:** If the buyers/borrowers are nearly broke, you don't want to have to sue and demonstrate that the money is not collectible from them before suing the person guaranteeing their loan. If the person guaranteeing the loan is merely a guarantor of collection, this is what your rights will be.

---

2. Costs.

Guarantor unconditonally guarantees to the Lender the payment of all costs, charges, and other expenses due under the Note and Mortgage, including but not limited to insurance, property taxes, and the costs of repairs. If this Guaranty is enforced by suit or otherwise, or if Lender exercises any remedies provided in the Note or Mortgage, Guarantor will reimburse the Lender for the expenses so incurred, including, but not limited to, reasonable attorney's fees. These amounts shall be payable by the Guarantor within Ten (10) days of receiving Notice that such amounts are due from the Lender.

3. Rights Waived by Guarantor.

The Guarantor hereby waives:

a. Presentment and demand for payment;

b. Protest of nonpayment;

c. Notice of acceptance of this Guaranty;

    d. Notice of any default under this Guaranty, the Note, or the Mortgage;

    e. Demand for performance or enforcement of any terms of this Guaranty, the Note, or the mortgage; All other notices and demands required by law which the Guarantor may lawfully waive; and

    f. Trial by jury.

4. Guarantor Loans to Mortgagor.

    If the Guarantor lends any money to the Mortgagor, or if the Mortgagor becomes indebted to the Guarantor, these loans and debts shall be subordinated to all amounts due and owing to the Lender, and nothing in this Guaranty shall be construed to give Guarantor any right of subrogation in the Note until all amounts owing the Lender have been paid in full.

5. Certain Rights of Lender.

    The Guarantor agrees that the Lender may, in the Lender's discretion, without notice to the Guarantor, and without in any way affecting the Guarantor's obligations and liabilities:

    a. Agree to the exchange, release, or disposition of all or any portion of the House referred to in the Mortgage;

    b. Modify or amend any provisions of the Note or the Mortgage;

    c. Grant extensions or renewals of the Note or the Mortgage;

    d. Effect any release, compromise, or settlement of the Note or Mortgage;

    e. Make advances for the purpose of performing any term or covenant contained in the Note or the Mortgage concerning the Mortgagor;

    f. Assign or otherwise transfer the Note, the Mortgage, or this Guaranty or any interest in any of these agreements;

    g. Waive compliance with, or any default under, the Note or the Mortgage; and

    h. Conduct matters with the Mortgagor, as if this Guaranty were not in effect.

---

**COMMENT:** Anything construed as changes made to the note or the mortgage could terminate the guaranty agreement and eliminate the protection it was supposed to provide. To prevent this from happening, the guaranty agreement should provide you with reasonable flexibility to take certain actions your lawyer considers necessary, without these being construed as changes.

6. Lender's Rights.

All rights and remedies afforded to Lender by reason of this Guaranty, whether under the terms hereof or by law, are separate and cumulative, and the exercise of one shall not in any way limit or prejudice the exercise of any other such rights or remedies. No delay or omission by Lender in exercising any right or remedy shall constitute a waiver of that right. No waiver of any rights and remedies under this Guaranty, and no modification or amendment hereof, shall be deemed made by Lender unless in writing and duly signed by Lender. Any written waiver shall apply only to the particular instance specified in that waiver and shall not impair the further exercise of any right or remedy of the Lender. No single or partial exercise of any right or remedy hereunder shall preclude other or further exercise thereof or any other right or remedy.

7. Construction.

This Mortgage shall be construed in accordance with the laws of Onestate. The use of masculine, feminine, or neuter, singular or plural, shall, wherever the context so requires, include the masculine or feminine or neuter, the singular or the plural. The captions shall not limit or affect the interpretation of this Guaranty.

8. Successors and Assigns.

This Guaranty shall inure to the benefit of, and be enforceable by, Lender and its successors and assigns as owners and holders of the Note and Mortgage, and shall be binding upon, and enforceable against, Guarantor and his heirs, executors, administrators, successors, and assigns.

9. Notice.

Any notice required to be given under this Guaranty, shall be a written notice, given by personal delivery, Federal Express, Express Mail, or certified mail with return receipt requested, postage and mailing costs prepaid, to the address of the parties listed above, unless notice of a different address is given as specified in this section ("Notice"). Notice by personal delivery shall be effective upon receipt, Notice by Federal Express or Express Mail shall be effective on the next business day following the day the Notice was sent, and Notice by certified mail shall be effective on the Fourth (4th) day following the day it was sent.

10. Termination.

This Guaranty shall not terminate until the Mortgagor makes the final payment in reduction of the principal indebtedness under the Note in the amount of Twenty-Five Thousand Dollars ($25,000.00), which payment is due and payable on November 30, 2000, and the payment of all other expenses then owing under the Note and Mortgage.

IN WITNESS WHEREOF, Guarantor has duly executed this Guaranty as of the day and year first above written.

_____

Gary Grandparent

_____

Gertrude Grandparent

STATE OF ONESTATE          )
                           :  ss.:
COUNTY OF OAKLAND          )

On this 1st day of December, 1990, before me personally came Gary Grandparent, to me known and known to me to be the individual described in and who execute the foregoing instrument, and he duly acknowledged to me that he executed the same.

_____

Notary Public

STATE OF ONESTATE          )
                           :  ss.:
COUNTY OF OAKLAND          )

On this 1st day of December, 1990, before me personally came Gertrude Grandparent, to me known and known to me to be the individual described in and who execute the foregoing instrument, and she duly acknowledged to me that she executed the same.

_____

Notary Public

# 20 TAX CONSEQUENCES OF SELLER FINANCING

There are important tax considerations in seller financing.

## THE INSTALLMENT METHOD OF REPORTING GAIN

The primary benefit to sellers (besides selling) of taking back a purchase-money mortgage, or selling on an installment contract, is the ability to use the installment method of reporting gain for tax purposes, if you will not be rolling over your house into an equally expensive replacement home. As long as you aren't a dealer in real estate (in the trade or business of buying and selling houses), this method should be available. (See Chapter 27 for tax consequences of selling by the conventional method, where you are rolling over your gain.)

If you were to sell your real estate for cash—all to be paid in the year of sale—you would have to recognize any gain (the proceeds less the investment or tax basis) in that year (if you don't buy an equally expensive replacement home). A very common alternative approach is for the buyers to pay some amount as a downpayment and the rest over a period of time (with interest on the unpaid balance). In this situation, it would seem unfair to tax you, the seller, on the entire proceeds in the year of sale. Not only would you not have received all the money due, but the tax you would owe could be more than the downpayment received.

The installment-sales rules address this problem. Sellers receiving payments over time generally will have to report income only as they get it. For most real estate sales this installment treatment is automatic any time at least one payment is made after the end of the year in which the sale occurs.

**EXAMPLE:** Howard Homeowner purchased a house in 1980 for $100,000. He sold it at the end of 1988 for $450,000. The buyer negotiated a deal in which Howard provided all of the financing and got only about an 11 percent downpayment, or $50,000, in cash at the closing. The balance was to be paid at the rate of $100,000 at the end of each year for four years with interest at prime plus 2 percent.

**CAUTION:** There is a lot of confusion concerning the status of the prime rate. "Prime" is generally the interest rate that banks charge their best customers. Whenever lending (or borrowing) money at a rate pegged to the prime rate, specify which bank's prime and perhaps even that bank's definition of prime. Or use a rate regularly set by the IRS.

The sale in the above example was automatically treated as an installment sale because at least one payment was made after the end of the tax year in which the sale occurred (1988). The installment-sales treatment will apply to any similar sale unless you specifically elect not to apply it.

When you receive installment payments under a purchase-money mortgage or an installment contract, only a portion of each payment is taxable. The basic rule is that the taxable portion of each payment is equal to the same proportion that your gross profit on the entire sale bears to the total contract price the buyer is to pay. That sounds more complicated than it is. The best way to explain this concept is to demonstrate it.

**EXAMPLE:** Continuing with the situation used above, Howard Homeowner sold his house for $450,000, and he had paid $100,000 for it. Thus, his taxable gain was $350,000. The contract price was $450,000, and this was the amount Howard was to receive over time. What portion of each of his installment payments has to be reported as income?

$$\frac{\text{Gross Profit}}{\text{Contract Price}} = \frac{\$350,000}{\$450,000} = 77.78\%$$

The following amounts of income had to, or have to be recognized on each of the scheduled payments:

| Year | Payment | Profit % | Profit Recognized |
|------|---------|----------|-------------------|
| 1988 | $50,000 | 77.78% | $38,889 |
| 1989 | 100,000 | 77.78% | 77,778 |
| 1990 | 100,000 | 77.78% | 77,778 |
| 1991 | 100,000 | 77.78% | 77,778 |
| 1991 | 100,000 | 77.78% | 77,777 |
| | $450,000 | | $350,000 |

## RULES AFFECTING INTEREST CHARGED

The tax laws require that a certain minimum interest rate be charged in transactions subject to the installment-sales rules. If the interest rate charged is too low, interest may have to be imputed at a rate set by the tax rules.

Assume that a fair-market interest rate at the time of the above transaction is 9 percent. Howard, however, only charged the purchaser interest at a 5 percent rate. Why would Howard have charged less than the going market rate? A below-market rate probably means the principal amount of the transaction (the $450,000 purchase price) was inflated. No seller would charge less than the going rate unless he or she got something for it—and that something is, according to the assumptions made by the tax laws, an excessive purchase price (principal amount).

If caught, the seller and the buyer would have to impute interest at a minimum rate required by law, say the 9 percent in the example. Howard would be required to report a lower gain on the sale and a higher annual interest income on the purchase-money mortgage (or on the unpaid installment obligation if an installment contract was used) than what the buyer was actually paying.

**EXAMPLE:**

| End Year | Payment Balance* | Actual Rate | Interest Paid | Total** Payment | Present Value at 9% Imputed |
|----------|------------------|-------------|---------------|-----------------|------------------------------|
| 1988 | $450,000 | 5% | — | $ 50,000 | $ 50,000 |
| 1989 | 400,000 | 5% | $20,000 | 120,000 | 110,088 |
| 1990 | 300,000 | 5% | 15,000 | 115,000 | 96,796 |

| End Year | Payment Balance* | Actual Rate | Interest Paid | Total** Payment | Present Value at 9% Imputed |
|---|---|---|---|---|---|
| 1991 | 200,000 | 5% | 10,000 | 110,000 | 84,942 |
| 1992 | 100,000 | 5% | 5,000 | 105,000 | 74,382 |
| | | | $50,000 | $500,000 | $416,208 |

\* Payment Balance is the amount of the installment notes outstanding for the year and thus the amount on which interest must be computed. Because the sale occurred on December 31, 1988, no interest was due in 1988. The payment balance is calculated by subtracting from the contract price the principal payments required by the contract—$50,000 at closing and $100,000 at the end of each of the next four years.

\*\* Total Payment is the sum to the principal payments required under the contract plus the interest payments at the 5 percent contract rate on the outstanding balance. The example assumes 5 percent simple interest with all payments made at the end of each year.

The payment schedule that would have to be used when the true 9 percent market interest rate is charged on the true imputed principal amount (sales price) is as follows:

| End Year | Principal Balance* | Imputed Rate | Interest Payment | Principal Payment | Total Payment |
|---|---|---|---|---|---|
| 1988 | $416,208 | 9% | — | $50,000 | $50,000 |
| 1989 | 366,208 | 9% | $32,959 | 87,041 | 120,000 |
| 1990 | 279,167 | 9% | 25,125 | 89,875 | 115,000 |
| 1991 | 189,292 | 9% | 17,036 | 92,964 | 110,000 |
| 1992 | 96,328 | 9% | 8,672 | 96,328 | 105,000 |
| | | | $83,792 | $416,208 | $500,000 |

## CONSEQUENCES OF SELLING THE PURCHASE-MONEY MORTGAGE

Assume in the above example that adequate interest was charged. The seller sold real estate for $50,000 down and took a purchase-money mortgage from the buyer for $400,000. The seller may have been willing to sell the real estate subject to a large purchase-money mortgage because he had no urgent need for the cash and was content to receive payments over four years with interest. On the other hand, he may have been willing to take back the purchaser's notes because it was the only way to make the deal. Suppose Howard Homeowner had had a strong need for cash shortly after the sale.

It may have been possible for him to sell the installment notes, but if he did, he would have been forced to report all the remaining gain for tax purposes. If Howard sold his $400,000 of installment notes right after the sale for the full price of $400,000, he would have had to recognize the remaining $311,111 of unreported profits.

How do we get this figure? The total profit on the sale transaction was $350,000. The seller had to report $38,889 in profit on the receipt of the $50,000 downpayment (see the chart above showing the gross profit to be reported on each scheduled payment). The remaining profit [$350,000–$38,889] would have had to be reported on his sale of the installment note for its face value of $400,000.

One more point: If you, as seller, pledge mortgage notes as collateral for loans, you will be denied the special benefits of the installment method and will have to pay tax on the portion of the notes pledged.

## CHAPTER SUMMARY

Besides earning interest, the next best benefit of taking back a mortgage is being able to report the gain in installments (as you get it), rather than all at once as in conventional transactions, assuming you're not rolling over the gain tax free into a replacement. For tax purposes, the installment treatment is automatic if at least one payment is made after the year in which the house is sold.

A certain minimum interest rate must be charged to buyers on installment transactions. If the PMM is sold, then the seller will have to recognize all of the remaining profit at once.

# 21 LEASE IT, WITH AN OPTION TO BUY

## WHY CONSIDER A LEASE-OPTION ARRANGEMENT?

In a lease-option arrangement, you don't sell your house—at least not now. You rent your house to a tenant who has also expressed some interest in buying the house. The lease agreement gives the buyer the right to buy the house at some future date.

It's not a sale, but if you haven't sold and you must move, it's an approach to minimizing your costs while waiting for a sale. When the market is tight and you can't find a buyer—or can't find a buyer at the price you want—a lease-option arrangement is a temporary step to consider. Unfortunately, as with any residential rental situation, there are a host of potential problems that you must consider before jumping into a rental.

## WHAT DISTINGUISHES A LEASE-OPTION ARRANGEMENT FROM A PLAIN LEASE?

Let's take the two components separately:

1. *Lease*: You rent your house to a tenant for a monthly fee. Generally, the tenant is also expected to pay the utilities, insurance, and other costs. Market conditions will largely dictate what you can and can't get the tenant to pay for.

2. *Option*: Included in the lease is the tenant's right to buy your house at certain times—perhaps at any time during the lease term, or only at the end of the lease.

Thus, the advantage over a standard lease, is that the tenant will have an incentive to purchase the house by the end of the lease term. This incentive could develop as a result of several factors.

- The tenant will grow attached to the house (the knowledge of the the option to purchase will help foster this attachment).

- A fixed purchase price has been set, which is rather favorable when the option can be exercised.

---

**EXAMPLE:** When you lease your house, you know that its estimated fair sales value is $175,000. You lease for one year, granting the tenant an option to purchase the house for $175,000. At the end of the year, the house has appreciated about 5 percent to $184,000. Now the house looks like a good deal to the tenant.

---

The problem with relying on a fixed purchase price as an incentive is that in many markets even a modest 5 percent appreciation may not be realized. If the price of the house stays flat or, worse, declines, it will almost ensure that the tenant won't excercise the option to purchase your house. (For another method of setting the price, see the Lease-Option Agreement, in "For Your Notebook," at the end of this chapter.)

- The terms of the lease provide an incentive for the tenant to purchase the house. The most common method of achieving this is to provide that some portion of each month's rental payment is to be credited against the ultimate purchase price the tenant will have to pay for the house.

---

**EXAMPLE:** You lease your house for one year to a tenant for $1,225 per month with an option to buy. You agree to give the tenant a credit toward the ultimate purchase price equal to 15 percent of the rent actually paid. Thus, if the tenant exercises the option a $2,205 credit [($1,225 × 12) × 15%] will reduce the $175,000 purchase price to $172,795. If this is combined with the scenario of an appreciating house value and a fixed purchase price (illustrated in the above example), the incentive is obviously even greater.

---

**TIP:** The tenant will also be able to apply the security deposit toward the purchase price, which will further reduce the cash needed at the closing if the option is exercised.

---

## WHAT'S THE DIFFERENCE BETWEEN THE LEASE-OPTION ARRANGEMENT AND A RIGHT OF FIRST REFUSAL?

A right of first refusal also gives the tenant an opportunity to purchase the house being rented, but it is different from an option in a very important way. If the tenant has a right of first refusal, you can't sell the house to anyone else without first giving the tenant an opportunity to buy the house from you at the same price and on the same terms.

---

**EXAMPLE:** You lease your house to Tom Tenant, and the lease agreement gives Tom a right of first refusal to buy your house at any time during the lease term. You finally get an offer of $187,500. You must now tell the potential buyers that they must wait, perhaps as long as 60 days, while you see if the tenant wants to buy the house at the same price. Then, if the tenant decides not to buy the house, you can sell it to the people who made the offer.

---

By that time, however, they will probably have their money in another house. A right of first refusal can make it very difficult to sell your house.

The right of first refusal is quite different from an option. With an option, if the tenant hasn't given you notice that the option is being exercised, depending on how the lease is drafted, you should be free to sell the house to anyone. Further, if the price of the house declines, you know that the tenant is unlikely to exercise an option. With a right of first refusal, the tenant must be consulted no matter what happens to the price of the house. Many potential lease-option tenant/buyers will try to negotiate both a right of first refusal and an option to buy. This gives the tenant/buyer the best of both worlds. If the price of the house increases, the tenant/buyer exercises the option (if the option is at a fixed price). If the price of the house declines, the tenant/buyer waits until you have an offer at a lower price and then exercise the right of first refusal to buy at that price.

---

**TIP:** Rights of first refusal can excessively restrict your ability to sell your house. If you can't avoid giving one to a buyer, make sure your lawyer negotiates by giving as limited a provision as possible—for example, by giving the tenant a short period of time in which to decide whether to buy.

---

## IS A LEASE-OPTION ARRANGEMENT REALLY A GOOD IDEA?

There are many negatives. While the incentives outlined above could increase the odds that the tenant will purchase the house, they are no guarantee. In a buyer's market, the tenant is likely to have many other opportunities to buy, perhaps at a better price. Because there are no guarantees on the tenant's buying, you shouldn't use a lease-option arrangement unless renting (without regard to the option to buy) is a reasonable course for you. If you believe that the rental income, potential appreciation in the house, and the possible tax benefits make renting worthwhile, then consider a lease-option arrangement. Don't fool yourself into thinking that leasing with an option to buy is some type of sale. It isn't.

---

**TIP:** The best time to offer a lease-option arrangement is when you can't find a buyer and would like a temporary rental while you continue to try and sell the house. In this scenario, the option portion of the lease may entice the tenant to buy. But if the tenant doesn't buy, you're no worse off because you were going to rent anyway.

---

One practical problem when you use a lease-option arrangement is that you take on all the risks and problems inherent in renting. There are endless horror stories of tenants who don't pay rent and trash your house before they finally move out or are evicted. If you end up with a bad tenant, it could cost you more in legal fees and repairs than the house is worth.

---

**CAUTION:** Don't expect any tenant to care for your house the way you did. If the tenant doesn't exercise the option to buy your house, you have it back on your hands after the lease ends, and the house is unlikely to be as good condition as when you were living there and trying to sell it. This can have a negative effect on the price the house will be able to command in the market.

---

There's another practical problem in using a lease-option arrangement (or any rental for that matter). You haven't sold your house. If you need the equity in your old house in order to buy your new house, a lease arrangement just may not be viable. There are two possible solutions to consider, with caution.

1.  You can remortgage your house and take out additional cash. This additional cash can then be applied toward the downpayment on your new house, or be used in whatever other way you were going to apply the sale proceeds. The biggest risk with this approach is that larger mortgage payments bring a greater potential for default.

2.  You could also rely on the additional monthly cash flow the rental generates to take out a bigger mortgage on your new house, instead of applying a larger downpayment the sale would have brought. The problem with this course is the uncertainty of your rental. What if the the tenant creates unexpected maintenance or other expenses for you? What if the tenant defaults on the rent? You could face a high mortgage payment on your new house and expenses you weren't counting on from your old one. You could risk losing both houses. Remember, higher leverage means risk.

## FIGURE IT OUT WITH A PENCIL

The only way to really know whether renting is a good idea is to push a pencil (or have your accountant do it for you). Calculate the rent you will earn over the lease period. Reduce the rent by all the costs involved. These include insurance, property taxes, maintenance and repairs, brokerage commissions on the lease, legal fees for having your lawyer review the lease, accounting fees for having your accountant prepare extra tax-return information, and any other costs you're likely to incur.

Remember, there are always unexpected costs when any residential property is leased, so factor in a "miscellaneous" or "contingency" expense to be safe. Also consider the tax benefit, if any, from leasing the house. This is discussed in Chapter 22.

Next, you should construct two financial scenarios: one for the tenant buying the house, and one for the tenant not buying the house. Determine what the tenant is likely to have to pay for the house. In case the tenant doesn't exercise the option, estimate the fair value you will receive if you have to sell to someone else.

In deriving the latter figure, take into account the effect on the price that the rental might have. If the tenant doesn't decorate the house as nicely as you did and doesn't take as good care of the house as you did, the house might sell for less than if you hadn't rented. Otherwise, estimate and deduct from the sale price the costs necessary to paint, clean, and prepare the house for sale to compensate for the tenant's wear and tear.

Finally, you must compare the results under each of these scenarios to the alternative of not renting.

---

**CAUTION:** Many homeowners simply compare the amount of rent they expect to get to the amount of their monthly mortgage payment and conclude that renting covers some of their out-of-pocket costs so it must be worthwhile. As the discussion above illustrates, this can be a costly mistake.

---

If, after working through all of the numbers, renting is only slightly better than not renting, considering all the risks involved, it may not pay to rent. On the other hand, if you must move, it may be preferable to rent, even if the numbers don't favor renting, rather than leaving your house empty and exposed to vandals.

## HOW TO PROTECT YOURSELF IF YOU RENT

If you pass all of the hurdles above and renting still makes sense, how can you protect yourself adequately? You can do due diligence—investigate the tenant. Get a lot of references and follow-up on all of them.

---

**CAUTION:** Be very careful not to violate any antidiscrimination or other laws when interviewing prospective tenants. Speak with your lawyer and your broker about the responsibilities you have. Your broker might even have an application form that has been checked out by attorneys that you can give to prospective tenants to complete. The last thing you want after the disappointment of not being able to sell your house is a lawsuit from a disgruntled prospective tenant.

---

The biggest risk you face with a tenant is the potential for damage that could cost a fortune to repair in order to get your house back into condition for selling. The impression from the tenant's references should indicate that the tenant is responsible. There should be references from one or more previous landlords. Also, run a credit check, to make sure this person pays bills on time. Your broker should be a very valuable source of information on how to check out a prospective tenant. Since the broker will be earning a fee for the rental, take advantage of the broker's expertise in this area.

Beyond that step, use the lease agreement for protection. See the sample lease-option agreement (with comments) in the "For Your Notebook" section at the end of this chapter.

## CHAPTER SUMMARY

The lease-option arrangement give a right to a tenant to buy your house under certain terms. It's not the same as a right of first refusal, which is too restrictive to a seller and is not recommended. Leasing your house with an option to buy, when you really want to sell, isn't likely to be a great alternative either. But if the market is very bad and you can't sell the house, you might have little choice. Figure out the economic picture with pencil and paper, setting out scenarios for (1) your tenant buying, (2) your tenant not buying, and (3) not having a tenant.

If you decide to lease while still hoping for a sale, make sure to take every step possible to protect your interests and your house. Both your broker and lawyer will prove valuable in guiding you.

# FOR YOUR NOTEBOOK

## SAMPLE RESIDENTIAL LEASE WITH OPTION TO BUY

**\*\*FOR DISCUSSION WITH YOUR LAWYER ONLY—
DO NOT USE AS A CONTRACT\*\***

I. <u>DATE OF LEASE.</u>
This Lease is made on this 22nd day of November, 1990, and the lease shall be effective on the date listed in the section entitled "TERM," below.

II. <u>THE LANDLORD AND TENANT.</u>
This Lease is made between Paul Purchaser and Pat Purchaser of 456 Redwood, Apt. 12E, Ridgewood, Onestate (the "Tenant"), and Sam and Sue Seller of 123 Main Street, Centerville, One State (the "Landlord").

III. <u>THE LEASE AND THE LEASED HOUSE.</u>
The Landlord has agreed to lease and does hereby lease to the Tenant, and gives possession and use of to the Tenant, and the Tenant hereby leases from the Landlord, for the term and upon the terms and conditions contained in this Lease, the house located at 123 Main Street, Centerville, Onestate, described more fully in Exhibit A annexed hereto (the "House"). The Tenant shall not use the House for any purpose other than as a residence for Tenant and Tenant's immediate family.

---

**COMMENT:** It's often simpler to attach a photocopy of the deed description as a full legal description of the property instead of having it retyped on the form.

---

**TIP:** If the house is leased with any furniture in it, have your lawyer add a section to the lease stating what furniture is included (or attach a list to the lease) and requiring the tenant to return it in good condition.

---

IV. <u>TERM.</u>
The Landlord leases the House to the Tenant for an initial term of Six (6) months commencing on December 1, 1990, and terminating on May 31, 1991, unless extended for an additional term of One (1) month in accordance with the terms herein.

**COMMENT:** Most tenants will insist on a longer lease. However, there are a number of important reasons why you might prefer to get the shortest lease possible: (1) You want to be able to terminate the lease and remove the tenant as soon as possible in case of any problem with the tenant. (2) If you are purchasing a new home and wish to qualify for the tax-free rollover of the sales proceeds on the old house into the new house, your old house must qualify as your "principal residence" when you sell it. The longer the lease the more likely for the IRS to argue that you've converted the old house into a rental property.

V. RENT.
  A. The Tenant covenants and agrees to pay to the Landlord a fixed monthly rent in the amount of One Thousand Two Hundred Dollars ($1,200) per month payable in advance on the first day of each month during the term hereof.
  B. The Tenant shall pay as additional rent to the Landlord any amounts due under this Lease, any costs paid by Landlord on Tenant's behalf that are required to be reimbursed to the Landlord under this Lease. Additional rent shall also include reasonable attorney's fees incurred by the Landlord as a result of the Tenant's violating any provision of this Lease. Any additional rent due shall be due on the same date as the next monthly rent payment is due. The Landlord has the same rights to enforce the payment of additional rent as the Landlord does to enforce the payment of rent under this Lease.

**COMMENT:** In many states, it's important that the lease say that the amounts due you are to be treated as rent. This is because you may have more rights and protections under the law to collect rent than to collect payments due you that are not rent.

  C. The Tenant shall pay the rent herein reserved, such payments to be made to the Landlord at the address listed above, or at such other place as the Landlord may designate by notice to the Tenant, without notice or demand.
  D. Even if the Lease term, or any extension or renewal of same, shall commence on a date other than the first day of the month, the rent for the first month shall not be

apportioned based upon the number of days remaining in said month.

E. The rent reserved herein shall be paid without abatement, deduction, counterclaim, or set-off, except as may be specifically set forth in this Lease.

---

**COMMENT:** It's important to specify to that the tenant has no right of set-off. This means if the tenant pays for a repair or other item that he or she believes to be your responsibility, the tenant can't just offset the rent by the amount of the repair. Instead, the tenant must pay the rent and discuss the claim for reimbursement separately.

---

VI. <u>LANDLORD'S LIABILITY.</u>
The Landlord shall not be liable for any loss, injury, or damage to any person or any property unless the loss, injury, or damage is due to Landlord's negligence or misconduct. Tenant shall hold Landlord harmless from and against all cost, expense, and liability arising out of or based upon any and all claims, accidents, injuries, and damages.

VII. <u>INSURANCE.</u>
Tenant shall obtain, and keep in full force and effect throughout the term of this Lease and any extensions, insurance against loss or damage by fire, with customary extended coverage, including vandalism and malicious mischief with liability of not less than $100,000 per incident, and property-damage insurance in an amount not less than $150,000 (and shall name Landlord as an additional insured). The insurance shall be carried with loss payable to Landlord and Tenant as their interests appear. Such insurance shall be maintained with a reputable insurance company rated "A" or better by Best's. Tenant shall furnish Landlord a copy of such insurance policy, with evidence satisfactory to the Landlord that such insurance has been obtained and is in effect. The Tenant shall procure renewals of such insurance at least twenty (20) days before the expiration of any policy.

---

**COMMENT:** It's critical that the tenant obtain proper and adequate insurance. Check with your lawyer and insurance agent as to the minimum coverage you should specify and the requirements you should have for the insurance company. Be certain to discuss what coverage you should maintain as landlord with your insurance agent. Don't rely on a lease clause requiring the tenant to buy insurance as sufficient protection.

## VIII. BROKER.

The Landlord and Tenant acknowledge that XYZ Realty Company arranged this Lease transaction and that the landlord shall be responsible for all commissions due such broker. The Tenant and Landlord represent that no other broker has been involved in this Lease and agree to indemnify each other for any breach of this representation.

**COMMENT:** You know the broker you dealt with, but what happens if the tenant/buyer had any dealings with another broker? You don't want to be on the hook for any other brokerage commissions, so the tenant must tell you in the contract that there were no other brokers, and if there turn out to be any, the tenant will pay.

## IX. SECURITY DEPOSIT.

The Tenant shall pay to the Landlord One Thousand Two Hundred Dollars ($1,200.00) to be held by the Landlord as a security deposit in the First National Bank of Onestate. The Landlord shall not be required to pay any interest earned on such account to the Tenant. At the termination of this Lease, the Landlord shall return the remaining security deposit to the Tenant. The Landlord may apply this security deposity to repair any damage done to the premises for which the Tenant is liable for repairs, or to reimburse Landlord for any amounts due to the Landlord under this Lease.

**COMMENT:** Check with your lawyer about local requirements concerning the security deposit. In many states, interest must be paid to tenants on residential leases. Also, inquire as to whether there are any requirements for reporting to the tenant, or how the money must be handled. Often the lease will address what you must do if you sell the house before the lease ends. This is not mentioned here because a tenant negotiating a purchase option is likely to object to your having the right to sell the house before the option expires.

**TIP:** Make sure to get enough of a security deposit to protect your interests. This sample agreement requires a security deposit equal to one month's rent. While this is typical, there is no reason not to request a larger deposit if you can get it. Remember, if the tenant damages the house and moves out, you might be much worse off than if you had simply continued trying to sell the house. In most lease-option arrangements the security deposit is credited against the purchase price if the tenant decides to buy the house. Stress this when negotiating the amount of security deposit with the tenant.

---

 X. REPRESENTATIONS AND WARRANTIES OF THE TENANT.
  Tenant represents and warrants:
  A. It shall during the term of this lease and any extensions hereunder, maintain and operate the House as a personal residence for the Tenant and the Tenant's immediate family, in a lawful manner in compliance with all local, state, federal, or other laws, regulations, statutes, ordinances and the like.
  B. It shall not at any time use, or permit others to use, the House for any business or nonresidential purpose.
  C. It shall not permit a pet to occupy the house.
  D. It assumes total and complete responsibility for any and all liabilities, suits, actions, and the like arising as a direct or indirect result of its use of the House.
  E. No improvements, including but not limited to painting, wallpapering, or other changes, shall be made to the House without Landlord's prior written consent.
  F. It shall take any actions requested by Landlord's counsel to effect the purposes of this Agreement.
 XI. REPRESENTATIONS AND WARRANTIES OF THE LAND-LORD.
  The Landlord warrants and represents that:
  A. It has full right and power to execute and perform this Lease and to grant the estate demised herein.
  B. It has good and marketable title to the House, free and clear of all encumbrances, liens, and restrictions except as set forth on Exhibit B.
 XII. REPAIRS AND ALTERATIONS.
  A. Tenant covenants throughout the term of this Lease, and any extension hereof, at its sole cost and expense, to maintain in good order and condition the House, including all shrubbery, appliances, and systems. Promptly at Tenant's own cost and expense, the Tenant shall make all repairs, ordinary or extraordinary, structural or non-

structural, foreseen or unforeseen. Repairs shall include replacements and renewals.

---

**COMMENT:** The tenant's lawyer is likely to object to such broad language, requiring the tenant to make extraordinary or structural repairs. At minimum, the tenant should be liable to make such improvements when the tenant has caused, or contributed to, the damage.

---

B. Tenant shall not commit or suffer, and shall use all reasonable precaution to prevent waste, damage, or injury to the House or anything contained in the House.

C. The Tenant shall not make any alterations or additions to the House except with the prior written consent of the Landlord, which may be withheld for any reason. The Tenant shall pay all costs, expenses, and charges for any alterations approved by the Landlord, and shall save Landlord harmless on account of any claims of mechanics, materialmen, or any other liens or liabilities arising out of alterations or additions to the House. Any buildings, improvements, alterations, or additions shall become the property of the Landlord, unless the Landlord directs the Tenant, in writing, to remove such improvements. Any costs of removal shall be borne by the tenant.

D. The Tenant shall pay all maintenance costs (including but not limited to any costs necessary to maintain the proper appearance of the House such as lawn mowing, weed and refuse removal, extermination to keep the premises free of rodents, insects and other pests, cleaning of chimney and furnace), and any expenses necessary to maintain the House in a safe condition and in accordance with the rules, regulations, and ordinances of any local government. The Tenant shall be responsible for all utility costs, including but not limited to electricity, sewer, water, oil, heat, and telephone.

XIII. GOVERNMENT REGULATIONS, ORDINANCES, ETC.

The Tenant shall comply with all ordinances, orders, judgments, statutes, laws, rules, regulations, decrees, injunctions, and other requirements of any federal, state, county, or local government, or any company insuring the House, which now or at any time during the term of this Lease apply to the House ("Law"). The Tenant shall not have the right to contest any such Law. The Tenant shall give the Landlord

prompt written notice of any notices received from any
government body or insurance company.

XIV. ASSIGNMENT AND SUBLET, ENCUMBRANCES.

The Tenant shall not have the right to assign or sublet the
House, or to place any mortgage or other encumbrance on
the House. The Landlord shall not be liable for any mechanic's or other lien for any labor or materials due to work
initiated by the Tenant. The Tenant shall promptly discharge
by payment, bond, or otherwise any such lien. The Tenant
shall not sell, transfer, mortgage, pledge, lease, license, or
encumber the House or this Lease without obtaining the
prior written consent of the Landlord, which consent shall
be in the sole discretion of the Landlord and which may
be withheld for any reason.

---

**COMMENT:** You probably don't want to give the tenant any right to lease
your house to anyone else. You should have completely investigated the
tenant you're renting to before signing the lease, but you probably wouldn't
ever meet the person the tenant would lease to. Absolute control of this
is essential. The tenant also must be prohibited from putting any mortgage
or other lien on the house. If the tenant doesn't buy the house, you don't
want more problems when you try to sell it to someone else after the
lease ends.

---

XV. SUBORDINATION.

Any mortgage placed on the House by Landlord shall not
be subject to or subordinate to this Lease. The Tenant's
possession of the House under this Lease shall be subject
to and subordinate to any such mortgage. Tenant shall take
all actions, and execute any documents, reasonably requested
by Landlord's lawyer to confirm the provisions of this Section.

XVI. INSPECTION.

The Landlord shall have the right to inspect the House for
any reason, and to show the House to any prospective purchaser or tenant at any reasonable time after 24 Hours' notice.

---

**COMMENT:** Liberal inspection rights are important to have in the lease,
and just as important to use. If the tenant is trashing your house, the
sooner you find out and can begin eviction proceedings, the better.

---

XVII. <u>TAXES AND ASSESSMENTS.</u>
Tenant shall pay all real property taxes and levies on the House. The Tenant shall promptly deliver to the Landlord all bills, notices, or assessments for taxes.

XVIII. <u>FIRE AND CASUALTY.</u>
A. In the event of any damage or loss to the House by fire or other casualty during the Lease term, the Tenant shall give prompt notice thereof to the Landlord. If the fire or other casualty is caused by the Tenant's act or neglect, the Tenant shall pay for the entire cost of repairing the House. If the House is partially damaged by fire or other casualty, the rent due by the Tenant shall be pro-rated to reflect the portion of the House that remains usable.
B. If the House if completely destroyed, this Lease shall terminate and rent shall be paid through the day prior to the destruction.
C. If the costs to repair damage due to fire or other casualty exceeds Fifteen Thousand Dollars ($15,000.00), or will reasonably require more than Sixty (60) days to repair, the Landlord may cancel this lease by giving Ten (10) days' Notice to the Tenant. Should the Landlord cancel the Lease pursuant to this section, the Tenant shall not be relieved of any liability for the costs to repair the House if the fire or casualty was due to Tenant's act or neglect.

XIX. <u>BANKRUPTCY.</u>
If the Tenant files a voluntary petition in bankruptcy, is adjudicated a bankrupt, claims benefit under any insolvency act, if a receiver is appointed for the Tenant's assets, or makes an assignment for the benefit of creditors, then the Landlord may cancel this lease with no further obligation to Tenant.

XX. <u>QUIET ENJOYMENT.</u>
So long as the Tenant pays the rent and complies with all other requirements of this Lease, the Tenant shall peaceably and quietly have the right to occupy and enjoy the House.

XXI. <u>DEFAULT BY TENANT.</u>
A. Each of the following shall constitute a default under this Lease by the Tenant:
  1. Failure of the Tenant to pay any installment of Rent within Five (5) days of when due, without notice or demand.

2. Failure to pay any additional Rent costs or expenses herein agreed to be paid by Tenant, within Five (5) days after written notice.

3. Failure of the Tenant to observe or perform any of the terms of this Lease and the failure continues for Twenty (20) days after Notice by the Landlord specifying the failure and demanding correction. The only exception to this Twenty (20) day period shall be when the failure requires acts to be done that cannot reasonably be done within such Twenty (20) day period. In this case no default shall exist so long as the Tenant shall have commenced correcting the failure within this period and shall diligently continue correcting the failure to completion.

B. If any Event of Default shall occur and shall not be corrected within the time specified above, the Landlord, at any time thereafter, may at its option give written notice to the Tenant stating that this Lease shall end on the date contained in the Notice (which shall be no earlier than Five (5) days after the mailing of the notice). On that date this Lease and all of the Tenant's rights shall terminate and the Tenant shall quit and surrender the House. The Landlord may also evict the tenant for any cause provided for by law. If this occurs, the Landlord may, without notice, re-enter and repossess the House, using such force for that purpose as may be necessary without being liable to indictment, prosecution, or damages. Tenant expressly waives: (i) the service of any notice of the Landlord's intention to re-enter provided for in any statute; (ii) the instituting of legal proceeding; and (iii) any right of redemption provided by any law presently in force or hereafter enacted, for re-entry or repossession or to restore the operation of this Lease.

---

**COMMENT:** It may be illegal for the tenant to waive all of these rights. Many laws tend to favor residential tenants over their landlords in order to protect them. Discuss this with your real estate lawyer and make sure that you reserve in the lease the maximum protection you are allowed under law. Local law may also require that specific types of notice be given to the tenant before you can sue or take other actions. In some areas, notice may not be required if the violation is the tenant's failure to pay rent. Be certain to engage a real estate attorney who does a considerable amount of landlord-tenant law. If you don't follow the required procedures your efforts could be severely hampered. You could even end up being liable to the tenant for damages.

A common procedure for removing a tenant is called eviction. You may have to give notice to the tenant and then file a suit (complaint) with the court, and serve a summons on the tenant. If you are successful in court, you will receive a warrant of removal (the name will vary). You might then have to have the sheriff remove the tenant.

---

**CAUTION:** The key point is, getting out a bad tenant can be an expensive and difficult process. It pays to know who you rent to. This is also why no-money down deals can prove to be very dangerous. You might have to incur substantial costs to get your house back. So make sure the down-payment is adequate.

---

C. Each right and remedy of Landlord provided for in this Lease shall be cumulative and shall be in addition to every other right or remedy provided for in this Lease, at law, or in equity.

---

**TIP:** Before deciding to lease you house, sit down with a real estate lawyer who knows the courts and is familiar with local landlord-tenant law. Ask what happens when you want to evict a tenant, how long it takes, how expensive it is. It is very important to understand your rights before you begin interviewing tenants. If you realize that the local laws and courts strongly favor tenants, so that it will be very difficult to evict a bad tenant, you will want to be all the more careful in selecting your tenant. The same lawyer should also be able to advise you as to what you can and cannot ask prospective tenants without violating the law.

---

XXII. CONDEMNATION.

If there is a condemnation of any part or all of the House, then either the Tenant or the Landlord shall have the right to terminate this Lease, and the Tenant's obligation to pay rent and taxes shall end as of the date the Tenant is required to vacate the House. Rent and other charges payable by the Tenant shall be apportioned. Any condemnation award shall be paid by the Landlord.

XXIII. TENANT'S PURCHASE OPTION.

A. The Landlord grants to the Tenant the option ("Option") to purchase the House at any time prior to the expiration of this Lease in accordance with the terms set forth in this Section.

B. The Tenant cannot exercise this Option if the Tenant is then in default under any term or provision of this Lease. The landlord may elect not to consummate the sale pursuant to this Option if, after the date of exercise by the Tenant, but prior to the date of closing on such purchase, the Tenant is in default under any provision of this Lease.

C. The Tenant must exercise this Option by providing the Landlord notice at least Thirty (30) days prior to the intended date of exercise. The notice must specify a closing date for the purchase. The closing date must be at least Thirty (30) days after the date of the notice, but not more than Ninety (90) days after the date of the notice.

D. Upon receiving notice of Tenant's election to exercise this Option, the Landlord shall:

1. Retain an appraiser at Landlord's expense to value the House. If the Tenant does not agree with the value set by the Landlord's appraiser, than the Tenant, at Tenant's sole expense, shall select another appraiser to value the House. If the two appraisers cannot agree on a value of the House, they shall select a third appraiser whose determination shall control. The cost of the third shall be borne equally by the Landlord and the Tenant.

2. Order a title report. The Tenant may not object to any exceptions listed in the title report, which is listed in Exhibit B to this Lease.

E. The purchase price to be paid at closing in bank or certified funds shall be equal to the appraised value of the House as determined in this Section, reduced by the credit provided in the following section (the "Credit").

F. The Tenant shall receive a Credit against the purchase price under this option, which equals Ten Percent (10%) of all of the monthly rental payments paid by the Tenant to the Landlord on a timely basis as required under this Lease.

---

**COMMENT:** The higher the credit, the bigger the incentive to the tenant. However, if the credit is too high, you could create a tax problem. The IRS might argue that you really sold the house when the lease was signed. This point is discussed more fully in the following chapter.

     G. The tenant shall be responsible for the costs of a survey,
title insurance policy, transfer taxes, recording fees, and
other charges.

     H. At the closing, the Landlord shall deliver to the Tenant
a general warranty deed.

---

**COMMENT:** See the discussion of deeds in Chapter 26.

---

XXIV. SURRENDER.

Upon the termination of this Lease, any improvements made
by the Tenant shall become the property of the Landlord.
The Landlord, however, shall have the right to require the
Tenant, by giving written notice at least Ten (10) days prior
to the termination of this Lease, to remove any improvement.
The Tenant shall, on or before the last day of this Lease, or
on the earlier termination thereof, peaceably and quietly
leave the House and surrender to the Landlord the House,
broom clean and in the same condition in which the House
was at the commencement of this Lease, ordinary wear and
tear excepted. The Tenant indemnifies the Landlord against
any damage or loss that the Landlord shall suffer by reason
of any delay in the Tenant's surrender of the House, or
failure to deliver the House free of changes or additions.
The provisions of this Section shall survive the termination
of this lease.

XXV. WAIVER.

The Landlord's failure to insist on the observance of any
term of this Lease shall not be deemed to be a waiver of
any provisions of the Lease. No failure on the part of the
Landlord to enforce any term of this Lease, and no waiver
of any right under this Lease by the Landlord, unless in
writing, shall constitute a waiver as to any future right of
the Landlord. The Landlord's receipt or acceptance of any
rent or any other money from the Tenant shall not reinstate
or extend the Lease.

XXVI. NOTICE.

Any notice under this Lease shall be in writing and shall
be sent by registered or certified mail, or by hand delivery
addressed to the addresses set forth above, or to such other
address or person as either party may designate by notice.
Any notice, demand, or request given hereunder shall be
deemed given Four (4) days after the date the notice is

properly mailed, or on the date the notice is delivered by hand.

XXVII. TENANT'S ESTOPPEL LETTER.

The Tenant shall within Ten (10) days after a written request by the Landlord, certify by written instrument, duly executed, acknowledged, and delivered, to any Mortgagee, assignee of any mortgagee or purchaser, or any proposed mortgagee, or any other person, firm, or corporation specified by Landlord, whether this Lease has been modified whether this lease is in full force and effect, and whether there are then existing any set-offs or defenses against the provisions of this Lease.

XXVIII. INTERPRETATION; CONSTRUCTION.

If any term or provision of this Lease is found invalid or unenforceable, the remainder of this Lease shall not be affected. The captions in this Lease are inserted only for convenience and in no way limit or affect the interpretation of any section of this Lease. This Lease constitutes the only agreement between the Landlord and Tenant concerning the lease of the House and all other matters discussed in this Lease. There are no oral agreements or understandings other than those contained in this Lease. This Lease shall be governed by and construed in accordance with the laws of Onestate.

XXIX. MISCELLANEOUS.

This Lease may not be changed except by a writing signed by the party against whom enforcement of any such change is to be enforced. The covenants and agreements contained in this Lease apply to, inure to the benefit of, and are binding upon, the Landlord and Tenant and their successors and assigns. The parties intend to create a landlord and tenant relationship, and no other relationship whatsoever, and nothing in this Lease shall be construed to make parties hereto partners or joint ventures, or to render either party hereto liable for any of the debts or obligations for the other party. The parties hereto waive the right to trial by jury in any issue involving the Lease. Tenant, for itself and all persons claiming under it, waives all present and future rights permitting it to redeem the House from Landlord after Tenant is disposed or ejected.

---

**COMMENT:** This last clause may not be permitted in your state. Check with your real estate lawyer.

---

### XXX. <u>RECORDING OF MEMORANDUM.</u>
The Tenant shall not record this Lease or any memorandum of this Lease.

---

**COMMENT:** You will not want the tenant to record a lease, if you can avoid it, because if the tenant doesn't buy the house, you'll have to record another document to cancel out the recorded lease. Generally, you don't want to create any potential for title problems with a house you're selling. The tenant however, might insist on a right to record the lease so that the purchase option will be in the public record. The issue will generally be taken up by the lawyers.

---

IN WITNESS WHEREOF, the parties hereto have duly executed this lease the day and year first above written.

---

**ADDITIONAL COMMENTS:** If the lease is prepared by a broker, there may be an attorney-review provision. When the contract is prepared by a broker, you have the right for a limited number of days to have the contract reviewed by your lawyer and to have your lawyer make objections. If this situation applies to you, immediately contact your attorney before the time period allowed runs out.

If you can get the tenant to have another person guarantee the lease, this can be a considerable help. This gives you another person to go after if the tenant defaults. See the discussion of guarantors in Chapter 19.

---

LANDLORD:

_____

Sam Seller

_____

Sue Seller

TENANT:

_____

Paul Purchaser

_____

Pat Purchaser

# 22 TAX CONSEQUENCES OF LEASING

## EFFECT ON THE ROLLOVER BENEFIT

There are a number of potentially important tax consequences of renting your house. The most important matter, which you must resolve before renting your home, is whether you risk losing the ability to roll over the gain on the eventual sale of your house into a replacement house. If you could lose that benefit, don't rent.

---

**CAUTION:** Consult with your tax adviser. This is a complicated issue, and you will probably have a substantial amount of money at stake. Don't rent until your tax adviser is comfortable with this risk.

---

The tax laws provide a very favorable tax break for homeowners that you probably don't want to risk losing. When you sell your principal residence, if you buy a replacement principal residence within two years which is at least as expensive as the house you sold, you can defer paying any tax on the sale. This is explained more fully in Chapter 27. There is a condition, however. To qualify for this great tax break, the house you sell and the house you buy both must be used as your principal residence.

The potential risk with renting your old house before you sell is that you will change its character from being your principal residence to being a rental property in IRS terms. And a rental property can't qualify for the tax-free rollover. The IRS will claim that you abandoned the house as your principal residence if you rented it for an extended period. However, the courts have permitted taxpayers to temporarily rent a house while trying to sell it.

But what is temporary? There are no exact guidelines as to what you can and can't do. The following list of suggestions will support your case that the house you rented out should still qualify for the tax-free rollover treatment:

- Rent for as short a lease term as possible—the shorter the better.
- Reserve the right in the lease to show the house to prospective buyers.
- Keep advertising the house for sale throughout the entire rental period.
- Include an option to buy in the lease.
- Sell the house (and buy your replacement house) within two years of moving out.

---

**CAUTION:** If there is any chance that you will not have sold the old house before two years from the date you move out, carefully evaluate the tax results with your accountant. The tax cost could be so horrendous that it may pay to cut the price of the house radically and just sell it.

---

---

**TIP:** If you're over age 55, the first $125,000 of gain can be excluded from tax. This may be enough so that you're not worried about the rollover rules. Check with your tax adviser before proceeding.

---

## TAX PROCEDURES AND DEPRECIATION

Once you've determined that the rental won't ruin your ability to roll over the gain on your house, you can then consider the tax effects of the rental itself. If you rent your house with the intent of earning a profit, you can deduct expenses that you pay against the rental income you realize. Expenses include all ordinary and necessary business expenses: insurance, property taxes (but not special assessments), maintenance and repairs (but not capital improvements that add to the value of the house), accounting, legal and other professional fees, and depreciation.

Depreciation is calculated by dividing your investment in the house (adjusted tax basis) by 27.5 years. Here is a definition of "adjusted tax basis": the price you paid for the house including all of the ancillary closing costs, *plus* any capital improvements you made (e.g., a new roof, a new porch), *minus* any losses from fire or other casualty and any depreciation deductions already claimed (e.g., on a home office you maintained in the house).

---

**EXAMPLE:**  Harry Homeowner (Howard's brother—see Chapter 19) paid $145,000 for his house. He also paid the lawyer $800 for the closing. He spent $3,200 on a new roof and $11,900 on a new den addition. His adjusted tax basis in the house is $160,900.

This amount, however, includes the value of the land (which can't be depreciated) and the house (which can be depreciated). So Harry must allocate his $160,900 adjusted tax basis between these two items. Harry's property-tax bill assesses his house at $135,000 and his land at $32,000. Harry can use this ratio as an estimate of how to allocate his adjusted tax basis to the house:

$$\frac{\$135,000}{\$135,000 + \$32,000} \times \$160,900 = \$133,069$$

Harry then calculates his depreciation deduction by dividing the $133,069 by 27.5, so his annual depreciation deduction is $4,839. For the first year, however, the deduction will probably be lower, because for the month in which you first start depreciating the property, you're only allowed to claim one-half month's depreciation, and because there probably will be only part of the year to claim.

---

With the deduction for depreciation, you can have a loss for tax purposes, or no gain, while still having a positive cash flow.

---

**EXAMPLE:**  Harry rents his house for $1,200 per month earning $14,400 for the year. Harry pays out $9,000 in mortgage interest, $2,400 in property taxes, and $650 in insurance. Harry earns a cash flow (cash he has available to spend) of $2,350 [$14,400 − ($9,000 + $2,400 + $650)]. But for tax purposes Harry will have a loss of $2,489 because he will deduct the $4,839 of depreciation calculated in the above example. If Harry is in a 28 percent tax bracket, deducting this loss will save him $697 in taxes [$2,849 × 28%]. Thus, Harry's total benefit from renting the house will be $3,047 [$697 + $2,350].

---

## WHAT BENEFIT CAN YOU GET FROM LOSS?

If you realize a loss on renting your house, you must satisfy a number of requirements in order to claim that loss for tax purposes. The most important of these are the passive loss limitation rules.

These rules say you cannot apply losses realized on a rental real estate investment (like your rented house) to offset other income (wages, dividends, interest, etc.) and reduce the tax due. However, there is one very important exception to this rule that many people will qualify for. Under certain conditions, you can deduct up to $25,000 of tax losses from certain rental properties without any limitation by the passive loss rules. The conditions are that (1) your modified adjusted gross income (your income on your tax return before deducting itemized deductions, subject to a number of adjustments—it will simply be referred to as income in the following discussion) must not be more than $150,000, and (2) you must actively participate in the leasing of the property.

---

**TIP:** If you hire a broker for a fee to find a tenant and oversee the property, make sure that your agreement with the broker gives you the final say in approving tenants, determining when repairs must be made, etc. Also, be sure to document the efforts you make in the rental process. Keep notes showing the days you check on the house and the phone calls you make to the broker and others, in order to demonstrate to the IRS that you were active.

---

This benefit is actually phased out as your income rises from $100,000 to $150,000: If your income is $100,000, you can use up to the full $25,000 of tax losses; if your income is $125,000, you can claim up to $12,500 in tax losses; once your income reaches the $150,000 mark, you will only be able to use the tax losses on your rental property to offset income you earn on other rental properties or other passive investments.

## IS IT A LEASE-OPTION ARRANGEMENT OR A SALE?

When you have an option included in the lease agreement, depending on how the arrangement is structured, there is a risk that the IRS will say that instead of leasing, you really sold the property immediately on the installment method. (See Chapter 19 on seller financing.) The IRS is most likely to make this claim when it is obvious that the tenant will exercise the option.

---

**EXAMPLE:** Harry Homeowner owns a house worth $145,000. Harry leases his house to Barbara Buyer for $3,500 per month. The fair rental is really $1,200 per month. At the end of the lease term, Barbara can buy that house from Harry for $10,000. It's obvious that the monthly payments are higher than any real tenant would ever pay. It's also obvious that nobody would fail to exercise such an option.

To the IRS it would be obvious that Harry has sold the house to Barbara on the installment method, and this will have a dramatically different tax consequence for Harry. He will not be entitled to claim any depreciation deductions because he won't be considered to own the hosue for tax purposes. If Harry doesn't qualify to roll over his gain, he will have to report taxable income from the sale proceeds as if he had sold the house.

---

In less extreme situations it can be unclear whether the IRS will respect the transaction as a lease-option arrangement or choose to treat it as a sale. To avoid a problem, consider the following points:

- The higher the percentage of the monthly rent that is credited toward the purchase price, the more it will look like a sale. Crediting 10 percent of the rent shouldn't create much problem. Crediting 75 percent will almost assuredly result in a sale treatment.

- If title to the house transfers to the "tenant" when the "lease" is signed, the transaction will be considered a sale. You wouldn't want this to happen anyway unless you had a mortgage or other legal documentation to protect your interests.

- The monthly payments by the tenant shouldn't exceed the fair rental value of the house by a significant amount.

- The purchase option shouldn't be much less than the fair market value of the property.

- The tenant shouldn't be required to make substantial improvements to the house. If the tenant had to invest substantial money, it would be obvious that the tenant would exercise the option.

## CHAPTER SUMMARY

There is a possible tax effect of renting out your house that you want to avoid: You could lose the valuable homeowner's benefit of rolling over the gain when you sell one house into the purchase of another house, so that you will have to pay tax on that gain. This could happen if the IRS characterized the house as a rental property instead of as your primary residence. Take steps to avoid this outcome and consult your tax adviser.

If you do rent, you might be able to deduct the expenses of maintaining the property, as well as depreciation. A loss, however, can be claimed only if you meet certain requirements.

Improper structuring of a rental with an option to buy can result in the IRS's treating the lease-option arrangement as an immediate sale on the installment method. Again, consult your tax adviser.

# Part Five

# WRAPPING UP THE DEAL

# 23 ONCE YOU GET AN OFFER: NEGOTIATING WITH AND CLOSING THE BUYER

## WHAT IS "CLOSING THE BUYER"?

You've made all the right preparations to sell your house. You've hired a lawyer and maybe contracted with an agent. You've cleaned, fixed, and decorated—your house looks so good you almost hate to move out; you've prepared a fact sheet, spread the word, and actually started showing the house. It's like being in the boat with a baited fishing rod and line. Whoops! You've got a bite. Now what? Now you've got to manage to get that fish in.

The objective is to get an agreement on a price, to get a deposit, and to get a signed preliminary contract. That's closing the buyer. It's not the same as closing the house (see later chapters), because a lot still will have to be done before the sale is complete. But at the present stage of selling your house, you're working on getting an agreement on price and terms with a ready, able, and almost willing buyer.

## NEGOTIATING TACTICS THAT WORK

The prospective buyer says, "Would you take $105,000?" Or: "Do the appliances and the fireplace equipment go with the house?" Or: "Could you move out in two months?" Or: "Would you consider renting to us and giving us an option to buy?" Or: "If we were thinking of buying, could you help us with a second mortgage?"

Welcome to the world of negotiating—sometimes known as bargaining or haggling. In this soft market, sellers aren't exactly in the catbird seat. You can't bargain bitterly over every last nickel, or stubbornly refuse to let any personal property, not even the old lawn furniture, out of your possession.

On the other hand, don't just give the house away. If the buyers are serious about wanting to live in your house and not steal it, they should be willing to give a little.

Keep in mind that the house price isn't the only thing you and the buyers can use to negotiate. You can also negotiate over the following:

- The move-in date (the buyers may want to move in quickly, because their lease is almost up, which gives you a bargaining point).

- Whether you'll help with financing. (See Chapter 19.)

- Whether you'll let them rent for a while, with an option to buy. (See Chapter 21.)

- Whether you'll permit certain contingencies—for example, the buyers will proceed to buy the house only if they can obtain a mortgage for the amount they need at a rate that's desirable.

  Your lawyer should guide you here. If you permit any contingencies, they should expire after a certain time—say, 30 days—and the terms should be realistic; the interest rate the buyers are seeking shouldn't be so low as to be miraculous. Certain contingencies are acceptable: The purchase may be subject to the approval of the buyer's spouse back home, or a house inspector's report, and so forth. Here, too, there should be specific expiration dates.

Other negotiating points are really ways to lower the price indirectly, which may allow you or the buyer to reap a tax savings— or to save face. You might offer the following:

- You'll give the buyers the value of whatever oil remains in the tank.

- You'll contribute an amount of money to lower the buyer's mortgage interest rate.

- You'll pay certain closing costs that, in your area, are not traditionally paid by the seller—like the cost of title insurance.

- You'll pay for a variety of small improvements—for having new wallpaper put up in the living room, for having the outside painted the color of the buyer's choice, or buying new kitchen appliances.

## SOME RULES OF SELLING

1. In a buyer's market, the first rule is, don't try so hard to win the bargaining contest that you lose the war—you don't sell your house.

You can tell that your ego is involved if you catch yourself straining over gnats. If you want to sell your house for $200,000, and the buyer offers $2,000 less, note that the difference is only 1 percent—the difference between 99 cents and one dollar. Not that $2,000 is a sniggling amount of money; just don't let it prevent your moving to a warmer climate, or a bigger house, or to a smaller house that will free up some of your equity in your current home.

The story is told of a woman who went to a used-car dealer and gave him $50 on the sly. She told the dealer, "When my husband bargains with you over the value of his car, at the last minute raise your bid by $50—so he thinks he won."

One house sale actually fell through because the seller wouldn't throw in an old washing machine!

Here's one way to reduce the pain of giving up some profit: You bought your house for $60,000 several years ago. Now you're offering it for $105,000, but you would settle for $100,000. A buyer bids $90,000. Is this a $10,000 loss (from your $100,000 rock-bottom price) or a $30,000 gain (above your purchase price)? If you think of it as a gain, perhaps you'll be more positive about the selling price.

In short, be prepared to lose the bargaining contest—to receive a little less than you wanted—in order to accomplish the goal, which is to sell your house at a reasonable price.

2. Become as well informed as you can. Is the market soft or is it reviving? Are mortgage interest rates going down, going up, or remaining the same? What about house prices? Is the type of house you're selling (style, number of rooms, location, price range) plentiful or scarce? (Even in a dreary market, a four-bedroom Tudor in the best area of the best school district could be in a class by itself.) If the market is reviving, interest rates are sinking, the inventory is shrinking, prices are going up, and your particular house doesn't

have much competition, you can be a little less accommodating when you bargain.

Also find out as much as you can about the buyers. Have they been looking for months, and are they ready to settle down? Do they have relatives and friends nearby? Do they have children, and are they attracted by the fact that a good school is a block away? Do they use public transportation to go to work, and are there buses or trains a block away from you? Must they buy a house soon because their lease is running out? Try to find out through the real estate agent, or, if you're selling on your own, by talking to them before showing them around your house. (See Chapter 16.)

3. Remember that the first offer is often the best offer. The reason is that when your house first comes on the market, the pool of buyers is the largest, and some of them have been looking for months. At that time, the chances of there being a "perfect" buyer for your house are unusually high. (A perfect buyer is someone for whom your house is almost perfectly suitable in all respects.) Therefore, if you reject the first offer because you want to gamble that another perfect buyer will come along and make a higher bid, you will likely be disappointed. A good deal of time may have to pass before a new pool of buyers (who haven't seen your house) builds up again.

---

**CAUTION:** No, the first offer isn't *always* from the perfect buyer. The first offer could be from a house stealer—someone who goes around making bids for houses at 20 percent to 25 percent below their fair-market value, and who plans to resell the house for a profit shortly thereafter. Let your agent guide you, and your lawyer, and your common sense.

---

4. Become familiar with the rules of the game. Often, in house sales, the buyer submits a written offer that's 10 percent below the asking price. The seller may reject the offer, and counteroffer with a price 3 percent below the asking price. The buyer returns with an offer 5 percent below the asking price—and, after a little give and take, it's a done deal.

---

**EXAMPLE:** If the house is going for $101,000, the first offer might be as low as $90,000. The seller counteroffers with $98,000. The buyer goes up to $95,000—and the sale might be made at $96,900.

---

An axiom about negotiations is that whoever makes the biggest "concessions," and makes them fastest, loses. (A buyer's concession is a boost in the bid; a seller's concession is a lowering of the asking price.) So, don't offer a house at $101,000, then offer to reduce it to $95,000 right away. The buyer may figure that, because you've lowered your price so drastically so quickly, he or she can get you down to $90,000.

Your concessions should be progressively smaller, to dampen the buyer's expectations. You might reduce your $101,000 price by $3,000, then by $1,500, then by $500. But the buyer should have boosted his or her concessions by similar amounts.

Have a target price in mind. If you offer your house for $101,000 and the market remains soft, you might decide to sell it for $96,000 (your rock-bottom price) to a buyer who (a) doesn't ask you to help out with the mortgage, and can certainly obtain a mortgage; and (b) can close at a time that's convenient to you. Three concessions— $3,000, $1,500, and $500—will bring you there.

If your buyer starts out with an offer of $90,000, though, and then makes the same concessions you made, his or her final price will be only $95,000. Depending on the circumstances, you might be wise to hold off on your concessions until it seems that both of you are heading toward the $96,000 figure rather than $95,000.

## MORE TIPS ON NEGOTIATING

Ignore statements like, "This is my final offer," or "Take it or leave it." Just continue negotiating. One agent has described a typical transaction as follows: The seller asks $300,000. The buyer bids $280,000. The seller counteroffers with $295,000, saying, "This is my final, rock-bottom offer. I'm not going one penny lower." The buyer raises his or her offering price to $285,000, saying, "Take it or leave it. I'm not going a nickel higher." They agree on $290,000.

If the buyer says, "Why don't we split the difference?" reply that you can't afford to. You need the money to buy the house you want, or to enjoy a comfortable retirement, or whatever. Otherwise, the buyer may offer $90,000, you counteroffer $98,000, and splitting the difference would leave you with only $94,000. Pleading poverty is always a good argument.

If the buyer says, "Be reasonable," reply: "I've thought it over carefully, and I really believe I am being reasonable. You won't find another house with all these amenities for less in the entire community." (If your agent says, "Be reasonable," maybe you aren't being reasonable. Your agent, remember, is legally and ethically obligated to sell your house for the best price and on the best terms.)

If you make any concessions, invoke the notion of fairness to win other favors. "Okay, I'll lower my price by another $1,000. But then it would be only fair if you change the move-in date, so I can move out earlier." Or: "How about you let us remain two weeks after the closing, free of charge?"

Remember that you can use cash substitutes. "Look, we're only $2,000 apart. How about I throw in the brass fireplace equipment and the lawn furniture? I had been planning to sell them at a tag sale. And you can keep the oil that's still in the tank."

If the buyers keep harping on minor imperfections in your house—a cracked window, a stain on the carpet, and so forth—offer to have them fixed. Buyers tend to overestimate the cost of repairs. By paying for such repairs yourself, you'll allay their worries—and you won't really be spending much money. This way, you may wind up selling your house for closer to your asking price, or even at your full asking price.

If the buyer refuses to budge, and you yourself can't budge, and if you have an agent, a last resort is to ask the agent to reduce his or her commission—just to guarantee that the sale goes through. Otherwise, decide if the amount is worth losing the sale over.

## THE FISH GIVES A MIGHTY JUMP (OR, THE BUYER ALMOST GETS AWAY)

Even if your prospects say yes, they put down a deposit, and they prepare to sign a contract (even if they sign the contract), the game isn't over. They may succumb to buyer's remorse, as it's called.

When they return for another visit, they may suddenly see flaws they overlooked. Or a serious issue may arise—whether they can get a mortgage, whether you will knock a little off the price, whether the appliances go with the house, and so forth. They just may get scared.

There's a way you can deal with their second-thoughts, however: Be reassuring. Some agents always tell nervous buyers, "Years from now, you'll thank me for helping you buy this house. We'll run into each other at the supermarket or bank, and you'll thank me."

You, as the seller, can say, "This house has been good to us, and I'm sure it will be good for you. We've raised a healthy family in a good neighborhood, and I'm sure you will, too. We've also made a decent profit on the place—not a big profit, mind you, but a decent one. And so will you. And if you ever have any problems, just call us. But as we've said, the basement's dry as a bone, the appliances are new, and the neighborhood's the best in town. We know you'll be as happy living here as we've been."

Or just use a one-sentence reassurance: "You're getting a good house at a good price, and you'll never have any regrets."

Before the closing takes place, keep on the best possible terms with the buyer. Give him or her a list of all the tradespeople and professionals you recommend in the area—physicians, lawyers, electricians, carpenters, plumbers, and so forth. Gather together all the warranties and guides; collect all the house keys, inside and outside, and label them. If they call with questions—even if they call over and over again—be cooperative.

If you must say no (they may have asked, "Could we move in a week before the closing?"), be as courteous as you can. Tell them you'll have to ask your lawyer, and then blame your lawyer for saying no. ("You know the way lawyers are.")

Whatever you can do to make the buyers feel they've bought a fine house, and that you're a decent, honest, above-board person, would be appropriate. In fact, when their lawyers present your lawyers with a check at the closing, shake their hands and say, "Congratulations. You've bought a darned good house at a darned good price."

## CHAPTER SUMMARY

Negotiate with other things besides money—like move-in dates and items that might remain with the house. Don't lose a sale by haggling over the small stuff, like $2,000 on a $200,000 house. Focus on what you paid for the house, not on what you might have received a few years ago, when the market was soaring.

In negotiating, ignore statements like, "I won't go one penny higher." When you make concessions, make them increasingly smaller, and head toward a number you're comfortable with. If you become deadlocked, and there's an agent, see if the agent will lower his or her commission.

Even after the buyers have signed on, you're not done. Keep reassuring them that you're helpful and honest, and that they have purchased a fine house at a good price.

# 24 THE PROSPECTIVE BUYER AS SLEAZEBAG

The more eager you are to sell (the more closely the word "desperate" describes your situation), the more wary you should become when you deal with buyers.

There are supposed house buyers out there you wouldn't want to touch with a 100-foot pole. And the more honest, fair, open, and decent you yourself are, the more likely you are to fall prey to their machinations—because you undoubtedly project your own essential decency into everyone you meet.

If you're selling your house by yourself, without a broker, you are especially likely to meet up with sleazy prospectors. You don't have a broker protecting your interest, and buyers know it, so fizzbos become their special prey. (Fizzbo: someone selling a house by himself or herself, from the initials for For Sale By Owner). The sleazy buyer will scan the advertisements and drive around town, looking precisely for fizzbos to fleece.

## THE VARIETIES OF UNDESIRABLE HOUSE BUYER

Some undesirable prospectors are not out to con you—only to waste your time. They are called "lookie-lookies." They have nothing better to do on weekend afternoons, so they drive from open house to open house, knowing they'll be welcomed warmly, and meanwhile they can help themselves to free coffee and cookies, or whatever you're serving.

Some lookie-lookies are just doing their own comparative market analysis, preparing to sell their own houses and checking out the competition.

And then there are the buyers as Hamlet—not much different from lookie-lookies, except that they think, someday, they really will buy a house. One man, a New York City musician, shopped around in New Jersey over the course of a year, seeing 143 houses. Yes, he finally bought one, but your chances of selling to such indecisive buyers are remote.

Descending a little lower into the circles of the inferno, we encounter the buyer as low-baller. This buyer figures you're desperate and offers an insultingly low bid for your house—either directly or through your agent (in the latter case, the agent must legally convey it to you). If you're selling your house for $200,000, the low-baller may offer $120,000. He or she knows that the house could certainly sell for over $180,000, so even with all the closing costs, the profit should be enormous. Desperate or disturbed sellers may say yes.

Low-ballers may work in pairs. Low-baller A may drop by and bid $120,000 for your $200,000 house. You slam the door. A day or two later, Low-baller B drops by and offers $150,000. Shaken and frightened by the first offer, you may be willing to sell, even at that outrageously low price.

A few, a very few, real estate agents collaborate with low-ballers. The agent persuades the seller to underprice the house, and then he or she has an associate, or a relative, buy it. If discovered, such an agent could lose his or her license. So make sure you deal with a reputable brokerage firm that has been around for many years.

A subvariety of the low-baller is the slow-baller. This character is willing to put in hours, and eat up yours. He or she visits your house a few or several times, bargains with you over the price and and terms, and finally agrees with you on a price. Then the buyer stalls, eventually submitting a far lower bid than what was agreed upon. "I found that I couldn't get the money I needed," he or she says apologetically. At this point, having counted on the house selling, and having firmed up your plans, you may feel forced to accept the lower price—which is what the slow-baller was counting on.

Descending even further into the pits, we meet sleazebags who really know their real estate. These con artists know the intricacies of the laws governing evictions, foreclosures, and everything else. They can run rings around real estate agents and even many lawyers. You can often identify them because they offer you unusual deals. They'll give you a little cash for your house, and throw in a plot of land down South or out West. They'll throw in a recreational vehicle. They want you to take back a second mortgage, and a third mortgage on top of that. They want to give you a postdated check, or out-of-state bonds. The operative word is "unusual."

Sometimes they manage to buy a house for no money down, live there a while (without paying rent), and walk away. Or they'll "sell" the house, at a bargain price, to other patsies. Sometimes they'll live in the house, default on their mortgages, and remain there until the poor seller has to spend thousands evicting them. Meanwhile, they'll have trashed the house—because they weren't willing to spend a cent on home maintenance—and they'll have hocked anything in there that was salable, from the appliances to the light fixtures.

## PROTECT YOURSELF FROM SLEAZY BUYERS

Warning sirens should go off in your head whenever prospective buyers suggest anything unusual. Can they live in your house before the actual closing? Can they trade you something other than plain cash for your house? Would you accept $500 down, and sign the contract provided by the buyer?

Your answer to all these questions should be "Let me check with my lawyer." If you don't have a lawyer, get one fast. Make sure you run these offers past a *practiced* lawyer—not a young attorney who draws up wills, defends drivers accused of drunkenness, and occasionally supervises a closing.

Another safety net: Demand a sizable amount of earnest money, or deposit, from any buyer. Not $50 or a few hundred. At least a few thousand.

Remember, finally, that con artists are successful in great part because of their personalities—they're warm, friendly, outgoing, cheerful, and charming. If a surly grouch suggested a strange-sounding, bizarre arrangement, you would be suspicious; you need to be just as suspicious when a sincere, likable buyer suggests a bizarre arrangment.

## CHAPTER SUMMARY

Some prospective house buyers are charming and, at the same time, utterly sleazy. You, the ordinary homeowner, are probably way out of your league in trying to deal with them. Call in an an experienced lawyer as soon as possible whenever any buyer makes an offer that's unusual—an offer other than the traditional one of just agreeing to pay you a lot of plain old money for your house.

# 25 UNDERSTANDING THE SALES CONTRACT

## WHY IT'S SO IMPORTANT TO UNDERSTAND THE CONTRACT

The most important document you will sign is the sales contract. The sales contract will describe in precise legal terminology exactly how much you are being paid, when you will be paid, and what you are selling. It sets forth most of the legal obligations that the seller and the buyer have concerning the sale of the house. (See the sample contract in the "For Your Notebook" section at the end of this chapter.)

Your real estate broker might review the contract (in some parts of the country the real estate broker will actually fill in the contract initially); you will then hire an attorney (if you haven't already), who will review the contract in detail; and, in some states, an escrow agent will review the contract as part of the closing procedures. The contract is generally signed well in advance of the closing. Between contract signing and closing is when the buyer gets a mortgage commitment and has house inspections completed.

With all these experts perusing it, is it really necessary for you to understand what's in the contract? Absolutely. The home you're selling is one of the biggest assets you'll ever own. The sum of money involved is tremendous. The emotional attachments are considerable. Also, if you live in one of the areas of the country where home sales have declined, prices are soft, and serious buyers are rare, you want to take every step you can in ensuring that no serious buyer will slip away over a minor contract dispute.

Understanding the contract is important for protecting your rights and for smoothing the sale to completion. You may have specific concerns that you neglected to tell your lawyer before he or she prepared the contract. The buyer's lawyer and your lawyer may argue over certain contract provisions. If you have an understanding of those contract provisions, you'll be in a much better position to decide with your lawyer whether you really need to fight the buyer, or whether you can give in and keep the deal moving toward closing.

---

**CAUTION:** The laws affecting real estate sales vary from state to state. Even within the same state, customs and conventions vary from county to county. Finally, the terms of every contract will differ somewhat to take into account the specific needs of the parties. Therefore, while the sample contract and suggestions offered below (in the "For Your Notebook" section) will prove a helpful starting point, always retain a lawyer to best protect your interests. If any of the information contained in the sample form conflicts with what your lawyer feels is appropriate, you might want to get a second opinion. But don't dismiss your lawyer's recommendations, because local laws and customs can be very important.

---

### EVEN THOUGH IT'S PRINTED, YOU CAN CHANGE IT— BUT USE RESTRAINT

Many homeowners, when confronted with a printed form, think the terms are inviolable, or that the printed portions of the agreement are to be accepted as standard. Quite to the contrary, as stated earlier; every provision of the sales contract is negotiable and can be changed. However, if you're trying to sell in a buyer's market, exercise restraint. The more changes made, the more opportunity for objection and the more potential time delays as the lawyers review each draft including the changes you've requested.

This doesn't mean you shouldn't ask your lawyer to change any provision you don't agree to. It means that if you're eager to close the sale, and you feel the buyer has the upper hand because of market conditions, choose your battles carefully. Earlier (see Chapter 5), we stressed the importance of hiring a lawyer whose attitude would not be so abrasive or niggling it could ruin a closing. Now, we offer the same advice to you: Only make changes that are really necessary to protect your interests. Don't lose the sale over a minor provision, or a matter of small-dollar value.

## COOPERATIVE APARTMENTS AND CONDOMINIUMS

If the "house" you're selling is really a cooperative or condominium, you will have to deal with some additional documents and points that aren't reflected in the contract that follows. Your lawyer undoubtedly will be familiar with the procedures for a cooperative or condominium and will advise you of the few extra steps that should be taken. The first thing for you to do, even before you hire a lawyer or find a buyer, is to contact officers of the cooperative corporation or the condominium association. Ask what procedures you must follow, what documents and other requirements they have for a prospective buyer, and what advice they can give you in selling. Most associations are quite helpful and will be able to guide you.

For a closing on a cooperative unit, your stock in the cooperative corporation may have to be canceled by the corporation, and new stock may have to be issued to the buyer. Also, your proprietary lease (which entitles you to live in the particular cooperative unit you own) will have to be assigned to the buyer.

## CHAPTER SUMMARY

Even though your lawyer and others will go over the sales contract, you should understand it yourself, so that the contract reflects the deal you want. You can ask for changes in the contract (every point is negotiable), but be judicious. Don't fight the buyer in a buyer's market unless your interests would really be jeopardized.

Cooperatives and condos will require some additional documents and steps.

# FOR YOUR NOTEBOOK

## SAMPLE CONTRACT TO SELL HOUSE

### ** FOR DISCUSSION WITH YOUR LAWYER ONLY— DO NOT USE AS A CONTRACT**

I. Opening Paragraph (Names of the Parties)

CONTRACT of sale dated December 1, 1990 between Sam and Sue Seller, residing at 123 Main Street, Centerville, Onestate (the "Seller"), and Paul and Pat Purchaser, residing at 456 Redwood, Apt. 12E, Ridgewood, Onestate (the "Purchaser").

---

**COMMENT:** Be certain that the buyer signs his or her full legal name at the end of the document. As noted earlier, any changes penned in on a printed form should be initialed by both you and the buyer in order to show that both of you have agreed to the changes. If the buyer is married, the buyer's spouse should sign as well. This makes the spouse liable as well in case the buyers default. If you've spent the time and legal fees to get to this stage, and have held your house off the market, you want to make sure that the buyers will be held to their end of the agreement. If the contract is not properly signed, this will be much more difficult.

Occasionally, someone other than the buyer may show up to sign papers at the closing. For example, the buyers live out of state and have authorized someone attend the closing in their behalf. Your primary concern is that the responsible party is obligated on the contract. You should obtain an agreement, such as a power of attorney, signed by the actual buyers and specifically giving the person attending the closing the right to sign documents on their behalf to buy real estate. Have your attorney review it to be sure it that meets any special state law requirements. If the buyer is a partnership, corporation, or other entity special problems are raised. You will need to be certain that the partnership or corporation has the right to buy the property. You will also have to ascertain who has the authority to bind the entity (e.g., the president, a general partner, etc.). Be certain to have a lawyer carefully review this issue and obtain all the additional documents necessary to assure that the buyer has the authority and competency to consummate the purchase (e.g., minutes of the corporation's board of directors approving the purchase and the name of the officer authorized to sign the contract, copy of a shareholders' agreement, a certificate of incorporation, etc.).

---

II. Sale.

The Seller agrees to sell, and the Purchaser agrees to buy the property, including all buildings and improvements thereon, erected, situated, lying, and being in the City of Centerville, County of Oakland, State of Onestate, more particularly described as follows:

ALL that tract or parcel of land and premises, situate, lying and being in the City of Centerville, in the County of Oakland, and State of Onestate. BEING known and designated as Lot No. 3 in Block No. 13 on a certain map entitled "Map of Elmora Manor, Centerville, Onestate, O.L.P. Jones, Surveyor, dated June 10, 1812" and filed in the Register's Office as Case #38-CH-4.

BEGINNING at a stake in the Northeasterly side of Main Street, at a point therein distant 50 feet Southeasterly from the intersection formed by the said Northeasterly side of Main Street and the Southeasterly side of Glenwood Road; thence running (1) North 36 degrees 01 minutes East, a distance of 100 feet to a stake for a corner; thence running (2) South 54 degrees 18 minutes East a distance of 48.02 feet to a point for another corner; thence running (3) South 35 degrees 42 minutes West a distance of 100 feet to a point in the aforesaid line of Main Street; thence running (4) North 54 degrees 18 minutes West a distance of 48.57 feet to the point or place of BEGINNING. BEING also known as 123 Main Street, Centerville, Onestate.

BEING known as Lot 3 in Block 13, Account No. 10-504B on the official tax map of the City of Centerville, Oakland County, Onestate (the "House").

---

**COMMENT:** The description should be complete and accurate. The complete legal description, not a mere address or lot and block number, should be included. Generally, it will come from a copy of the deed you obtained when you purchased the house. However, the description on the old deed shouldn't be accepted without question. It should be carefully compared to the description contained in the survey done of the property, and any differences should be investigated.

---

**TIP:** If there are any problems with the title to the property, or with the information reflected in the survey, discuss them with your lawyer before you complete negotiations with any potential buyer. If the problems can be resolved ahead of time, it may facilitate the sale of the property. If the defects can't be changed (for example, a neighbor has an easement to use your driveway to reach his house), it's probably best to be up-front with prospective buyers. If problems are discovered after the transaction has progressed, the buyers may suspect your honesty, which could affect the entire transaction.

III. Street Rights.

This sale includes all the right, title, and interest, if any, of the Seller in and to any land lying in the bed of any street, in front of or adjoining the House, to the center line of such street.

IV. Condemnation.

This sale also includes any right of the Seller to any unpaid award by reason of any taking by condemnation any damages to the House. The Seller shall deliver, at no additional cost to the Purchaser, at the closing, or after the closing, on demand, any document which the Purchaser may require to collect any such award.

---

**COMMENT:** Condemnation rarely occurs. However, if it does, it is critical to provide for exactly what should happen. If the contract is vague, drawn-out legal battles could ensue as the parties negotiate whether the sale should be concluded, who is entitled to the condemnation proceeds, what the sales price should be, and so forth. This provision should be read in conjunction with the section below discussing what your obligations are as a seller when you can't deliver to the buyers the property they were intending to buy.

---

V. Personal Property.

A. Included in this sale are all fixtures and articles of personal property attached to or used in connection with the House, unless specifically excluded. The Seller represents that the fixtures and personal property are paid for and owned by the Seller free and clear of any security interests or liens other than the existing mortgage, or they shall be satisfied at the time of the closing from the proceeds of the sale in order to convey an unencumbered property. Fixtures and personal property included in this sale are the following: heating, air conditioning, plumbing, electrical and lighting fixtures (except the breakfast-room ceiling fixture), bathroom and kitchen fixtures and cabinets, storm windows and doors, screens, shades, mail box, wall-to-wall carpets, sump pump, shrubbery, fences, range, refrigerator, freezer, washing machine, clothes dryer, dishwasher, and drapery in the dining room, including the hardware and rods.

B. Not included in this sale are the following: furniture, drapes (other than the dining room), curtains, microwave oven, fireplace equipment, breakfast-room ceiling fixture, and lawn ornaments.

---

**COMMENT:** This section specifies precisely which items of personal property are included and which are excluded from the sale. Personal property is generally movable property, such as furniture. Personal property that is not permanently attached to the house or land is not included in the sale unless the contract says it is. This is distinguished from real property, the house and the land, which are automatically included in the sale. Property known as fixtures is personal property that is attached to the house or land. Fixtures are generally included automatically in the sale. The law is not always clear as to what property is personal property or fixtures, and even if the law is clear, your buyer may not be. Therefore, the best approach is to list everything in detail.

Although this is probably the simplest provision in a sales contract, in many sales it can cause the most problems. Too often, the buyer and seller disagree as to what items should and should not be included in the sale. Keep your perspective. Don't risk losing a sale over what personal property is and is not included. It's rarely wise to cancel a sale over a personal property dispute. Even if the bookcase the buyer wants is worth $500, that's probably a pittance in comparison to the sales price of the house. (See the "For Your Notebook" section of Chapter 2 for more information and a checklist.)

---

VI. Purchase Price.

The purchase price is One Hundred Forty-Two Thousand Dollars ($142,000).

---

**COMMENT:** Make sure the purchase price properly reflects what you've agreed with the buyer. If the price was to be, for example, $142,000, but the buyer has agreed to pay you an additional $250 for a bookcase, list the price as $142,250, or perhaps detail that the price is $142,000 for the house and $250 for the bookcase, for a total of $142,250. This will make it easier for everyone involved to understand the final number.

VII. Payment of Purchase Price.
A. The Purchase Price shall be paid as follows:
1. By check on the signing of this Contract, to
   be held in escrow by Seller's attorney  ...... $    5,200
2. By allowance for the principal amount
   remaining unpaid on the Assignable
   Existing Mortgage  ............................... $  23,569
3. By a Purchase Money Mortgage and Note
   from Purchaser to Seller  ....................... $  25,000
4. Certified, bank, escrow, or lawyer's
   trust account check at closing
   (from buyer's mortgage)  ........................ $  85,000
5. Balance due and payable at closing  .......... $    3,231
   Total  ................................................. $142,000

---

**COMMENT:** If significant money is held in escrow, request an interest-bearing account with the interest paid to the seller.

Sellers should generally try to obtain as large a downpayment as possible. In many parts of the country a larger downpayment than that illustrated in the contract is customary.

---

**EXAMPLE:** Assume you will be receiving $150,000 at the closing of the house you're selling in the morning and will be going to the closing for the house you will be buying that afternoon, you might want to ask your buyer, prior to closing (since you probably won't have exact numbers when the contract is signed), for two checks totaling $150,000 rather than one check. Assume that the seller of the house you will be buying in the afternoon owes his bank approximately $105,468 and that the purchase price of the house you'll be buying is $265,000. If you will be getting a mortgage for $100,000 and paying $165,000 in cash, ask your buyer for two checks: (1) one for $105,468, which you will sign over at the afternoon closing to the bank which holds the mortgage on the house you'll be buying; and (2) one for $44,532, which you'll sign over to the seller of the house you'll be buying. You will also give the seller of the house you're buying $100,000 from the new mortgage you'll be getting and $15,000 in a certified check of your own funds. The total of all the payments to the seller of the house you're buying in the afternoon is $265,000 [$105,468 + $44,532 + $100,000 + $15,000]. Make sure to coordinate all of this with the buyer of the house you're selling and the seller of the house you're buying. You want to make certain that the checks will be acceptable to the bank of the seller whose house you are buying.

---

**TIP:** Specifying the exact payments above is not sufficient. It is critical that detailed provisions be included elsewhere in the contract and the closing statement or the RESPA (HUD-1) form of sale specifying all of the details of a mortgage assumption, etc.

---

B. All money payable under this contract shall be paid, unless otherwise specified, as follows:
   1. Cash, but not over $1,000,
   2. Certified check of the Purchaser, or an official check of any bank, savings bank, trust company or savings and loan association having a banking office in the State, payable to the order of the Seller,
   3. Money other than the purchase price, payable to the Seller at closing, may be by check of the Purchaser up to the amount of $1,000, or
   4. As the Seller or Seller's attorney may otherwise agree in writing.

---

**COMMENT:** It's very important to specify the type of payment that will be acceptable. If the contract doesn't state that a bank or certified check if required, the buyer may try to pay with a regular check. If you're planning to close on a new house you're buying shortly after the closing on the house you're selling, you must have ready available funds from the buyer. This obviously isn't the case in the sample clause above since the seller isn't getting much cash out of the transaction. When you are to receive a substantial amount of payment at closing and are going to close shortly on a new home you're buying, you might want to have the buyer break payment down into more than one check so that you can endorse the checks over at the closing for the house you're buying.

---

**TIP:** Make sure to get photocopies of all checks used at the closing and to save them in your house file. You should also make an extra copy of the contract and give it to your accountant to make sure everything is properly reported for tax purposes.

---

C. All monies held in escrow shall be held in interest-bearing accounts, and Purchaser shall be entitled to all interest earned.

**COMMENT:** Escrow is when a third party (someone other than the buyer or seller) holds monies and papers pending completion of the closing of the sale of the house. Specify whether the monies will be held in an interest-bearing account and who should get the interest—buyer or seller. Occasionally, the buyer and seller split the interest. The contract should also make clear when the escrow ends in the event that the contract doesn't close; and, who should get the money and other documents held in escrow? What are the obligations and responsibilities of the escrow agent?

VIII. <u>Seller Financing—Purchase Money Mortgage.</u>
   A. The Purchaser shall give to the Seller, and Seller shall accept, a purchase money mortgage and a note (the "Purchase Money Mortgage and the Note"). The Purchase Money Mortgage and the Note shall be drawn by the attorney for the Seller at the expense of the Purchaser, and shall be substantially in the form of the Purchase Money Mortgage and the Note attached to this Contract. Purchaser shall pay the mortgage recording tax, recording fees, and the attorney's fee in the amount of $250 for the preparation of these documents.
   B. The Purchase Money Mortgage and Note shall each state that it is subject to the prior lien to the Big City Bank (the "Existing Mortgage"), and to any extension or modification of the Existing Mortgage made in good faith. If any required payments are made on an Existing Mortgage between now and Closing, which reduce the unpaid principal amount of an Existing Mortgage below the amount shown in this agreement, then the balance of the price payable at closing will be increased accordingly. The interest rate on the Purchase Money Mortgage shall be Thirteen percent (13%), and principal and interest shall be payable based on a Twenty-Five (25) year amortization schedule with any remaining principal and interest payments due Ten (10) years from the date which is the last day of the first full month following the Closing of this Contract.

**COMMENT:** If you will be helping the buyer finance part of the purchase (taking back "paper" from the buyer), be certain that the amount of purchase-money mortgage is properly reflected in the contract. In addition, the key terms of the loan you will make to the buyer should also be noted in the contract so that these items will be agreed to before the closing. The key terms, in addition to the amount of the loan, include: maturity date (when the loan comes due), amortization period (period over which payments are calculated, which can exceed the maturity date), interest rate, and any personal guarantees.

IX. Existing Mortgage.
   A. The House shall be conveyed subject to the lien of an assumable existing mortgage to Big City Bank, which at the date of this Contract has an unpaid principal amount of approximately $23,569, and on which interest is paid at the rate of Ten percent (10%) per year (the "Existing Mortgage"). Payments are in monthly installments in advance, on the first day of each month, beginning with January 1, 1991. Such payments include principal, interest, hazard insurance, and real property taxes. Any balance of principal and interest shall be due and payable on December 1, 1997.
   B. Seller shall assign the mortgage escrow account that is held for the payment of taxes, insurance, and other expenses to the Purchaser, if it can be assigned, and the Purchaser shall pay the amount of the escrow account to the Seller at the Closing.
   C. The Seller represents and warrants that: (i) The principal amount shown above for the Existing Mortgage is reasonably correct and that only the payments required pursuant to the Existing Mortgage shall be made; (ii) The Existing Mortgage does not contain any provision allowing the holder of the mortgage to require its immediate payment in full or to change the interest rate or any other term by reason of the transfer of title or closing; and (iii) The Existing Mortgage shall not be in default at the time of closing.

---

**COMMENT:** When it's possible for the buyer to assume your mortgage, this can be a substantial help to making a sale. If you have a low-rate fixed mortgage that is assumable, it may be possible for the buyer to afford a larger downpayment or purchase price than if the buyer had to pay market interest rates on all borrowed monies. Unfortunately, most fixed-rate mortgages aren't assumable. The only way to be certain is to have your lawyer review your loan agreement and to check with the bank that is holding your mortgage. (See Chapter 19, Endnote.)

Instead of making the representation in section C. (ii), you could have the buyer satisfy his or her own concerns by having his or her lawyer review your mortgage agreement. Check with your lawyer.

---

## X.  Mortgage Contingency Clause.

This contract of sale is contingent upon the buyer's obtaining a written mortgage commitment by November 15, 1990, from a reputable bank, savings and loan association, credit union, or mortgage company, in an amount not less than Eighty-Five Thousand Dollars ($85,000.00). The terms of the mortgage shall not be less favorable than an interest rate of Ten and One Half percent (10.5%), with an amortization period of not less than Fifteen (15) years, and points not in excess of Three (3) percent of the principal balance borrowed. The loan must be a conventional, Conventional-MGIC, or adjustable-rate loan and mortgage. The buyers shall make an immediate application to a lending institution, and shall endeavor in good faith to obtain mortgage loan on terms at least as favorable as those set forth herein. Buyers shall pay the application, appraisal and credit report, and other fees relating to such mortgage application. The buyers shall promptly supply all information and forms requested by the lending institution. If the buyers, after reasonable and diligent efforts, are unable to obtain a mortgage commitment, this sale contract shall be void and all funds and documents shall be returned to the respective parties, and neither the buyers nor the sellers shall have any rights against each other.

---

**COMMENT:** In almost all home sales the buyer will have to get a mortgage to complete the sale. In order to avoid being in default under the sale contract, buyers will insist on a mortgage-contingency clause. This provides that if the buyer, after reasonable efforts, can't get the required mortgage, the sale doesn't go through.

Although buyers will insist on such a clause, you should keep the provisions as reasonable as possible. If the buyers state a mortgage amount that is unreasonably high (for example, too large a percentage of purchase price), or an interest rate that is too low in comparison with current market rates, or any other terms that are not likely to be obtained in the current market environment, negotiate a change. If the buyers are sincere, they shouldn't object to terms that are in line with current market conditions.

It may be preferable to use the phrase "at the prevailing interest rate" than agree to a fixed maximum-interest rate that the buyer may not be able to obtain.

If you permit the buyer to use FHA- or VA-financing, which might make it easier for the buyer to get financing and close the deal, you may have to pay points and meet other requirements.

## XI. Flood Area.

If the House is located in a state or federal flood hazard area, Purchaser may cancel this Contract on written notice to Seller within Ten (10) days from the date of this Contract, in which case the provisions of Section XVI of this Contract shall apply.

**COMMENT:** Find out in advance if your house is located in a flood area. Assume that most buyers will find out, and disclose up-front if you are. If you try to sell a house hoping the buyers will miss this point, all you're likely to accomplish is to have the sale fall through. Worse yet, if the buyer doesn't find out until after the closing, you might have a lawsuit! Not a productive approach.

## XII. Assessments.

If, at the time of closing, the House is subject to any assessment that is, or may become, payable in annual installments for improvements which have been made, and the first installment is then a lien, or has been paid, then for the purposes of this contract all the unpaid installments shall be deemed to be due, and shall be paid, by the Seller at closing.

**COMMENT:** If an assessment by the local town or county has become a lien on the property you, as the seller, will be responsible for it, unless the contract states otherwise. Because this is fairly standard, it may be difficult in a buyer's market to change it.

## XIII. Mortgage Estoppel Certificate.

Seller agrees to deliver to the Purchaser at the Closing a certificate dated not more than Thirty-One (31) days before closing signed by Big City Bank, the holder of the Existing Mortgage, in a form appropriate for recording, certifying the amount of the unpaid principal and interest, date of maturity, and rate of interest of the Existing Mortgage. The Seller shall pay the fees for recording this certificate.

XIV.  Violations.

All notices of violations, any regulations, codes, laws, ordinances, orders, or other requirements by any governmental agency affecting the House at the date of this contract, shall be complied with by the Seller, at Seller's expense, subject to the limitations contained in Section XIX.C., and the House Shall be conveyed free of any violations. This provision shall survive closing.

---

**COMMENT:** Some municipalities require that a certificate of occupancy or some other type of inspection certificate be obtained. (See XIX.C.) As a precondition to issuing the certificate, an inspection might have to be performed, and specified repairs might have to be made. You probably can't avoid this requirement, but discuss with your lawyer putting a limit on the amount you would have to spend. If you have to make extensive repairs, a dollar limit might enable you to cancel the sale contract and then sell the house at a higher price to another buyer (i.e., a price reflecting the work you've done).

---

XV.  Adjustments At Closing.
  A.  The following items are to be apportioned as of midnight of the day before closing: (i) interest on the Existing Mortgage; (ii) taxes; (iii) water charges; (iv) sewer rents, if any, on the basis of the fiscal year for which assessed; and (v) heating oil, if any.
  B.  The adjustment on account of the mortgage escrow account on the Existing Mortgage shall be made as required in Section 8(b) of this Contract.
  C.  If the Closing shall occur before a new tax rate is fixed, the apportionment of taxes shall be based upon the old tax rate for the prior period applied to the latest assessed valuation.
  D.  If there is a water, electric, or other utility meter on the premises, the Seller shall furnish a reading to a date not more than Ten (10) days prior to the Closing, and the charges, if any, shall be apportioned on the basis of the last reading.

---

**TIP:** Get the readings within a week of the closing and write all of the utility companies and notify them of the date of the closing to cut off future liability.

---

E. The Seller may credit the Purchaser, as an adjustment to the purchase price, with the amount of any unpaid taxes, assessments, water charges and sewer rents, together with any interest and penalties, to a date not less than Ten (10) days after the Closing, provided that the official bills, computed to that date, are provided to the Purchaser at Closing.

---

**COMMENT:** Consider whether adjustments will have to be made for insurance premiums. If there is a tenant renting the house, there may also have to be adjustments for rent and security deposits. Be sure to comply with any applicable lease terms and advise the tenant to pay rent to the new owner.

---

## XVI. Default by Seller.

If the Seller is unable to convey title in accordance with the terms of this Contract, the sole liability of the Seller will be to refund to the Purchaser the amounts paid on account of this Contract, plus all reasonable charges made for examination of title and any additional searches made under this Contract, including the survey, termite and structural inspection charges, such expenses in the aggregate being not more than Five Hundred Dollars ($500.00). Upon such refund and payment this Contract shall be considered canceled, and neither the Seller nor the Purchaser shall have any further rights against the other by reason of this Contract.

---

**COMMENT:** Title is the ownership interest in the real estate that you are selling to the buyer. If the title defect (for example, an easement or lien) can be corrected without a substantial cost, it may pay to do so instead of your canceling the sale, especially in a tough market. It may be wise to state in the contract that the seller has the option of curing the title defect, if possible.

---

## XVII. Closing.

The closing of this transaction shall include the payment of the purchase price to the Seller and the delivery to the Purchaser the deed described in Section 16 below (the "Closing"). The Closing will take place at the office of the Buyer's attorney's, or the mortgagee's office at 100 Legal Street, Clawson, Onestate, on or about 11:00 A.M., January 15, 1990.

**COMMENT:** The closing is the final meeting, when escrow is broken and all monies and documents evidencing the title to the property are transferred. Although you might prefer the transaction to be at your lawyer's office (which would keep your lawyer's costs down), be flexible. The buyer's lender may want the closing to take place in its office, or in the office of its lawyer. If the property is a cooperative, the closing may have to take place in the office of the cooperative corporation's management company. If you've gotten this far with the deal, don't worry about where the closing is, be happy you'll have one.

XVIII.  Deed.

At the Closing the Seller shall deliver to the Purchaser a bargain and sale with covenants against grantor's acts deed in the proper statutory form for recording to transfer full ownership, fee simple title, to the Premises, free of all encumbrances except as stated in this Contract (the "Deed").

**COMMENT:** The deed is the legal document that transfers the title to (the ownership of) the land to the buyer. There are a number of types of deeds. A bargain and sale deed with covenants against grantor's acts transfers all of your right, title, and interest in the property to the buyer. You also promise to the buyer that you haven't done anything while you owned the property that could jeopardize the buyer's obtaining good title. You do not, however, make any promises about what prior owners have done to the property. A warranty deed goes beyond those rights granted in the bargain and sale deed and is not something you would wish to agree to.

Deeds have different names in different parts of the country, so if there is any question as to what is appropriate, consult with your lawyer.

XIX.  Quality of Title.

A.  The Seller shall give and the Purchaser shall accept such title as a reputable title company which regularly conducts business in this State will be willing to approve and insure at standard rates with their standard form of title insurance policy. This title insurance policy must transfer ownership of the property to the Purchaser free of any rights and claims except the following: (i) restrictive covenants of record which do not and will not impair the normal use of the property; (ii) utility and similar easements which do not impair the normal use of the property or inhibit the

Purchaser from constructing any reasonable improvements or additions to the House; (iii) laws and government regulations that affect the use and maintenance of the House, provided that they are not violated by the existing house and improvements or by their current use; (iv) consents by the Seller or any former owner of the House for the erection of any structure or structures on, under, or above any street or streets on which the House may abut but which are not within the boundary lines of the House.

---

**COMMENT:** A court will generally require a buyer to accept marketable title. This assures the buyer the right to sell the property if he or she so chooses, the right to use the property, and the right to hold the property peacefully. The buyer is basically assured by marketable title that he or she shouldn't have to be subject to litigation in order to take and use the property. A number of factors could affect marketability: liens, mortgages, judgments, past due real estate taxes, physical encroachments (e.g., a neighbor's fence that extends three inches over your property line), an improperly handled probate proceeding, an invalid divorce proceeding, etc. Again, if it's a buyer's market and you want to sell, it's in your interest to clear up these problems as early as possible to assure a smooth closing.

---

B. Seller shall deliver to Purchaser an affidavit of title at Closing. If a title examination discloses judgments, bankruptcies, or other returns against other persons having names the same as or similar to that of the Seller, the Seller shall state in the affidavit showing that they are not against the Seller.

---

**COMMENT:** If your name is John Smith, there might be another John Smith who has a judgment against him for failing to pay a debt. You will have to give a sworn statement (affidavit) to the buyer stating that you're a different John Smith, and that the judgment isn't against you.

---

C. If required pursuant to local law, Seller shall deliver to Purchaser, at Seller's sole expense, a certificate of occupancy. Seller shall make any repairs necessary to obtain the certificate of occupancy at Seller's sole expense up to a maximum of One Thousand Dollars ($1,000). If repairs in excess of such amount are required and Purchaser is unwilling to assume the cost, then either party hereto may cancel this

Contract, and the provisions of Section XIV of this Contract shall apply.

XX. Risk of Loss.

The risk of loss or damage to the premises by fire or other casualty until the delivery of the deed is assumed by the Seller. If there is a fire or other casualty to the House prior to the Closing and the cost of repairing the damage exceeds Ten Thousand Dollars ($10,000) Purchaser may cancel this Contract and the provisions of the section "Default By Seller" shall apply.

---

**COMMENT:** Many contracts are written using a percentage of the purchase price, with 10 percent being common. You want a fairly high threshold in order to make it more difficult for the buyer to back out of the contract.

---

XXI. Transfer and Recording Taxes.

The Seller shall deliver a check at the Closing payable to the order of the appropriate State, City, or County officer in the amount of any applicable transfer tax, recording tax, or both, payable by reason of the delivery or recording of the Deed together with any required tax return. The Purchaser's attorney, at Purchaser's expense, shall complete any tax return and cause the check and the tax return to be delivered to the appropriate office promptly after Closing.

XXII. Broker.

The Purchaser and Seller state that neither has dealt with any broker in connection with this sale other than Joe's Real Estate Company, Inc., and the Seller agrees to pay the broker the commission earned pursuant to a separate agreement at the rate of Five Percent (5%). Each party agrees to hold the other party hereto harmless in the event of any misrepresentation as to the use of brokers.

---

**COMMENT:** See Chapter 7 for a discussion of brokers and the brokerage agreement.

---

XXIII. Condition of the House.

The Purchaser agrees to purchase the Premises, buildings and personal property as is, which shall mean in their present condition subject to reasonable use, wear, tear, and natural deterioration between the date of this Contract and Closing, except as specifically provided otherwise in the section "Inspections." The Premises and personal property shall be delivered in broom-clean condition, and all personal property not included in this sale shall be removed. All systems and appliances shall be in working order. The roof shall be free of leaks and the basement free of seepage. Purchaser shall have the right to inspect the House prior to the Closing to verify the condition of the House.

---

**COMMENT:** You may want to make the buyer negotiate for some of the language in this section rather than including it automatically. The buyer should have had an inspector go through the house and should rely on the report of the inspector, or on the professional home inspection you obtained, not on your representation as to the house's condition.

Be careful of making a representation that appliances and systems are in "good" working order. Working order probably means if you turn them on they work. You may have a 25-year-old freezer that works, but could it ever be in "good" working order?

---

**CAUTION:** You may be required by law to make certain disclosures to the buyers as to defects of the house or other problems. Discuss with your lawyer whether the disclosures should be made in the contract. The advantage is that then you are on record as having made any required disclosures, and the buyer can't claim that he or she wasn't aware of the problems when the contract was signed.

---

XXIV. Inspections.

The Purchaser has Ten (10) days from the signing of this contract to obtain a termite inspection of the Premises, and a structural inspection by a qualified home inspection service or engineer, at the Purchaser's sole cost and expense if Purchaser so chooses. If the inspection reports indicate the presence of termite infestation or any structural problem, the Seller shall eliminate the infestation or correct the structural problem at Seller's expense, if the cost does not exceed One Thousand Dollars ($1,000). If the costs exceed such amount, and Purchaser is unwilling to bear the additional cost, this Contract will be canceled and the provisions of the section

"Default by Seller" shall apply. Notice of the Seller's intent to cancel this Contract must be given to the Purchaser's attorney within Ten (10) days after Seller's receipt of the termite or structural inspection report. If notice is not given to the Purchaser's attorney within this Ten (10) day period, it shall be the Seller's responsibility to eliminate the reported problem at the Seller's sole cost and expense. If the attorney for the Seller has not received the termite or structural inspection reports within Ten (10) days from the signing of this contract, this paragraph shall be unenforceable and of no effect.

---

**COMMENT:** Home inspections for structural problems are almost universal. Inspections for radon and termites are a necessity in some parts of the country. Your concerns as a seller are that the buyer not delay the closing for any lengthy period, since your house will be off the market during that time. If the buyer doesn't notify you, then he will have waived his rights to object based on an inspection. Although sellers have preferred not to be responsible for repairing items found by inspectors or reducing the purchase price, in areas of the country where buyers are scarce, sellers may not have much choice.

---

XXV. <u>Entire Agreement</u>.

All prior understandings and agreements between the Purchaser and the Seller are superseded by this Contract which contains their entire agreement. This Contract is entered into after full investigation by both parties and no reliance is made on any matter not set forth in this Contract.

XXVI. <u>Modification</u>.

This Contract may not be changed or terminated except in a writing signed by both parties. However, each of the parties authorizes their respective attorneys to agree in writing to any change in dates and time periods provided for in this Contract.

XXVII. <u>Binding Effect</u>.

This Contract shall apply to and bind the heirs, executors, administrators, successors, distributees, and assigns of the respective parties.

XXVIII. IN WITNESS WHEREOF, this contract hs been executed by the parties:

| | |
|---|---|
| Purchaser | Seller |

| | |
|---|---|
| Purchaser | Seller |

STATE OF ONESTATE    )

                                :  ss.:

COUNTY OF OAKLAND    )

On this 1st day of December, 1990, before me personally came PAUL PURCHASER, to me known and known to me to be the individual described in and who execute the foregoing instrument, and he duly acknowledged to me that he executed the same.

/s/ Nancy Notary

---

Notary Public

STATE OF ONESTATE    )

                                :  ss.:

COUNTY OF OAKLAND    )

On this 1st day of December, 1990, before me personally came PAT PURCHASER, to me known and known to me to be the individual described in and who execute the foregoing instrument, and she duly acknowledged to me that she executed the same.

/s/ Nancy Notary

---

Notary Public

STATE OF ONESTATE    )

                                :  ss.:

COUNTY OF OAKLAND    )

On this 1st day of December, 1990, before me personally came SAM SELLER, to me known and known to me to be the individual described in and who execute the foregoing instrument, and he duly acknowledged to me that he executed the same.

/s/ Nancy Notary
_____
Notary Public


STATE OF ONESTATE          )
                           :   ss.:
COUNTY OF OAKLAND          )

On this 1st day of December, 1990, before me personally came SUE SELLER, to me known and known to me to be the individual described in and who execute the foregoing instrument, and she duly acknowledged to me that she executed the same.

/s/ Nancy Notary
_____
Notary Public

# 26 WHAT HAPPENS AT A HOUSE CLOSING AND ALL THE LISTS YOU'LL NEED TO GET THROUGH YOURS

The buyer has been found, the deposit received, the sale contract signed, and the buyer's financing obtained. The next (and, you hope, last) big step is the closing.

The closing is when the seller receives the sales price for the house, and title (ownership) passes to the buyer. The closing is the culmination of the entire transaction; it's when you turn the keys over. A sheaf of other documents and checks will likely change hands. But exactly what happens, and in what order, will depend on state law and local custom. Therefore, the following discussion should be regarded as a general guideline. You'll have to rely on your lawyer, escrow agent, and broker for specifics.

One important point is relevant to all closings. If everyone does his and her "homework" in advance, the closing should be a relatively simple and smooth process. The objective is to avoid last-minute negotiations and fights in which emotions could ruin an otherwise "done deal."

### WHAT CAN GO WRONG?

Estimates are that around 5 percent of all house closings are called off after contracts have been signed. Sometimes lawsuits ensue—

long-lasting, expensive lawsuits. Yet, in many cases, the problems could have been headed off. Sometimes closings are canceled because buyers and sellers disagree over who should pay for repairs that a house inspector has recommended.

Or a mechanic's lien turns up during a title search—someone who worked on the house claims that he or she hasn't been paid. Or the buyer's mortgage lender decides to raise the interest rate or lower the length of the mortgage—or, worst of all, decides that the buyers shouldn't get all the money they wanted to borrow.

Still other reasons why house closings have fallen through are related to special, maybe oddball, circumstances:

- At one closing, with lawyers, bankers, sellers, and real estate agent in attendance, the buyer began examining all the bills he had to pay—for this, that, etc. He turned pale, excused himself from the room, and was never seen again.
- The charming little pond in the backyard turned out to be an overflowing septic tank.
- The seller had told the buyer that a railroad track behind the house was abandoned. When the buyer came around one day and heard a train, she bowed out.
- According to Irving Price, author of *How to Get Top Dollar for Your Home*, the seller removed three antique light fixtures that were supposed to go with the house and replaced them with three flashlights.
- The night before the closing, the buyer's mother-in-law was mugged in front of the house.
- The woman whom the seller had introduced as his wife, and who had signed all of the sale documents, turned out to be a close friend of the seller but not his wife. His real wife, and the real co-owner of the house, hadn't signed any of the sale documents.

These are not normal situations, but it *is* normal for closings to be fraught with tension and anxiety. For buyers and sellers, large sums of money are at stake. For lawyers and agents, there are serious responsibilities, which could lead to costly lawsuits. Trivial things, like a pile of trash discovered in the basement, or missing fireplace equipment noticed a few days before the closing, can cause turmoil because everyone is on edge. That's why absolutely everything that can be done before the closing should be done.

## WHAT SHOULD BE DONE BEFORE CLOSING?

Almost everything. Some steps should be taken care of well in advance, because they take time, and some at the last minute. Here is what should be done well in advance:

1. The buyer should secure mortgage financing and should advise his or her bank of the closing date well in advance. You or your lawyer should keep checking on the progress being made.

2. Your lawyer should give all the calculations and amounts to be paid to the buyer's lawyer. (If the buyer owes you $130,000, you might want four checks in different amounts instead of a check for the lump sum, so that you can sign over some of the checks for other uses, such as buying a replacement house.) These should be paid in certified or bank and not personal checks.

3. Your lawyer should review every document and letter received from the buyer's lawyer and should notify the buyer's lawyer of any questions or problems.

4. The buyer should obtain all necessary inspections, or waive the right to do so.

5. If you were required to clear any problems with title, or complete any repairs, everything should be taken care of in advance of the closing.

6. Your lawyer should estimate all of the closing costs and adjustments and discuss these with the buyer's lawyer so that any questions or disagreements can be resolved ahead of time.

7. You should review the contract and make sure any items that the closing is contingent upon have been properly dealt with.

8. You should obtain certificates of occupancy for all improvements or additions you made on the house. Obtain a flood-hazard or other necessary certificate. Double-check with your lawyer what else you must bring with you to the closing—like a termite-inspector's report and the keys to the house. Also find out what closing costs you must pay, and bring checks to cover them.

Here are last-minute things to do before the closing:

9. Arrange with utility companies to shut off all water, gas, and electricity in your name and to issue final bills to your new address. Concurrently the buyer should notify the utility companies of the purchase, so that service will be continued in the buyer's name. If the utilities are a lien on the house being sold, some of your money may be held in escrow pending payments of the bills. In this case,

the utilities should be directed to send their final bills to the escrow agent.

10. Get a written confirmation from your bank of the principal balance remaining on your mortgage. Also have the bank notify you of the amount of interest that accrues (becomes due) each day. This is important because if the final payment is mailed to the bank instead of handed over at the closing, additional interest should be paid to cover the day or two the mail will take to reach the bank.

11. Confirm by telephone a few days before the closing that everyone who must attend the closing will, in fact, be there and has the correct address, time, and directions.

12. File a change of address form with the post office.

13. Have your phone disconnected, or have your calls forwarded.

14. Arrange for your oil company to estimate the value of any oil remaining in your tank.

15. Notify your bank or savings and loan of your change of address.

## WHERE IS THE CLOSING HELD?

The closing can be held at any one the following places: the office of your lawyer, the office of the buyer's lawyer, the office of the title company, the office of the buyer's bank, the office of the bank's lawyer, etc. Be flexible. The location will often be governed by the lender or some other party. Usually, the sale contract will specify where the closing will take place.

## WHO ATTENDS THE CLOSING?

Although custom, local law, and convenience of the parties all dictate who will be present at the closing, the following are possible candidates:

1. Seller's Lawyer. Your lawyer should be present at the closing to represent your interests. Documents that may not have been available before the closing might have to be reviewed. Often minor, last-minute decisions must be made.

2. Buyer's Lawyer. The buyer's lawyer will have to be present for the same reasons as the above. In some states the buyer's lawyer represents the mortgagee/lender and, possibly, the title company (which insures the buyer's title to your house). In these instances,

the buyer's lawyer may have to be approved by the lender and/or title company to perform the necessary functions.

---

**TIP:** Although the house closing may be simple enough for one lawyer to handle competently, this is rarely advisable. You and the buyer have different interests, which will best be represented by different lawyers.

---

3. Seller's Mortgagee. If you have a mortgage outstanding, your bank may require that its representative (perhaps its lawyer) attend the closing to obtain the check from the buyer for the amount of outstanding mortgage due. It may be possible to avoid having your bank's representative present (thus saving any fee you might be charged) by having the buyer's lawyer represent your bank (the buyer is concerned that your mortgage be paid off so it doesn't remain a lien on the house he or she is buying) and forward documents and payments to your bank after the closing. The drawback of this is that the buyer won't be able to obtain written confirmation at the closing that your mortgage has been satisfied.

4. Escrow Agent. This is usually an independent party, perhaps a representative of the title insurance company or of the bank. Whether you'll use an escrow agent depends on the custom in your part of the country. If present, the escrow agent will handle all of the money and paperwork associated with the closing, using the sales contract as a guide to ensure that all terms are adhered to and all monies are appropriately applied (e.g., to pay outstanding real estate taxes, utility bills, etc.).

Sometimes a list of steps to be taken by the escrow agent (sometimes called the escrow instructions) is prepared to summarize the escrow agent's responsibility and the money and documents the buyer and seller each must furnish to the escrow agent. The escrow agent may arrange for the recording of documents, payment of repair or insurance costs, proration of insurance or taxes, and other matters necessary to effect the closing.

5. Real Estate Agent. The agent will be there to pick up the commission check and to provide you with a statement indicating that the commission has been paid in full. He or she may assist in resolving any questions or disputes between the buyer and seller concerning the condition of the property, personal property involved, or other matters.

6. Buyer's mortgage lender. A representative may attend to advance the buyer the funds for closing (if the buyer is closing simultaneously on the mortgage and house).

7. Title insurance company. A representative may be present to provide the buyer with the title insurance binder, to resolve any title exceptions, and to collect the payment owed to the title company.

## DOCUMENTS THAT ARE INVOLVED AT THE CLOSING

Again, the nature of the transaction, local custom, and state law will affect which documents will be used. However, the following papers are usually involved:

1. Deed to the house. This is prepared by your attorney and given to the buyer by you. The deed must be the specific type of deed required in the sales contract. The legal description of your house in the deed should match the information contained in the title insurance binder the buyer receives.

2. Title insurance reports and searches (as contained in the buyer's title insurance binder).

3. Payoff statement from the seller's lenders (first mortgage, second mortgage, home-equity lender, etc.).

4. Survey. If an old survey is relied upon, the title insurance company, lender or buyer may require the seller to sign an affidavit stating that there have not been any material changes since the date of the prior survey.

5. Settlement sheet or closing summary. Sometimes a RESPA (Real Estate Settlement and Procedures Act—a form required by the U.S. Department of Housing and Urban Development) is used. This contains all the insurance, property tax, real estate transfer fees, fuel and other adjustments, and reconciles all payments and amounts due to the seller and paid from the buyer.

6. Affidavit of Title (given by the seller to the buyer in some states). The seller represents to the buyer that the seller has owned the property, is the sole owner, has never used any names other than those listed, has paid for all fixtures on the property, is not subject to any lawsuits, etc.

---

**EXAMPLE:** There may be a judgment against another person with the same name as you. The buyer will want you to provide a statement, under oath, that the judgment is not against you but is against another person with the same name.

---

7. In states and counties where there are real estate transfer taxes there will typically be forms and affidavits to complete for filing. For example, if the sale of your house is exempt from the tax, an affidavit to that effect may have to be filed.

8. A signed receipt by the broker acknowledging payment of the commission and stating that such payment discharges the seller from all liabilities to the broker.

9. Your insurance policy (if you are turning it over to the buyer).

10. Bill of Sale. You give this to the buyer as evidence that the buyer has taken title to the personal property sold in the transaction.

---

**TIP:** Check with your accountant in case any sales tax has to be paid on the amount of property transferred with the bill of sale.

---

11. Mortgage and note (for the buyer's loan used to buy your house).

12. Inspection reports (house, radon, termite, other pests).

## PAYMENTS

Every transaction has its own nuances; however, the following payments are often involved (a single statement, the RESPA form, may be used to calculate many of the expenses listed above, so that fewer checks may be needed to cover the net due as result of all the amounts listed).

---

**TIP:** Double-check to see that all checks total the required amounts, that every check is properly made out as payable to the correct party, that the checks which are supposed to be bank or certified checks are, and that every check has been properly endorsed. At some closings the escrow agent completes all of the checks involved and only a single check must be paid to the escrow agent.

---

1. Deposit monies initially paid by the buyer. Depending on the area's custom, these funds may have been held by your attorney, in his or her attorney escrow account. In other areas, the real estate broker, the title insurance company, or an independent escrow agent will hold the funds.

2. Payment of the broker's commission. The seller generally pays the commission unless alternative arrangements have been made.

3. Payments of any outstanding liens on the property.

4. Checks to or from the buyer or seller to reconcile the proration of taxes, insurance, rental income, etc.

5. Payment of the lawyer's and escrow agent's fees.

6. Payments for property and other taxes.

7. Insurance (fire and hazard) payment by the buyer. If you are holding a purchase-money mortgage on the property, you want to be sure the buyer has adequate insurance coverage to protect your mortgage.

8. Title insurance premium. This is paid by the buyer to the title insurance company selected by the buyer.

9. Pay-off of the seller's outstanding mortgage on the property.

---

**TIP:** In many cases the cost of using an overnight mail carrier to get the check to the bank the next day will be cheaper than the interest cost you would incur during the three or four days it would take regular mail to reach the bank.

---

10. Balance of payments due to the buyer's mortgage lender. This can include points for origination and discount fees.

11. Fee to the mortgage lender's review attorney for the preparation and review of the documents.

12. Payments of charges for document recording.

13. Mortgage-recording fee or tax.

14. Realty transfer tax.

### THINGS TO DO AFTER THE CLOSING

Even though the closing is the consummation of the transaction, there are a number of steps that the seller should take after the closing. You might consider the following:

1. Send your insurance policy back to the insurance company with a request that the policy be canceled and a refund issued. (The bank that held the mortgage on the house you sold might have the policy.)

2. Send copies of the closing statements and of all checks to your accountant. Indicate in your covering letter the address of the house

you will be purchasing as a replacement and the date and amount of purchase.

3. Collect all files and papers from the transaction, put them in a single binder, and store them with your tax and financial records.

4. Follow up with the bank that held the mortgage on the house you sold. Make sure the mortgage and note were canceled and that you received a mortgage satisfaction statement from the bank.

5. Record the mortgage satisfaction.

## CHAPTER SUMMARY

Closing procedures vary considerably depending on where in the country a house is located. The common point is that advance preparation and care will make the closing go more smoothly and, most importantly, avoid last-minute problems that can derail a sale. Communicate regularly with the parties involved to make sure everything is taking place on schedule. Let the checklists serve as guidelines and "homework" prompts.

# FOR YOUR NOTEBOOK

## SAMPLE CLOSING STATEMENT

The following is illustrative of a closing statement, which some lawyers prepare following a closing. Whether or not this is your lawyer's practice, the following example is a helpful summary of some of the people, checks, and documents that might be involved at a closing.

I. THE CLOSING.

Bill and Barbara Buyer purchased the house located at 1234 Main Street, Big City, Onestate, from Sam and Sue Seller. The closing took place at the law offices of Smith, Smith and Jones, 567 Big Avenue, Big City, Onestate 94848 on January 10, 1990.

II. PEOPLE IN ATTENDANCE AT THE CLOSING.

  A. Allen Attorney, attorney for buyers.

  B. Steven Smith, attorney for sellers.

  C. Bill and Barbara Buyer, the buyers.

  D. Sam and Sue Seller, the sellers.

  E. Bob Stevens, for Kaszvitz, Isaacson, counsel to Bigbank, lender to buyers.

  F. Jon Hunter, real estate broker.

III. DOCUMENTS PRESENTED AT CLOSING.

  A. Deed.

  B. 1099-B—reporting to be completed by Steven Smith.

  C. Mortgage—4 original signed copies.

  D. Certificate of Occupancy No. 38ZN3.

  E. Certificate of Transfer.

  F. Tax Information Worksheet.

  G. Mortgage Loan Commitment.

  H. Affidavit of Title—Buyers.

  I. Affidavit of Title—Sellers—3 copies.

  J. Survey.

  K. RESPA.

  L. Survey Affidavit.

  M. Notice of New Escrow Account—Tax Bill Authorization—Onestate Attachment A.

  N. Tax Certification of Your Mortgage Escrow Agreement.

  O. Copy of Downpayment Check.

  P. XYZ Title Insurance Corporate Commitment or Binder Endorsement.

Q. Mortgage for Jones (prior owner) cancelled.

R. Notice of Settlement.

S. National Bigcity Bank Payoff Statement.

T. Insurance Binder #1BBS66-018.

U. Mortgage Disclosure Statement.

V. Mortgage Loan Closing Statement.

IV. <u>PAYMENTS MADE AT CLOSING.</u>

A. Bigcity National Bank Tellers' Check—check #55998—to Bill and Barbara Buyer for $3,353.00, paid to Allen Attorney's escrow account.

B. Smith, Smith and Jones Escrow Account—check #95—to Allen Attorney, Esq. Trust Account for $146,400.00.

C. Suzy Relative—check #4782—to Bill Buyer for $3,000.00, signed over to Allen Attorney's escrow account.

D. Allen Attorney Trust Account check #1017—to National Bigcity Bank for $101,477.44, payoff Sellers mortgage.

E. Allen Attorney Trust Account check #1018 to Smith, Smith and Jones for $450.00, bank's counsel's fee.

F. Allen Attorney Trust Account check #1019 to Tax Collector, City of Wayne for 569.69.

G. Allen Attorney Trust Account check #1020 to Tax Collector, City of Wayne for $699.95.

H. Allen Attorney Trust Account check #1021 to Mortgage Finders Funding, Ltd. for $1,664.00, points.

I. Allen Attorney Trust Account check #1022 to Bigcity Lawyers Services for $774.60.

J. Allen Attorney Trust Account check #1024 to Steven Smith for $130.00, costs.

K. Allen Attorney Trust Account check #1024 to Wayne County Register for $590.00.

L. Allen Attorney Trust Account check #1028 to Jon Hustler for $3,000.00, brokerage commission.

M. Allen Attorney Trust Account check #1026 to Sam and Sue Seller for $42,219.31, balance of sales price.

N. Allen Attorney Trust Account check #1027 to Safe Insurance Company, Inc. for $570.00, insurance binder (not at closing).

O. Rich National Bank Tellers' Check #590097 to National Bigcity for $1,647.00, paid to Allen Attorney's trust account.

P. Suzy Relative check #703 to Allen Attorney's Trust Account for $5,000.00.

# 27 AFTER THE SALE: WHAT ABOUT THE TAX EFFECTS?

## WHY TAX PLANNING IS SO IMPORTANT FOR SELLERS

Once you decide to sell your home, the primary concern if you're in a soft market is getting a buyer at a reasonable price. No matter what type of market you're in, you want to get the most money you can from the sale, either to help pay for a new home, or to put into your pocket. The chapters discussing how to fix up and market your house, and how to help the buyer with financing, were aimed at getting your house sold and at the best price possible. But there's another important factor that might come into play when you've completed the sale: Uncle Sam. Understanding the tax consequences of selling a home can save you many dollars.

Although in many cases you can avoid paying any tax on selling your home by buying a more expensive replacement home within two years, the rules are complex and contain many traps. Ideally, you're reading this book before you sell your house and will be able to take advantage of the tax-planning information contained here when you meet with your tax adviser. In the "For Your Notebook" section of this chapter, sample tax forms illustrate how you should report your sale to the IRS under different circumstances. Even if you don't fill out your own tax return, these forms can serve as checklists of the kinds of information you'll have to give your accountant.

## THE BASIC TAX RULE AFFECTING SELLERS

The general rule that most homeowners take advantage of is this: If you sell a house that qualifies as your principal residence and, within two years, buy or build another principal residence for a cost at least as great as the adjusted sales price (defined later) of the home you've sold, you don't have to report any of the gain on the sale of the first house to the IRS.

---

**EXAMPLE:** Hilton and Hilda Homeowner bought a starter home for $85,000 five years ago, just after they got married. Although the real estate market where they live has slowed considerably, the house is still worth $145,000. If the Homeowners sell for that price and move to a rental apartment, they will have a $60,000 gain [$145,000 sales proceeds − $85,000 cost or tax basis]. Given the Homeowners' 28 percent tax bracket, the sale would cost them $16,800 in taxes. However, if the Homeowners buy a new home for $150,000, they won't have to pay any tax to the IRS. They will have to report the sale to the IRS in all cases, on Form 2119.

---

Unfortunately, the calculations involved are rarely so simple. It is often quite complicated to determine what your tax basis is in the home you've sold. There will be brokerage commissions and other expenses that must be considered. Perhaps the replacement home you buy costs somewhat less than the house you've sold so that only part of the gain will be taxed. These and many other common situations that sellers encounter are discussed below.


## CALCULATING YOUR GAIN WHEN YOU SELL YOUR HOUSE

The basic steps for calculating the amount of gain (or "amount realized") you have to report are as follows:

1. Determine the "amount realized" from the sale of your home. This is the total of all cash you were paid from the sale minus the costs of selling. The amount realized includes payments received directly from the buyer and from the buyer's bank, the amount received from an escrow agent or your lawyer relating to monies due you on the sale, and the fair value of any property the buyer gave you as consideration for the sale. For example, if the buyer is an art dealer and gave you a painting worth $5,000 as part of the payment, the

$5,000 must be added in. Also add to the amount realized the amounts of any debts on your house that the buyer has assumed as part of the purchase.

---

**EXAMPLE:** Harry and Hilda Homeowner from the example above decide to sell their house to Bill and Betty Buyer for only $95,000. However, the Homeowners have a mortgage of $50,000 still on their home, which the Buyers are assuming. The Homeowners calculate the amount they receive as follows: Cash and payments received ($95,000) plus mortgage assumed ($50,000). Thus, the total amount realized by the Homeowners is $145,000 [$95,000 + $50,000]. This is the same amount they would have received by selling the house for $145,000. The logic behind this rule is that there should be no difference in the result to the Homeowners whether the Buyers assume their $50,000 mortgage, or pay the Homeowners $50,000 more and the Homeowners then pay off the mortgage.

---

There are a number of items that will generally have to be subtracted to determine the amount you've realized. These include: brokerage commissions, legal fees, advertising costs, and other costs of actually making the sale (not costs to fix your home up for sale—those fall into another category).

2. Calculate your investment (tax basis) in the home. Start with the amount you paid for the home. This can be found on the sale contract used when you bought the house. Add to this the cost of any capital improvements you made while living in the house. These are permanent improvements that add to the value of the house. Examples include a new porch, roof, furnace, storm or replacement windows, siding, etc. Ancillary costs incurred when you purchased the house, such as legal bills, are also counted.

If, instead of buying your home, you received it as a gift or you inherited it, special rules apply to determine your tax basis. If you received your home as a gift, your tax basis is generally the tax basis of the person who gave it to you. If you inherited your home, its tax basis to you is generally the fair value of the house on the day the person who bequeathed it to you died.

There might also be a number of negative adjustments to be made to calculate your tax basis. If you've ever suffered a casualty loss (theft, fire, condemnation, etc.) to your home, the amount of the loss reduces your tax basis. Note that if you received insurance or other proceeds and used them to rebuild the damage, these expenditures would be added back above as capital improvements, so that the net result on your tax basis from a casualty in your home might be a wash.

If you've used part of your home as an office or for rental, the depreciation you've declared will reduce your tax basis. (Note, however, that the effect of having an office or rental unit in your home will be much more severe than that, because any portion of the sales proceeds allocable to a home office or rental can't qualify for the tax-free rollover. Some planning ideas for these situations will be discussed later.)

Another common adjustment is for sellers who have owned prior homes. Your tax basis must be reduced by the amount of gain deferred on a prior sale by having rolled over that gain into your present home. This reduction is the mechanism whereby the tax laws permit you to avoid tax on the home you sell if you roll your gain over into a new home for an equal or greater price. But the rollover provision isn't a free lunch. The gain will eventually have to be reported when you sell and don't roll over (the $125,000 exclusion discussed below is the only exception to this rule).

---

**EXAMPLE:** It's years after the last example and Harry and Hilda Homeowner have bought a home for $120,000, which they sell for $170,000, realizing a $50,000 gain [$170,000 − $120,000]. They roll this gain over by buying a replacement home for $190,000. Therefore, no tax is due on the $50,000 gain. If the Homeowners had to pay tax on the gain their tax cost would be $14,000 [$50,000 gain × 28% tax rate]. What happens to the $50,000 gain that isn't taxed? It is applied to reduce their tax basis in the replacement home. Therefore, the Homeowners' tax basis in the replacement home is $140,000 [$190,000 cost − $50,000 gain deferred]. This is exactly equal to their tax basis in their old home plus the new cash (or mortgage) they added to buy the new home [$120,000 + $20,000].

---

3. Calculate the amount realized on the sale by subtracting (2) from (1). This is the most you'll ever have to report as a gain on your tax return. Fortunately, there are a number of special rules that may save you some or all of the tax that would otherwise be due.

4. Consider the following special rules to reduce the gain you would otherwise have to report from item 3, above:

**Special Rule #1:** If the amount you realized on the sale of your home (item 3), less fix-up expenses you incur to make your home more salable, is not more than the price of your replacement home, no tax will be due. That is, you can deduct fix-up costs from the amount realized as gain for tax purposes.

**COMMENT:** Fix-up expenses are the costs you've incurred to repair and fix up your home in order to sell it. Fix-up expenses include the cost of wallpapering, painting, landscaping, gardening, making plumbing repairs, repairing appliances, cleaning and repairing broken gutters and leaders, and so forth. To qualify, *these costs must be incurred no more than 30 days before you sell your home.* You must also pay for these costs *no later than 30 days after you sell your home.*

**Special Rule #2:** If you are 55 or older when you sell your home, you may qualify for a once-in-a-lifetime exclusion of up to $125,000 of the gain realized. If the amount in item 3 is less than $125,000, then no tax would be due.

**CAUTION:** You must be age 55 or older *at the time of the sale;* merely turning 55 in the year of the sale isn't sufficient to qualify. Make sure that the closing is after your birthday.

**COMMENT:** A number of requirements must generally be met to qualify for the $125,000 exclusion. You must have owned and used the property as your *principal residence for at least three of the five years before the date of the sale.* Only your principal home qualifies. A summer or vacation home won't qualify. Also, the sale must be a sale of your entire house. You can't sell someone a 50 percent interest in the house and use the exclusion. *Husband and wife are entitled to only one $125,000 exclusion.* Filing separate tax returns won't avoid this limitation, because each of you will be entitled to only a $62,500 exclusion. Also, you can't divide up the exclusion and use it at different times; you can't, for example, use $100,000 now and use the $25,000 "remaining" on another house sale. The $25,000 isn't remaining. The exclusion, regardless of the amount excluded, *can be claimed only once.*

## SOME INDIVIDUAL SITUATIONS

Generally, applying the rollover rules is fairly simple: You, or you and your spouse, own a home; you sell it and buy a new home, and the gain is rolled over tax free. However, a number of different circumstance can arise in which, without careful tax planning, the tax benefits can be lost.

**First Situation:** You and your fiancé are getting married. You each own separate condominiums that you plan to sell so you can buy one home, which is more expensive than the two condominiums. You can both roll over your separate gains into the single new home, but you must attach a statement to your joint tax return (which, presumably, you'll file once you're married).

---

**CAUTION:** These favorable rollover rules do not apply to nonmarried people who live together.

---

**Second Situation:** You live with your parents, and the house is in their name. You sell the house, and everyone agrees to put the new house in your name. Bad move: The rollover provision won't be available. A better approach would be to have your parents take the new house in their name and then present the house to you as a gift.

---

**CAUTION:** There may be gift-tax consequences with the latter approach. Although your parents can gift up to $600,000 each without incurring a tax, they will use up a portion of their unified estate and gift tax credit, which may not be advisable. Check with your tax adviser before any transfer is completed.

---

**Third Situation:** Your home has a lot of land around it. If the market is tight, one way to maximize your sales proceeds might be to subdivide the land. You can sell your house with a smaller yard and sell the rest of the land as a vacant lot to another buyer. But if you do this, can you still roll over all of the proceeds? Another way to ask that is: Will the amount you receive for the vacant lot you split off still be considered proceeds from the sale of your home? The answer is that if the land, including the lot you split off, was always used solely as your principal residence, you should be able to qualify.

### IMPORTANT EXCLUSIONS FROM THE ROLLOVER TREATMENT

If you've had a home office or rental unit in your home, the portion of the gain allocable to these nonpersonal residence uses will not qualify for the favorable tax-deferred treatment. This is because rental units and home offices are characterized as business rather than personal-residence uses, and the rollover rules are available only for personal residences.

If 15 percent of your home was occupied by a home office, then 15 percent of the sales proceeds will be allocated for the sale of your home office. You must also allocate a portion of the tax basis in your home to the home office to calculate your actual taxable gain.

---

**EXAMPLE:** Hilton Homeowner purchased a house for $150,000. Hilton uses 15 percent of the house as an office for his consulting business. Hilty sells his home for $220,000 and purchases a replacement home for $225,000. The amount of gain realized (ignoring depreciation on the home office to simplify the example) attributable to his home office is calculated as follows:

(1) Multiply the sale proceeds by 15 percent [$220,000 × 15% = $33,000]. (2) Multiply the tax basis by 15 percent [$150,000 × 15% = $22,500]. (3) Subtract (2) from (1) to get the answer: [$33,000 − $22,500 = $10,500]. The amount of gain attributable to the home office is $10,500, and this amount must be excluded from the gain Hilton rolls over into his new home purchase.

---

**TIP:** There is one planning opportunity available to avoid this tax. If you stop using your home office the year before the sale, you shouldn't have to pay tax on the allocable gain, because then you would be using the entire house as a personal residence for the year of the sale. However, if you've claimed home office deductions for some time, there should be some external evidence proving that you actually discontinued using the home office as an office. Examples of evidence would be if you rent office space elsewhere, or completely close down your business. Also, make sure that your home office space is being used regularly for personal purposes, to fully nullify its business use.

---

If you've rented out a portion of your home (whether it's a duplex or has a basement apartment), similar rules apply.

Another potential problem area is one that affects many senior citizens—that is, when the replacement home is a nursing, life-care, or retirement facility. Depending on the legal arrangements, buying into such a facility may, or may not, qualify for the tax-free rollover provisions. The key is that you must be acquiring an interest in the real estate in order to roll over the gain on the house you're selling.

If you're not (i.e., if you're merely acquiring a right to meals, living quarters, etc.), the rollover provisions won't be available, and you could get hit with a whopping tax on the home you sell.

There's another trap that many homeowners aren't aware of: There is a limit to how frequently you can use the rollover provisions.

---

**CAUTION:** *You can use the tax-free rollover provisions only once every two years.* If you've sold another home during the period two years before the date you're selling your current home, a tax may be due. There is one very important exception to this rule. If you are moving because of a work-related matter, and can meet the requirements to qualify for a moving-expense deduction, this limitation won't apply.

---

## MOVING EXPENSES CAN PROVIDE TAX BENEFITS

At the same time you're trying to sell your current home, you're often looking for a new home. Whenever you're moving, consider carefully whether you can qualify to deduct moving expenses, because these can generate valuable tax benefits. The basic requirements for deducting moving expenses are the following:

1. The distance between the location of your new job and your old home must be at least thirty-five miles more than the distance between the location of your old job and your old home.

2. During the 12-month period immediately after the move, you must work full time for at least 39 weeks. Or, if you're self employed, you must work full time for a minimum of 78 weeks in the 24-month period immediately after the move.

3. Your move must be connected with your work at the new location. Thus the move must take place at approximately the same time that you begin your new job.

4. Only reasonable expenses can be deducted.

Once you meet these requirements, you can deduct the direct costs of moving and certain indirect costs up to prescribed limits. The cost of moving household goods (furniture, clothing, dishes, etc.) from the home you're selling to your new home are fully deductible. This includes the cost to pack, insure, and ship them.

The cost of traveling for you and your family is deductible.

The costs of house hunting and temporary living expenses while your new home is being readied are indirect costs, which can be deducted only up to a $1,500 limit. Other indirect costs are the expenses of selling your old home, including brokerage fees, legal fees, survey costs, and so forth. However, the total amount of indirect costs you can deduct is limited to $3,000. Many of the indirect costs in excess of this amount can be added to your tax basis in your new home. If you qualify for moving-expense deductions, claim them on Form 3903.

## CHAPTER SUMMARY

Although the focus of this book has been on helping you sell your home at a decent price, the most important number ultimately is the amount of money you have left when the sale is complete. Although taxes aren't likely to be uppermost in your mind when you're fighting to sell a house in a buyer's market, you can't overlook the tax consequences, because they can have a dramatic impact on what you will net on the sale of your home. This chapter has highlighted some of the many traps and rules you must be aware of. However, it's always best to check with your tax adviser if you'll be involved in anything but a simple rollover.

Homeowners get one of best tax benefits available—the ability to roll the gain from the house you're selling over into another, more expensive house within two years. In order to take advantage of this benefit, sellers need to be sure they understand the limitations and exclusions, as on a home office or rental situation. They need to know how to reduce the amount of gain they must report by deducting fix-up expenses, or how much they can exclude because they are 55 or older. They need to know when and how to use moving-expense deductions.

# FOR YOUR NOTEBOOK

## SAMPLE TAX FORMS FOR REPORTING A HOUSE SALE

The following scenarios and tax returns were prepared by the New York City office of the international accounting firm Ernst & Young. These sample tax returns include most of the tax forms your accountant will complete for the year in which you sell your house.

### CASE 1

**The Facts:** A married couple, ages 58 and 52, sell their home for $276,000. They purchased the home in 1973 for $74,300. They made various improvements over the years of $23,190. They move into a retirement apartment and do not roll over the gain. What are the consequences of these transactions, and how are they reported?

**Comments:** Because one of the homeowners is more than 55 years of age when the sale occurs, and the sellers have met the other requirements, the couple will qualify for the special once-in-a-lifetime $125,000 exclusion. However, since the couple is not buying a replacement home, the $53,510 gain above this exclusion amount is taxable.

Case 1

| Form **2119** | **Sale of Your Home** | OMB No. 1545-0072 |
|---|---|---|

Department of the Treasury
Internal Revenue Service (x)

▶ See Separate Instructions.

▶ Attach to Form 1040 for year of sale.

**1989**

Attachment Sequence No. **22**

**Please Type or Print**

Your first name and initial (If joint, also give spouse's name and initial.)      Last name

Marc & Kelly      Minker

Your social security number

060 : 99 : 8888

Present home address (no., street, and apt. no., or rural route) (or P.O. box no. if mail is not delivered to street address)

123 Argyle Drive

Spouse's social security number

001 : 19 : 7224

City, town or post office, state, and ZIP code

Millneck,　MI　　72850

---

**Part I**    **Facts About You and Your Home**

| | | | Yes | No |
|---|---|---|---|---|
| **1a** | Date former main home was sold ▶       September 30, 1989 | | | |
| **b** | Enter the face amount of any mortgage, note (for example, second trust), or other financial instrument on which you will receive periodic payments of principal or interest from this sale. (See Instructions for line 1b.)▶   $    - 0 - | | | |
| **2a** | Have you bought or built a new main home? | | | X |
| **b** | Are any rooms in either main home rented out or used for business for which a deduction is allowed? (If "Yes," see Instructions.) | | | X |
| **3a** | Were you 55 or older on date of sale? | | X | |
| **b** | Was your spouse 55 or older on date of sale? If you answered "No" to 3a and 3b, do not complete 3c through 3f or Part III. | | | X |
| **c** | Did the person who answered "Yes" to 3a or 3b own and use the property sold as a main home for a total of at least 3 years (except for short absences) during the 5-year period before the sale? | | X | |
| **d** | If you answered "Yes" to 3c, do you choose to take the one-time exclusion of the gain on the sale? | | X | |
| **e** | At time of sale, who owned the home ?   ☐ you   ☐ your spouse   ☒ both of you | | | |
| **f** | Social security number of spouse, at time of sale, if different from above ▶ (Enter "None" if you were not married at time of sale.) | | | |

---

**Part II**    **Figure Your Gain (Do not include amounts that you deduct as moving expenses.)**

| | | | |
|---|---|---|---|
| **4** | Selling price of home. (Do not include personal property items.) | **4** | 276,000 |
| **5** | Expense of sale. (Include sales commissions, advertising, legal, etc.) | **5** | |
| **6** | Subtract line 5 from line 4. This is the amount realized | **6** | 276,000 |
| **7** | Basis of home sold. (See Instructions.) | **7** | 97,490 |
| **8a** | Subtract line 7 from line 6 (gain on sale). If zero or less, enter zero and do not complete the rest of the form. Enter the gain from this line on Schedule D, line 3 or 10,* unless you bought another main home or checked "Yes" to 3d. Then continue with this form | **8a** | 178,510 |
| **b** | If you haven't replaced your home, do you plan to do so within the replacement period?    ☐ Yes ☒ No (If "Yes," see Instructions under When and Where To File.) | | |

---

**Part III**    **If Age 55 or Older, Figure Your One-Time Exclusion**    *Complete this part only if you checked "Yes" to 3d.)*

| | | | |
|---|---|---|---|
| **9** | Enter the **smaller** of line 8a or $125,000 ($62,500 if married filing separate return) (See instructions.) | **9** | 125,000 |
| **10** | Subtract line 9 from line 8a (gain). If zero, do not complete rest of form. Enter the gain from this line on Schedule D, line 10,* unless you bought another main home. Then continue with this form | **10** | 53,510 |

---

**Part IV**    **Figure Gain To Be Postponed and Adjusted Basis of New Home**    *(Complete this part if you bought another main home.)*

| | | | |
|---|---|---|---|
| **11** | Fixing-up expenses. (See Instructions for time limits.) | **11** | |
| **12** | Subtract line 11 from line 6 (adjusted sales price) | **12** | |
| **13a** | Cost of new home | **13a** | |
| **b** | Enter the date you moved into your new main home ▶ ............................................. | | |
| **14** | Subtract line 13a plus line 9 (if applicable) from line 12. If result is zero or less, enter zero. Do not enter more than line 8a or line 10 (if applicable). This is the gain taxable this year. Enter the gain from this line on Schedule D, line 3 or 10*. | **14** | |
| **15** | Subtract line 14 from line 8a. **However**, if you completed Part III, subtract line 14 from line 10. (This is the gain to be postponed.) | **15** | |
| **16** | Subtract line 15 from line 13 (adjusted basis of new main home) | **16** | |

**\*Caution:** If you completed Form 6252 for the home in line 1a, do not enter your taxable gain from Form 2119 on Schedule D.

**Please Sign Here**

Under penalties of perjury, I declare that I have examined this form, including attachments, and to the best of my knowledge and belief, it is true, correct, and complete.

Your signature      Date      Spouse's Signature      Date

▶

(If joint return, both must sign.) (Sign and date only if not attached to your tax return.)

For Paperwork Reduction Act Notice, see separate Instructions.      Form **2119** (1989)

PREPARED BY ERNST & YOUNG, NEW YORK

307  10-89                                          Case 1

2045-5

| SCHEDULE D | **Capital Gains and Losses** | OMB No 1545-0074 |
|---|---|---|
| **(Form 1040)** | **(And Reconciliation of Forms 1099-B)** | 19**89** |
| Department of the Treasury<br>Internal Revenue Service   (4) | ▶ Attach to Form 1040.    ▶ See Instructions for Schedule D (Form 1040).<br>▶ For more space to list transactions for lines 2a and 9a, get Schedule D-1 (Form 1040). | Attachment<br>Sequence No. **12A** |

| Name(s) shown on Form 1040 | Your social security number |
|---|---|
| Marc & Kelly Minker | 060 ⋮ 99 ⋮ 8888 |

1  Report here the total sales of stocks, bonds, etc., reported for 1989 to you on Form(s) 1099-B or on an equivalent substitute statement(s). If this amount differs from the total of lines 2c and 9c, column (d), attach a statement explaining the difference. See the Instructions for line 1 for examples . . . . . | 1

**Part I   Short-Term Capital Gains and Losses—Assets Held One Year or Less**

| (a) Description of property<br>(Example, 100 shares 7%<br>preferred of "Z" Co.) | (b) Date acquired<br>(Mo., day, yr.) | (c) Date sold<br>(Mo., day, yr.) | (d) Sales price (see<br>Instructions) | (e) Cost or other<br>basis (see<br>Instructions) | (f) LOSS<br>If (e) is more than (d),<br>subtract (d) from (e) | (g) GAIN<br>If (d) is more than (e),<br>subtract (e) from (d) |
|---|---|---|---|---|---|---|
| **2a Stocks, Bonds, and Other Securities (Include all Form 1099-B transactions. See Instructions.)** | | | | | | |
| | | | | | | |
| | | | | | | |
| | | | | | | |
| | | | | | | |
| | | | | | | |
| **2b** Amounts from Schedule D-1, line 2b (attach Schedule D-1) . | | | | | | |
| **2c Total** (add column (d) of lines 2a and 2b).   ▶ 2c | | | | | | |
| **2d Other Transactions (Include Real Estate**<br>**Transactions From Forms 1099-S.)** | | | | | | |
| | | | | | | |
| | | | | | | |

| | | | | |
|---|---|---|---|---|
| 3 | Short-term gain from sale or exchange of your home from Form 2119, line 8a or 14 . | **3** | | |
| 4 | Short-term gain from installment sales from Form 6252, line 22 or 30 . . . . | **4** | | |
| 5 | Net short-term gain or (loss) from partnerships, S corporations, and fiduciaries . . | **5** | | |
| 6 | Short-term capital loss carryover . . . . . . . . . . . . . . | **6** | | |
| 7 | Add all of the transactions on lines 2a, 2b, and 2d and lines 3 through 6 in columns (f) and (g) . . | **7** (                      ) | | |
| 8 | Net short-term gain or (loss), combine columns (f) and (g) of line 7 . . . . . . | | **8** | |

**Part II   Long-Term Capital Gains and Losses—Assets Held More Than One Year**

**9a Stocks, Bonds, and Other Securities (Include all Form 1099-B transactions. See Instructions.)**

| | | | | | | |
|---|---|---|---|---|---|---|
| | | | | | | |
| | | | | | | |
| | | | | | | |
| | | | | | | |
| | | | | | | |
| **9b** Amounts from Schedule D-1, line 9b (attach Schedule D-1) . | | | | | | |
| **9c Total** (add column (d) of lines 9a and 9b).   ▶ 9c | | | | | | |
| **9d Other Transactions (Include Real Estate**<br>**Transactions From Forms 1099-S.)** | | | | | | |
| | | | | | | |

| | | | | |
|---|---|---|---|---|
| 10 | Long-term gain from sale or exchange of your home from Form 2119, line 8a, 10, or 14 . | **10** | | 53510 |
| 11 | Long-term gain from installment sales from Form 6252, line 22 or 30 . . . . | **11** | | |
| 12 | Net long-term gain or (loss) from partnerships, S corporations, and fiduciaries . . | **12** | | |
| 13 | Capital gain distributions . . . . . . . . . . . . . . . | **13** | | |
| 14 | Enter gain from Form 4797, line 7 or 9 . . . . . . . . . . . . | **14** | | |
| 15 | Long-term capital loss carryover . . . . . . . . . . . . . | **15** | | |
| 16 | Add all of the transactions on lines 9a, 9b, and 9d and lines 10 through 15 in columns (f) and (g) | **16** (                      ) | | 53510 |
| 17 | Net long-term gain or (loss), combine columns (f) and (g) of line 16 . . . . . . . . | | **17** | 53510 |

For Paperwork Reduction Act Notice, see Form 1040 Instructions.                                          Schedule D (Form 1040) 1989

**2045-6**

Case 1

307  10-89

Schedule D (Form 1040) 1989      Attachment Sequence No. **12A**      Page **2**

Name(s) shown on Form 1040. (Do not enter name and social security number if shown on other side.)      Your social security number

### Part III    Summary of Parts I and II

| | |
|---|---|
| 18 | Combine lines 8 and 17, and enter the net gain or (loss) here. If result is a gain, **stop here** and also enter the gain on Form 1040, line 13. If the result is a (loss), go on to line 19 . . . . . . . . . | **18** |
| 19 | If line 18 is a (loss), enter here and as a (loss) on Form 1040, line 13, the **smaller** of: | |
| a | The (loss) on line 18; **or** | |
| b | ( \$3,000) or, if married filing a separate return, (\$1,500) . . . . . . . . . . . | **19** ( ) |
| | Note: *When figuring whether 19a or 19b is* **smaller***, treat both numbers as if they are positive.* | |
| • | Go on to Part IV if the loss on line 18 is more than \$3,000 (\$1,500, if married filing a separate return), OR if taxable income on Form 1040, line 37, is zero. | |

### Part IV    Figure Your Capital Loss Carryovers From 1989 to 1990

#### Section A.—Figure Your Carryover Limit

| | |
|---|---|
| 20 | Enter taxable income or loss from Form 1040, line 37. (**If Form 1040, line 37, is zero, see the Instructions for the amount to enter.**)    **20** |
| | Note: *For lines 21 through 36, treat all amounts as positive.* |
| 21 | Enter the loss shown on line 19 . . . . . . . . . . .    **21** |
| 22 | Enter the amount shown on Form 1040, line 36    **22** |
| 23 | Combine lines 20, 21, and 22. If zero or less, enter zero . . .    **23** |
| 24 | Enter the **smaller** of line 21 or line 23 . . . . . . . . . .    **24** |

#### Section B.—Figure Your Short-Term Capital Loss Carryover
(Complete this section only if there is a loss shown on line 8 and line 19. Otherwise, go on to Section C.)

| | |
|---|---|
| 25 | Enter the loss shown on line 8 . . . . . . . . . . .    **25** |
| 26 | Enter the gain, if any, shown on line 17 . . . . . . .    **26** |
| 27 | Enter the amount shown on line 24 . . . . . . .    **27** |
| 28 | Add lines 26 and 27 . . . . . . . . . . . . .    **28** |
| 29 | Subtract line 28 from line 25. If zero or less, enter zero. This is your **short-term capital loss carryover from 1989 to 1990.** . . . . . . . . . . . . .    **29** |

#### Section C.—Figure Your Long-Term Capital Loss Carryover
(Complete this section only if there is a loss shown on line 17 and line 19.)

| | |
|---|---|
| 30 | Enter the loss shown on line 17 . . . . . . . . . . .    **30** |
| 31 | Enter the gain, if any, shown on line 8 . . . . . . . .    **31** |
| 32 | Enter the amount shown on line 24 . . . . . . . . .    **32** |
| 33 | Enter the amount, if any, shown on line 25 . . . . . .    **33** |
| 34 | Subtract line 33 from line 32. If zero or less, enter zero . . .    **34** |
| 35 | Add lines 31 and 34 . . . . . . . . . . . . . . .    **35** |
| 36 | Subtract line 35 from line 30. If zero or less, enter zero. This is your **long-term capital loss carryover from 1989 to 1990** . . . . . . . . . . .    **36** |

### Part V    Complete This Part Only If You Elect Out of the Installment Method and Report a Note or Other Obligation at Less Than Full Face Value

| | |
|---|---|
| 37 | Check here if you elect out of the installment method . . . . . . . . . . . . . ▶ ☐ |
| 38 | Enter the face amount of the note or other obligation . . . . . . . . . . . ▶ .................... |
| 39 | Enter the percentage of valuation of the note or other obligation . . . . . . . . . ▶ |

### Part VI    Reconcile Forms 1099-B for Bartering Transactions

(Complete this part if you received one or more Form(s) 1099-B or an equivalent substitute statement(s) reporting bartering income.)

Amount of bartering income from Form 1099-B or equivalent statement reported on form or schedule

| | |
|---|---|
| 40 | Form 1040, line 22 . . . . . . . . . . . . . . . . . .    **40** |
| 41 | Schedule C (Form 1040) . . . . . . . . . . . . . . . .    **41** |
| 42 | Schedule D (Form 1040) . . . . . . . . . . . . . . . .    **42** |
| 43 | Schedule E (Form 1040) . . . . . . . . . . . . . . . .    **43** |
| 44 | Schedule F (Form 1040) . . . . . . . . . . . . . . . .    **44** |
| 45 | Other form (identify) (if not taxable, indicate reason—attach additional sheets if necessary) ▶ ......... |
| | ----------------------------------------------------------------------------- |
| | -----------------------------------------------------------------------------    **45** |
| 46 | Total (add lines 40 through 45) . . . . . . . . . . . . . . . .    **46** |
| | Note: *The amount on line 46 should be the same as the total bartering income on all Forms 1099-B and equivalent statements received.* |

## CASE 2

**The Facts—Case 2(a):** A homeowner purchased a home for $76,500. Two years ago the home was worth $175,000. Now the market is soft and the home can be sold for only $155,000. The seller decides to rent the house for one year, hoping the market will come back, and then sell. The house is rented for $1,200 per month. After 12 months the house is sold for $169,500. Assuming that the seller rolls over the entire gain into a new house costing $174,000, how is the gain reported?

**Comments:** The seller temporarily rents the home, waiting for the market to firm up, which it does. Depreciation claimed during this rental period (see Form 4562) of $2,666 must be applied to reduce the tax basis in the home when the seller calculates the adjusted basis of the new home on Form 2119. Thus the taxpayer's basis in the home sold is the original $76,500 purchase price, less the $2,666 of depreciation claimed, or the $73,834 reported on line 7 of Form 2119.

**The Facts—Case 2(b):** Assume the same general facts as in Case 2(a). What would happen if the home were characterized as a rental property and the gain couldn't be rolled over?

**Comments:** In this variation of Case 2(a), the seller didn't take the necessary precautions, and the home became a rental property. Form 2119 is therefore not applicable, because the taxpayer is not selling a home. Instead, Form 4797, "Sale of Business Property," must be used, and a tax will be due.

Case 2(a)

| Form **2119** | **Sale of Your Home** | OMB No. 1545-0072 |
|---|---|---|
| Department of the Treasury Internal Revenue Service (x) | ▶ See Separate Instructions. ▶ Attach to Form 1040 for year of sale. | 19**89** Attachment Sequence No. **22** |

| | Your first name and initial (If joint, also give spouse's name and initial.) | Last name | Your social security number |
|---|---|---|---|
| **Please** | Roy & Ellen | Jones | 793 : 65 : 4321 |
| **Type** | Present home address (no., street, and apt. no., or rural route) (or P.O. box no. if mail is not delivered to street address) | | Spouse's social security number |
| **or** | 2175 Perth Hill Terrace | | 998 : 77 : 1001 |
| **Print** | City, town or post office, state, and ZIP code | | |
| | Twin Cities, VA 01776 | | |

**Part I    Facts About You and Your Home**

**1a** Date former main home was sold ▶ ___January 15, 1989___

| | | | Yes | No |
|---|---|---|---|---|
| **b** | Enter the face amount of any mortgage, note (for example, second trust), or other financial instrument on which you will receive periodic payments of principal or interest from this sale. (See Instructions for line 1b.) ▶  $ – 0 – | | | |
| **2a** | Have you bought or built a new main home? . . . . . . . . . . . . . . . . . . . . . | | X | |
| **b** | Are any rooms in either main home rented out or used for business for which a deduction is allowed? . . . . (If "Yes," see Instructions.) | | | |
| **3a** | Were you 55 or older on date of sale? . . . . . . . . . . . . . . . . . . . . . . | | | X |
| **b** | Was your spouse 55 or older on date of sale? . . . . . . . . . . . . . . . . . . . If you answered "No" to 3a and 3b, do not complete 3c through 3f or Part III. | | | X |
| **c** | Did the person who answered "Yes" to 3a or 3b own and use the property sold as a main home for a total of at least 3 years (except for short absences) of the 5-year period before the sale? . . . . . . . . . . | | | |
| **d** | If you answered "Yes" to 3c, do you choose to take the one-time exclusion of the gain on the sale? . . . . . | | | |
| **e** | At time of sale, who owned the home ? ☐ you    ☐ your spouse    ☐ both of you | | | |
| **f** | Social security number of spouse, at time of sale, if different from above ▶ (Enter "None" if you were not married at time of sale.) | | | |

**Part II    Figure Your Gain (Do not include amounts that you deduct as moving expenses.)**

| | | | |
|---|---|---|---|
| **4** | Selling price of home. (Do not include personal property items.) . . . . . . . . . . | **4** | 169,500 |
| **5** | Expense of sale. (Include sales commissions, advertising, legal, etc.) . . . . . . . . | **5** | |
| **6** | Subtract line 5 from line 4. This is the amount realized . . . . . . . . . . . . . | **6** | 169,500 |
| **7** | Basis of home sold. (See Instructions.) . . . . . . . . . . . . . . . . . . . | **7** | 73,834 |
| **8a** | Subtract line 7 from line 6 (gain on sale). If zero or less, enter zero and do not complete the rest of the form. Enter the gain from this line on Schedule D, line 3 or 10,* unless you bought another main home or checked "Yes" to 3d. Then continue with this form . . . . . . . . . . . . . | **8a** | 95,666 |
| **b** | If you haven't replaced your home, do you plan to do so within the replacement period? . . . . . . . . . ☐ Yes ☐ No (If "Yes," see Instructions under When and Where To File.) | | |

**Part III    If Age 55 or Older, Figure Your One-Time Exclusion   (Complete this part only if you checked "Yes" to 3d.)**

| | | | |
|---|---|---|---|
| **9** | Enter the **smaller** of line 8a or $125,000 ($62,500, if married filing separate return) (See Instructions.) | **9** | |
| **10** | Subtract line 9 from line 8a (gain). If zero, do not complete rest of form. Enter the gain from this line on Schedule D, line 10,* unless you bought another main home. Then continue with this form . . . . | **10** | |

**Part IV    Figure Gain To Be Postponed and Adjusted Basis of New Home   (Complete this part if you bought another main home.)**

| | | | |
|---|---|---|---|
| **11** | Fixing-up expenses. (See Instructions for time limits.) . . . . . . . . . . . . . | **11** | – 0 – |
| **12** | Subtract line 11 from line 6 (adjusted sales price) . . . . . . . . . . . . . . . | **12** | 169,500 |
| **13a** | Cost of new home . . . . . . . . . . . . . . . . . . . . . . . . . . . | **13a** | 174,000 |
| **b** | Enter the date you moved into your new main home ▶ ___January 31, 1989___ | | |
| **14** | Subtract line 13a plus line 9 (if applicable) from line 12. If result is zero or less, enter zero. Do not enter more than line 8a or line 10 (if applicable). This is the gain taxable this year. Enter the gain from this line on Schedule D, line 3 or 10*. . . . . . . . . . . . . . . . . . . . | **14** | – 0 – |
| **15** | Subtract line 14 from line 8a. **However**, if you completed Part III, subtract line 14 from line 10. (This is the gain to be postponed.) . . . . . . . . . . . . . . . . . . . . . | **15** | 95,666 |
| **16** | Subtract line 15 from line 13 (adjusted basis of new main home) . . . . . . . . . . | **16** | 78,334 |

*****Caution:** If you completed Form 6252 for the home in 1a, do not enter your taxable gain from Form 2119 on Schedule D.

| **Please Sign Here** | Under penalties of perjury, I declare that I have examined this form, including attachments, and to the best of my knowledge and belief, it is true, correct, and complete. |
|---|---|
| | Your signature          Date          Spouse's Signature          Date |
| | ▶ |
| | (If joint return, both must sign.) (Sign and date only if not attached to your tax return.) |

For Paperwork Reduction Act Notice, see separate Instructions.          Form **2119** (1989)

3C7   10-89

Case 2(a)

**2045-5**

| SCHEDULE D | **Capital Gains and Losses** | OMB No. 1545-0074 |
|---|---|---|
| (Form 1040) | **(And Reconciliation of Forms 1099-B)** | **1989** |
| Department of the Treasury Internal Revenue Service   (4) | ▶ Attach to Form 1040.    ▶ See Instructions for Schedule D (Form 1040). ▶ For more space to list transactions for lines 2a and 9a, get Schedule D-1 (Form 1040). | Attachment Sequence No. **12A** |

Name(s) shown on Form 1040

Roy & Ellen          Jones

Your social security number

793 ⋮ 65 ⋮ 4321

1  Report here the total sales of stocks, bonds, etc., reported for 1989 to you on Form(s) 1099-B or on an equivalent substitute statement(s). If this amount differs from the total of lines 2c and 9c, column (d), attach a statement explaining the difference. See the Instructions for line 1 for examples . . . . . |1|

**Part I   Short-Term Capital Gains and Losses—Assets Held One Year or Less**

| (a) Description of property (Example, 100 shares 7% preferred of "Z" Co.) | (b) Date acquired (Mo., day, yr.) | (c) Date sold (Mo., day, yr.) | (d) Sales price (see Instructions) | (e) Cost or other basis (see Instructions) | (f) LOSS If (e) is more than (d), subtract (d) from (e) | (g) GAIN If (d) is more than (e), subtract (e) from (d) |
|---|---|---|---|---|---|---|
| **2a  Stocks, Bonds, and Other Securities (Include all Form 1099-B transactions. See Instructions.)** | | | | | | |
| | | | | | | |
| | | | | | | |
| | | | | | | |
| | | | | | | |
| | | | | | | |
| | | | | | | |
| | | | | | | |

2b  Amounts from Schedule D-1, line 2b (attach Schedule D-1) .

2c  Total (add column (d) of lines 2a and 2b) . ▶ **2c**

**2d  Other Transactions (Include Real Estate Transactions From Forms 1099-S.)**

| | | | | | | |
|---|---|---|---|---|---|---|
| | | | | | | |
| | | | | | | |

| | | |
|---|---|---|
| 3  Short-term gain from sale or exchange of your home from Form 2119, line 8a or 14 . | **3** | |
| 4  Short-term gain from installment sales from Form 6252, line 22 or 30 . . . . . | **4** | |
| 5  Net short-term gain or (loss) from partnerships, S corporations, and fiduciaries. . | **5** | |
| 6  Short-term capital loss carryover  . . . . . . . . . . . . . . . | **6** | |
| 7  Add all of the transactions on lines 2a, 2b, and 2d and lines 3 through 6 in columns (f) and (g) . | **7** ⎥( ⎥ ) | |
| 8  Net short-term gain or (loss), combine columns (f) and (g) of line 7 . . . . . . . . . . | **8** | |

**Part II   Long-Term Capital Gains and Losses—Assets Held More Than One Year**

9a  Stocks, Bonds, and Other Securities (Include all Form 1099-B transactions. See Instructions.)

| | | | | | | |
|---|---|---|---|---|---|---|
| | | | | | | |
| | | | | | | |
| | | | | | | |
| | | | | | | |
| | | | | | | |

9b  Amounts from Schedule D-1, line 9b (attach Schedule D-1) .

9c  Total (add column (d) of lines 9a and 9b). ▶ **9c**

**9d  Other Transactions (Include Real Estate Transactions From Forms 1099-S.)**

| | | | | | | |
|---|---|---|---|---|---|---|
| | | | | | | |
| | | | | | | |

| | | | |
|---|---|---|---|
| 10  Long-term gain from sale or exchange of your home from Form 2119, line 8a, 10, or 14 . | **10** | | – 0 – |
| 11  Long-term gain from installment sales from Form 6252, line 22 or 30  . . . . | **11** | | |
| 12  Net long-term gain or (loss) from partnerships, S corporations, and fiduciaries . . | **12** | | |
| 13  Capital gain distributions  . . . . . . . . . . . . . . . . . | **13** | | |
| 14  Enter gain from Form 4797, line 7 or 9  . . . . . . . . . . . . . | **14** | | |
| 15  Long-term capital loss carryover . . . . . . . . . . . . . . . | **15** | | |
| 16  Add all of the transactions on lines 9a, 9b, and 9d and lines 10 through 15 in columns (f) and (g) . | **16** ⎥( ⎥ ) | | – 0 – |
| 17  Net long-term gain or (loss), combine columns (f) and (g) of line 16 . . . . . . . . . . | **17** | | – 0 – |

For Paperwork Reduction Act Notice, see Form 1040 Instructions.                    Schedule D (Form 1040) 1989

**2045-6**

Case 2(a)

307  10-89

Schedule D (Form 1040) 1989                                          Attachment Sequence No. **12A**          Page **2**

Name(s) shown on Form 1040. (Do not enter name and social security number if shown on other side.) | Your social security number

### Part III  Summary of Parts I and II

| | | |
|---|---|---|
| 18 | Combine lines 8 and 17, and enter the net gain or (loss) here. If result is a gain, **stop here** and also enter the gain on Form 1040, line 13. If the result is a (loss), go on to line 19 . . . . . . . . . | 18 |
| 19 | If line 18 is a (loss), enter here and as a (loss) on Form 1040, line 13, the **smaller** of: | |
| a | The (loss) on line 18; **or** | |
| b | ( $3,000) or, if married filing a separate return, ($1,500) . . . . . . . . . . . . . | 19 ( ) |
| | **Note:** *When figuring whether 19a or 19b is **smaller**, treat both numbers as if they are positive.* | |
| | Go on to Part IV if the loss on line 18 is more than $3,000 ($1,500, if married filing a separate return), OR if taxable income on Form 1040, line 37, is zero. | |

### Part IV  Figure Your Capital Loss Carryovers From 1989 to 1990

**Section A.—Figure Your Carryover Limit**

| | | |
|---|---|---|
| 20 | Enter taxable income or loss from Form 1040, line 37. (**If Form 1040, line 37, is zero, see the instructions for the amount to enter.**) . . . . . . . . . . . . . . . . . | 20 |
| | **Note:** *For lines 21 through 36, treat all amounts as positive.* | |
| 21 | Enter the loss shown on line 19 . . . . . . . . . . . . . . . . . . . . | 21 |
| 22 | Enter the amount shown on Form 1040, line 36 . . . . . . . . . . . . . | 22 |
| 23 | Combine lines 20, 21, and 22. If zero or less, enter zero . . . . . . . . . . . . | 23 |
| 24 | Enter the **smaller** of line 21 or line 23 . . . . . . . . . . . . . . . . | 24 |

**Section B.—Figure Your Short-Term Capital Loss Carryover**
(Complete this section only if there is a loss shown on line 8 and line 19. Otherwise, go on to Section C.)

| | | |
|---|---|---|
| 25 | Enter the loss shown on line 8 . . . . . . . . . . . . . . . . . . . . | 25 |
| 26 | Enter the gain, if any, shown on line 17 . . . . . . . . . | 26 | |
| 27 | Enter the amount shown on line 24 . . . . . . . . . . | 27 | |
| 28 | Add lines 26 and 27 . . . . . . . . . . . . . . . . . . . . . . . | 28 |
| 29 | Subtract line 28 from line 25. If zero or less, enter zero. This is your **short-term capital loss carryover from 1989 to 1990** . . . . . . . . . . . . . . . . . . . . . . . . . | 29 |

**Section C.—Figure Your Long-Term Capital Loss Carryover**
(Complete this section only if there is a loss shown on line 17 and line 19.)

| | | |
|---|---|---|
| 30 | Enter the loss shown on line 17 . . . . . . . . . . . . . . . . . . . . | 30 |
| 31 | Enter the gain, if any, shown on line 8 . . . . . . . . . . . . . . . . . | 31 |
| 32 | Enter the amount shown on line 24 . . . . . . . . . . | 32 | |
| 33 | Enter the amount, if any, shown on line 25 . . . . . . . | 33 | |
| 34 | Subtract line 33 from line 32. If zero or less, enter zero . . . . . . . . . . . . | 34 |
| 35 | Add lines 31 and 34 . . . . . . . . . . . . . . . . . . . . . . . . . | 35 |
| 36 | Subtract line 35 from line 30. If zero or less, enter zero. This is your **long-term capital loss carryover from 1989 to 1990** . . . . . . . . . . . . . . . . . . . . . . . | 36 |

### Part V  Complete This Part Only If You Elect Out of the Installment Method and Report a Note or Other Obligation at Less Than Full Face Value

| | | |
|---|---|---|
| 37 | Check here if you elect out of the installment method . . . . . . . . . . . . . . . . . . ▶ ☐ |
| 38 | Enter the face amount of the note or other obligation . . . . . . . . . . . . ▶ . . . . . . . . . . . . |
| 39 | Enter the percentage of valuation of the note or other obligation . . . . . . . . . ▶ |

### Part VI  Reconcile Forms 1099-B for Bartering Transactions

(Complete this part if you received one or more Form(s) 1099-B or an equivalent substitute statement(s) reporting bartering income.)

Amount of bartering income from Form 1099-B or equivalent statement reported on form or schedule

| | | |
|---|---|---|
| 40 | Form 1040, line 22 . . . . . . . . . . . . . . . . . . . . . . . . | 40 |
| 41 | Schedule C (Form 1040) . . . . . . . . . . . . . . . . . . . . . . | 41 |
| 42 | Schedule D (Form 1040) . . . . . . . . . . . . . . . . . . . . . . | 42 |
| 43 | Schedule E (Form 1040) . . . . . . . . . . . . . . . . . . . . . . | 43 |
| 44 | Schedule F (Form 1040) . . . . . . . . . . . . . . . . . . . . . . | 44 |
| 45 | Other form (identify) (if not taxable, indicate reason—attach additional sheets if necessary) ▶ . . . . . . . . | |
| | . . . . . . . . . . . . . . . . . . . . . . . . . . . . . . . | |
| | . . . . . . . . . . . . . . . . . . . . . . . . . . . . . . . | 45 |
| 46 | Total (add lines 40 through 45) . . . . . . . . . . . . . . . . . . . . | 46 |
| | **Note:** *The amount on line 46 should be the same as the total bartering income on all Forms 1099-B and equivalent statements received.* | |

11-7-89

Case 2(a)

4562 1

| Form **4562** | **Depreciation and Amortization** | OMB No. 1545-0172 |
|---|---|---|
| Department of the Treasury Internal Revenue Service (4) | ▶ See separate instructions. ▶ Attach this form to your return. | 19**89** Attachment Sequence No. 67 |

Name(s) as shown on return
Roy & Ellen Jones

Identifying number
793-65-4321

Business or activity to which this form relates
Residential Rental Property

**Part I**   **Depreciation** *(Use Part III for automobiles, certain other vehicles, computers, and property used for entertainment, recreation, or amusement.)*

**Section A.—Election To Expense Depreciable Assets (Section 179)**

| | | |
|---|---|---|
| 1 Maximum dollar limitation | 1 | $10,000 |
| 2 Total cost of section 179 property placed in service during the tax year (see instructions) | 2 | |
| 3 Threshold cost of section 179 property before reduction in limitation | 3 | $200,000 |
| 4 Reduction in limitation (Subtract line 3 from line 2, but do not enter less than -0-.) | 4 | |
| 5 Dollar limitation for tax year (Subtract line 4 from line 1, but do not enter less than -0-.) | 5 | |

| (a) Description of property | (b) Date placed in service | (c) Cost | (d) Elected cost |
|---|---|---|---|
| 6 | | | |

| | | |
|---|---|---|
| 7 Listed property—Enter amount from line 28 | 7 | |
| 8 Tentative deduction (Enter the lesser of: (a) line 6 plus line 7; or (b) line 5.) | 8 | |
| 9 Taxable income limitation (Enter the lesser of :(a) Taxable income; or (b) line 5) (see instructions) | 9 | |
| 10 Carryover of disallowed deduction from 1988 (see instructions) | 10 | |
| 11 Section 179 expense deduction (Enter the lesser of: (a) line 8 plus line 10; or (b) line 9.) | 11 | |
| 12 Carryover of disallowed deduction to 1990 (Add lines 8 and 10, less line 11.) ▶ | 12 | |

**Section B.—MACRS Depreciation**

| (a) Classification of property | (b) Date placed in service | (c) Basis for depreciation (Business use only—see instructions) | (d) Recovery period | (e) Convention | (f) Method | (g) Depreciation deduction |
|---|---|---|---|---|---|---|
| **13 General Depreciation System (GDS) (see instructions):** *For assets placed in service ONLY during tax year beginning in 1989* | | | | | | |
| a   3-year property | | | | | | |
| b   5-year property | | | | | | |
| c   7-year property | | | | | | |
| d   10-year property | | | | | | |
| e   15-year property | | | | | | |
| f   20-year property | | | | | | |
| g   Residential rental property | 01-01-88 | 76,500 | 27.5 yrs. | MM | S/L | 2666 |
| | | | 27.5 yrs. | MM | S/L | |
| h   Nonresidential real property | | | 31.5 yrs. | MM | S/L | |
| | | | 31.5 yrs. | MM | S/L | |
| **14 Alternative Depreciation System (ADS) (see instructions):** *For assets placed in service ONLY during tax year beginning in 1989* | | | | | | |
| a   Class life | | | | | S/L | |
| b   12-year | | | 12 yrs. | | S/L | |
| c   40-year | | | 40 yrs. | MM | S/L | |

| | | |
|---|---|---|
| 15 Listed property—Enter amount from line 27 | 15 | |
| 16 GDS and ADS deductions for assets placed in service before 1989 (see instructions) | 16 | |

**Section C.—ACRS and/or Other Depreciation**

| | | |
|---|---|---|
| 17 Property subject to section 168(f)(1) election (see instructions) | 17 | |
| 18 ACRS and/or other depreciation (see instructions) | 18 | |

**Section D.—Summary**

| | | |
|---|---|---|
| 19 Total (Add deductions on line 11 and lines 13 through 18.) Enter here and on the appropriate line of your return (Partnerships and S corporations—see instructions.) | 19 | 2666 |
| 20 For assets shown above and placed in service during the current year, enter the portion of the basis attributable to section 263A costs (see instructions). | 20 | |

For Paperwork Reduction Act Notice, see page 1 of the separate instructions.

Form **4562** (1989)

**4562** <sup>2</sup>

Case 2(a)

11-7-89

Form 4562 (1989)

| **Part II** | **Amortization** | | | | | |
|---|---|---|---|---|---|---|
| (a) Description of property | (b) Date amortization begins | (c) Cost or other basis | (d) Code section | (e) Amortization period or percentage | (f) Amortization for this year | |
| 21 Amortization for property placed in service **only** during tax year beginning in 1989 | | | | | | |
| | | | | | | |
| | | | | | | |

22 Amortization for property placed in service before 1989 . . . . . . . . . . . **22**

23 Total. Enter here and on "Other Deductions" or "Other Expenses" line of your return . . . . . . **23**

**Part III** **Listed Property.—Automobiles, Certain Other Vehicles, Computers, and Property Used for Entertainment, Recreation, or Amusement**

If you are using the standard mileage rate or deducting vehicle lease expense, complete columns (a) through (d) of Section A, all of Section B, and Section C if applicable.

**Section A.—Depreciation** (Caution: See instructions for limitations for automobiles.)

24a Do you have evidence to support the business use claimed? ☐ Yes ☐ No  24b If "Yes," is the evidence written? ☐ Yes ☐ No

| (a) Type of property (list vehicles first) | (b) Date placed in service | (c) Business use percentage (%) | (d) Cost or other basis (see instructions for leased property) | (e) Basis for depreciation — business use only | (f) Recovery period | (g) Method | (h) Depreciation deduction | (i) Elected section 179 cost |
|---|---|---|---|---|---|---|---|---|
| 25 Property used more than 50% in a trade or business: | | | | | | | | |
| | | | | | | | | |
| | | | | | | | | |
| | | | | | | | | |
| 26 Property used 50% or less in a trade or business: | | | | | | | | |
| | | | | | | | S/L | |
| | | | | | | | S/L | |
| | | | | | | | S/L | |

27 Total (Enter here and on line 15, page 1.) . . . . . . . . . . . . . . . . **27**

28 Total (Enter here and on line 7, page 1.) . . . . . . . . . . . . . . . . . . **28**

**Section B.—Information Regarding Use of Vehicles—**If you deduct expenses for vehicles:

• Always complete this section for vehicles used by a sole proprietor, partner, or other "more than 5% owner," or related person.

• If you provided vehicles to your employees, first answer the questions in Section C to see if you meet an exception to completing this section for those vehicles.

| | (a) Vehicle 1 | | (b) Vehicle 2 | | (c) Vehicle 3 | | (d) Vehicle 4 | | (e) Vehicle 5 | | (f) Vehicle 6 | |
|---|---|---|---|---|---|---|---|---|---|---|---|---|
| 29 Total business miles driven during the year (DO NOT include commuting miles) . . | | | | | | | | | | | | |
| 30 Total commuting miles driven during the year | | | | | | | | | | | | |
| 31 Total other personal (noncommuting) miles driven . . . . . . . . . | | | | | | | | | | | | |
| 32 Total miles driven during the year (Add lines 29 through 31) . . . . . . | | | | | | | | | | | | |
| | Yes | No | Yes | No | Yes | No | Yes | No | Yes | No | Yes | No |
| 33 Was the vehicle available for personal use during off-duty hours? . . . . . . . | | | | | | | | | | | | |
| 34 Was the vehicle used primarily by a more than 5% owner or related person? . . . | | | | | | | | | | | | |
| 35 Is another vehicle available for personal use? . . . . . . . . . . . | | | | | | | | | | | | |

**Section C.—Questions for Employers Who Provide Vehicles for Use by Their Employees**

(Answer these questions to determine if you meet an exception to completing Section B. Note: Section B must always be completed for vehicles used by sole proprietors, partners, or other more than 5% owners or related persons.)

| | Yes | No |
|---|---|---|
| 36 Do you maintain a written policy statement that prohibits all personal use of vehicles, including commuting, by your employees? . . . . . . . . . . . . . . . . . . . . . . . . . . . . . . . . . . . . | | |
| 37 Do you maintain a written policy statement that prohibits personal use of vehicles, except commuting, by your employees? (See instructions for vehicles used by corporate officers, directors, or 1% or more owners.) . . . . . | | |
| 38 Do you treat all use of vehicles by employees as personal use? . . . . . . . . . . . . . . . . | | |
| 39 Do you provide more than five vehicles to your employees and retain the information received from your employees concerning the use of the vehicles? . . . . . . . . . . . . . . . . . . . . . . . . . . | | |
| 40 Do you meet the requirements concerning qualified automobile demonstration use (see instructions)? . . . . | | |

Note: If your answer to 36, 37, 38, 39, or 40 is "Yes," you need not complete Section B for the covered vehicles.

Case 2(a)

| SCHEDULE E (Form 1040) | **Supplemental Income and Loss** | OMB No. 1545-0074 |
|---|---|---|

Department of the Treasury
Internal Revenue Service    (X)

**Supplemental Income and Loss**
(From rents, royalties, partnerships, estates, trusts, REMICs, etc.)
▶ Attach to Form 1040 or Form 1041.
▶ See Instructions for Schedule E (Form 1040).

**1989**
Attachment
Sequence No. **13**

Name(s) shown on return: Roy & Ellen    Jones

Your social security number: 793 : 65 : 4321

**Part I    Income or Loss From Rentals and Royalties**    Caution: *Your rental loss may be limited. See Instructions.*

1 Show the kind and location of rental property:
A  Residential property
B  ............................................
C  ............................................

2 For each rental property listed on line 1, did you or your family use it for personal purposes for more than the greater of 14 days or 10% of the total days rented at fair rental value during the tax year?

| | Yes | No |
|---|---|---|
| A | | X |
| B | | |
| C | | |

3 For each **rental real estate property** listed on line 1, did you **actively participate** in its operation during the tax year? (See Instructions.)

| | Yes | No |
|---|---|---|
| A | X | |
| B | | |
| C | | |

| Rental and Royalty Income: | | Properties | | | D Totals |
|---|---|---|---|---|---|
| | | A | B | C | (Add columns A, B, and C) |
| 4 Rents received | 4 | 14,400 | | | 4 |
| 5 Royalties received | 5 | | | | 5 |
| **Rental and Royalty Expenses:** | | | | | |
| 6 Advertising | 6 | 150 | | | |
| 7 Auto and travel | 7 | 100 | | | |
| 8 Cleaning and maintenance | 8 | 450 | | | |
| 9 Commissions | 9 | 1200 | | | |
| 10 Insurance | 10 | 1500 | | | |
| 11 Legal and other professional fees | 11 | | | | |
| 12 Mortgage interest paid to banks, etc. (see Instructions) | 12 | | | | 12 |
| 13 Other interest | 13 | | | | |
| 14 Repairs | 14 | | | | |
| 15 Supplies | 15 | | | | |
| 16 Taxes | 16 | 1950 | | | |
| 17 Utilities (see Instructions) | 17 | | | | |
| 18 Wages and salaries | 18 | | | | |
| 19 Other (list) ▶ ............ | 19 | | | | |
| 20 Add lines 6 through 19 | 20 | 5350 | | | 20 |
| 21 Depreciation expense or depletion (see Instructions) | 21 | 2666 | | | 21 |
| 22 Total expenses. Add lines 20 and 21 | 22 | 8016 | | | |
| 23 Income or (loss) from rental or royalty properties. Subtract line 22 from line 4 (rents) or line 5 (royalties). If the result is a (loss), see Instructions to find out if you must file **Form 6198** | 23 | 6384 | | | |
| 24 Deductible rental loss. **Caution:** *Your rental loss on line 23 may be limited. See Instructions to find out if you must file Form 8582* | 24 | ( | )( | )( | ) |

25 **Income.** Add rental and royalty income from line 23. Enter the total income here . . . . . . . . | 25 | 6384

26 **Losses.** Add royalty losses from line 23 and rental losses from line 24. Enter the total losses here . . . | 26 | ( | )

27 Combine amounts on lines 25 and 26. Enter the net income or (loss) here . . . . . . . . . . | 27 | 6384

28 Net farm rental income or (loss) from Form 4835. (Also complete line 43 on page 2.) . . . . . . | 28 |

29 Total rental and royalty income or (loss). Combine amounts on lines 27 and 28. Enter the result here. If Parts II, III, and IV on page 2 do not apply to you, enter the amount from line 29 on Form 1040, line 18. Otherwise, include the amount from line 29 in the total on line 42 on page 2 . . . . . . . . | 29 | 6384

For Paperwork Reduction Act Notice, see Form 1040 Instructions.                                Schedule E (Form 1040) 1989

11-7-89

Case 2(b)

4797 ¹

| Form **4797** | **Sales of Business Property** | OMB No. 1545-0184 |
|---|---|---|

(Also, Involuntary Conversions and Recapture Amounts Under
Sections 179 and 280F)

**1989**

Department of the Treasury
Internal Revenue Service   (4)

▶ Attach to your tax return. See separate Instructions.

Attachment
Sequence No. 27

| Name(s) shown on return | Identifying number |
|---|---|
| Roy & Ellen Jones | 793-65-4321 |

**Part I   Sales or Exchanges of Property Used in a Trade or Business and Involuntary Conversions From Other Than Casualty and Theft—Property Held More Than 1 Year**

1 Enter here the gross proceeds from the sale or exchange of real estate reported to you for 1989 on Form(s) 1099-S (or an equivalent statement) that you will be including on lines 2 or 10 (column d), or on line 20. (Form 1099-S is a Statement for Recipients of Proceeds From Real Estate Transactions.) . . . . . . . . . . . . . . . . . **1**   169,500

| (a) Description of property | (b) Date acquired (mo., day, yr.) | (c) Date sold (mo., day, yr.) | (d) Gross sales price | (e) Depreciation allowed (or allowable) since acquisition | (f) Cost or other basis, plus improvements and expense of sale | (g) LOSS ((f) minus the sum of (d) and (e)) | (h) GAIN ((d) plus (e) minus (f)) |
|---|---|---|---|---|---|---|---|
| **2** | | | | | | | |
| | | | | | | | |
| | | | | | | | |
| | | | | | | | |
| | | | | | | | |
| | | | | | | | |

3 Gain, if any, from Form 4684, Section B, line 21 . . . . . . . . .

4 Section 1231 gain from installment sales from Form 6252, line _ or 30 . . . . . . . .   95,666

5 Gain, if any, from line 32, from other than casualty and theft . . . . . . . . . . . (          )   95,666

6 Add lines 2 through 5 in columns (g) and (h). . . . . . . . . . . . . . . . . . .

7 Combine columns (g) and (h) of line 6. Enter gain or (loss) here, and on the appropriate line as follows (partnerships see the Instructions for line references): . . . . . . . . . . . . . . . . . . . . . .   95,666

If line 7 is zero or a loss, enter the amount on line 11 below and skip lines 8 and 9. (S corporations enter the loss on Schedule K (Form 1120S), line 5.) If line 7 is a gain and you did not have any prior year section 1231 losses, or they were recaptured in an earlier year, enter the gain as a long-term capital gain on Schedule D and skip lines 8, 9, and 12 below.

8 Nonrecaptured net section 1231 losses from prior years (see Instructions) . . . . . . . . . .

9 Subtract line 8 from line 7. If zero or less, enter zero . . . . . . . . . . . . . . .

If line 9 is zero, enter the amount from line 7 on line 12 below. If line 9 is more than zero, enter the amount from line 8 on line 12 below, and enter the amount from line 9 as a long-term capital gain on Schedule D. See Line-by-Line Instructions for line 9.

**Part II   Ordinary Gains and Losses**

| (a) Description of property | (b) Date acquired (mo., day, yr.) | (c) Date sold (mo., day, yr.) | (d) Gross sales price | (e) Depreciation allowed (or allowable) since acquisition | (f) Cost or other basis, plus improvements and expense of sale | (g) LOSS ((f) minus the sum of (d) and (e)) | (h) GAIN ((d) plus (e) minus (f)) |
|---|---|---|---|---|---|---|---|
| 10 Ordinary gains and losses not included on lines 11 through 16 (include property held 1 year or less): | | | | | | | |
| | | | | | | | |
| | | | | | | | |
| | | | | | | | |
| | | | | | | | |
| | | | | | | | |

11 Loss, if any, from line 7 . . . . . . . . . . . . . . . . . . . . . .

12 Gain, if any, from line 7, or amount from line 8 if applicable . . . . . . . . . . .

13 Gain, if any, from line 31 . . . . . . . . . . . . . . . . . . . . .

14 Net gain or (loss) from Form 4684, Section B, lines 13 and 20a . . . . . . . . .

15 Ordinary gain from installment sales from Form 6252, line(s) 21 and/or 29 . . . . . .

16 Recapture of section 179 deduction for partners and S corporation shareholders from property dispositions by partnerships and S corporations (see Instructions) . . . . . . . . . . . . . . . . (          )

17 Add lines 10 through 16 in columns (g) and (h) . . . . . . . . . . . . . .

18 Combine columns (g) and (h) of line 17. Enter gain or (loss) here, and on the appropriate line as follows: . . . . . .
  a   For all except individual returns: Enter the gain or (loss) from line 18 on the return being filed.
  b   For individual returns:
    (1) If the loss on line 11 includes a loss from Form 4684, Section B, Part II, column (b)(ii), enter that part of the loss here and on line 21 of Schedule A (Form 1040). Identify as from "Form 4797, line 18b(1)" . . . . . . . .
    (2) Redetermine the gain or (loss) on line 18, excluding the loss (if any) on line 18b(1). Enter here and on Form 1040, line 15 . . . . .

For Paperwork Reduction Act Notice, see page 1 of separate Instructions.                    Form **4797** (1989)

**4797** 2                                    Case 2(b)                                    11-7-89

Form 4797 (1989)                                                                          Page 2

| Part III | Gain From Disposition of Property Under Sections 1245, 1250, 1252, 1254, and 1255 |

| 19 | Description of sections 1245, 1250, 1252, 1254, and 1255 property: | | Date acquired (mo., day, yr.) | Date sold (mo., day, yr.) |
|---|---|---|---|---|
| | **A** Residential real estate | | 8/01/81 | 1/1/89 |
| | **B** | | | |
| | **C** | | | |
| | **D** | | | |

| Relate lines 19A through 19D to these columns ▶ | Property A | Property B | Property C | Property D |
|---|---|---|---|---|
| 20 Gross sales price | 169,500 | | | |
| 21 Cost or other basis plus expense of sale | 76,500 | | | |
| 22 Depreciation (or depletion) allowed (or allowable) | 2,666 | | | |
| 23 Adjusted basis, subtract line 22 from line 21 | 73,834 | | | |
| 24 Total gain, subtract line 23 from line 20 | 95,666 | | | |

**25 If section 1245 property:**

a Depreciation allowed (or allowable) (see Instructions)

b Enter the **smaller** of line 24 or 25a

**26 If section 1250 property:** If straight line depreciation was used, enter zero on line 26g unless you are a corporation subject to section 291.

a Additional depreciation after 12/31/75

b Applicable percentage multiplied by the **smaller** of line 24 or line 26a (see Instructions)

c Subtract line 26a from line 24. If line 24 is not more than line 26a, skip lines 26d and 26e

d Additional depreciation after 12/31/69 and before 1/1/76

e Applicable percentage multiplied by the **smaller** of line 26c or 26d (see Instructions)

f Section 291 amount (for corporations only)

g Add lines 26b, 26e, and 26f        — 0 —

**27 If section 1252 property:** Skip this section if you did not dispose of farmland or if you are a partnership.

a Soil, water, and land clearing expenses

b Line 27a multiplied by applicable percentage (see Instructions)

c Enter the **smaller** of line 24 or 27b

**28 If section 1254 property:**

a Intangible drilling and development costs, expenditures for development of mines and other natural deposits, and mining exploration costs (see Instructions)

b Enter the **smaller** of line 24 or 28a

**29 If section 1255 property:**

a Applicable percentage of payments excluded from income under section 126 (see Instructions)

b Enter the **smaller** of line 24 or 29a

**Summary of Part III Gains** (Complete property columns A through D, through line 29b before going to line 30.)

| 30 Total gains for all properties (add columns A through D, line 24) | 95,666 |
|---|---|
| 31 Add columns A through D, lines 25b, 26g, 27c, 28b, and 29b. Enter here and on line 13. (see the Instructions for Part IV if this is an installment sale) | — 0 — |
| 32 Subtract line 31 from line 30. Enter the portion from casualty and theft on Form 4684, Section B, line 15. Enter the portion from other than casualty and theft on Form 4797, line 5 | 95,666 |

| Part IV | Complete This Part Only if You Elect Out of the Installment Method and Report a Note or Other Obligation at Less Than Full Face Value |

33 Check here if you elect out of the installment method ▶ ☐

34 Enter the face amount of the note or other obligation ▶............

35 Enter the percentage of valuation of the note or other obligation ▶

| Part V | Computation of Recapture Amounts Under Sections 179 and 280F When Business Use Drops to 50% or Less (See Instructions for Part V.) |

| | (a) Section 179 | (b) Section 280F |
|---|---|---|
| 36 Section 179 expense deduction or section 280F recovery deductions | | |
| 37 Depreciation or recovery deductions (see Instructions) | | |
| 38 Recapture amount (subtract line 37 from line 36) (see Instructions for where to report) | | |

307  10-89                              Case 2(b)                              **2045-5**

| SCHEDULE D | **Capital Gains and Losses** | OMB No 1545-0074 |
|---|---|---|
| **(Form 1040)** | (And Reconciliation of Forms 1099-B) | **1989** |
| Department of the Treasury<br>Internal Revenue Service  (4) | ▶ Attach to Form 1040.   ▶ See Instructions for Schedule D (Form 1040).<br>▶ For more space to list transactions for lines 2a and 9a, get Schedule D-1 (Form 1040). | Attachment<br>Sequence No. 12A |

| Name(s) shown on Form 1040 | Your social security number |
|---|---|
| Roy & Ellen   Jones | 793 : 65 : 4321 |

1  Report here the total sales of stocks, bonds, etc., reported for 1989 to you on Form(s) 1099-B or on an equivalent substitute statement(s). If this amount differs from the total of lines 2c and 9c, column (d), attach a statement explaining the difference. See the Instructions for line 1 for examples . . . . .  **1**

**Part I   Short-Term Capital Gains and Losses—Assets Held One Year or Less**

| (a) Description of property<br>(Example. 100 shares 7%<br>preferred of "Z" Co.) | (b) Date acquired<br>(Mo . day. yr ) | (c) Date sold<br>(Mo . day. yr ) | (d) Sales price (see<br>Instructions) | (e) Cost or other<br>basis (see<br>Instructions) | (f) LOSS<br>If (e) is more than (d),<br>subtract (d) from (e) | (g) GAIN<br>If (d) is more than (e),<br>subtract (e) from (d) |
|---|---|---|---|---|---|---|
| **2a Stocks, Bonds, and Other Securities (Include all Form 1099-B transactions. See Instructions.)** | | | | | | |
| | | | | | | |
| | | | | | | |
| | — | | | | | |
| | | | | | | |
| | | | | | | |
| | | | | | | |
| **2b** Amounts from Schedule D-1, line 2b (attach Schedule D-1) . | | | | | | |
| **2c Total** (add column (d) of lines 2a and 2b). ▶ **2c** | | | | | | |
| **2d Other Transactions (Include Real Estate**<br>**Transactions From Forms 1099-S.)** | | | | | | |
| | | | | | | |
| | | | | | | |

3  Short-term gain from sale or exchange of your home from Form 2119, line 8a or 14 .  **3**
4  Short-term gain from installment sales from Form 6252, line 22 or 30  . . . .  **4**
5  Net short-term gain or (loss) from partnerships, S corporations, and fiduciarie_.  **5**
6  Short-term capital loss carryover  . . . . . . . . . . . . .  **6**
7  Add all of the transactions on lines 2a, 2b, and 2d and lines 3 through 6 in columns (f) and (g)  **7** ( )
8  Net short-term gain or (loss), combine columns (f) and (g) of line 7  . . . . . . . .  **8**

**Part II   Long-Term Capital Gains and Losses—Assets Held More Than One Year**

**9a Stocks, Bonds, and Other Securities (Include all Form 1099-B transactions. See Instructions.)**

| | | | | | | |
|---|---|---|---|---|---|---|
| | | | | | | |
| | | | | | | |
| | | | | | | |
| | | | | | | |
| | | | | | | |
| **9b** Amounts from Schedule D-1, line 9b (attach Schedule D-1) . | | | | | | |
| **9c Total** (add column (d) of lines 9a and 9b). ▶ **9c** | | | | | | |
| **9d Other Transactions (Include Real Estate**<br>**Transactions From Forms 1099-S.)** | | | | | | |
| | | | | | | |
| | | | | | | |

| | | |
|---|---|---|
| 10  Long-term gain from sale or exchange of your home from Form 2119, line 8a, 10, or 14 .  **10** | | |
| 11  Long-term gain from installment sales from Form 6252, line 22 or 30  . . . .  **11** | | |
| 12  Net long-term gain or (loss) from partnerships, S corporations, and fiduciaries . .  **12** | | |
| 13  Capital gain distributions . . . . . . . . . . . . . . . .  **13** | | |
| 14  Enter gain from Form 4797, line 7 or 9 . . . . . . . . . . . .  **14** | | 95,666 |
| 15  Long-term capital loss carryover . . . . . . . . . . . . . .  **15** | | |
| 16  Add all of the transactions on lines 9a, 9b, and 9d and lines 10 through 15 in columns (f) and (g)  **16** ( ) | | 95,666 |
| 17  Net long-term gain or (loss), combine columns (f) and (g) of line 16  . . . . . . . . . .  **17** | | 95,666 |

For Paperwork Reduction Act Notice, see Form 1040 Instructions.                    Schedule D (Form 1040) 1989

**2045-6**                             Case 2(b)                                    307  10-89

Schedule D (Form 1040) 1989                            Attachment Sequence No  **12A**              Page **2**

Name(s) shown on Form 1040. (Do not enter name and social security number if shown on other side.) | Your social security number

| **Part III** | **Summary of Parts I and II** |

**18**  Combine lines 8 and 17, and enter the net gain or (loss) here. If result is a gain, **stop here** and also
enter the gain on Form 1040, line 13. If the result is a (loss), go on to line 19 . . . . . . . .  **18**

**19**  If line 18 is a (loss), enter here and as a (loss) on Form 1040, line 13, the **smaller** of:
**a**  The (loss) on line 18; **or**
**b**  ( $3,000) or, if married filing a separate return, ($1,500) . . . . . . . . . .  **19** |(                        )
  Note: *When figuring whether 19a or 19b is* **smaller**, *treat both numbers as if they are positive.*
**.**  Go on to Part IV if the loss on line 18 is more than $3,000 ($1,500, if married filing a separate return),
  OR if taxable income on Form 1040, line 37, is zero.

| **Part IV** | **Figure Your Capital Loss Carryovers From 1989 to 1990** |

**Section A.—Figure Your Carryover Limit**

**20**  Enter taxable income or loss from Form 1040, line 37. **(If Form 1040, line 37, is zero, see the
Instructions for the amount to enter.)** . . . . . . . . . . . . . . . . . . . . .  **20**
  Note: *For lines 21 through 36, treat all amounts as positive.*
**21**  Enter the loss shown on line 19 . . . . . . . . . . . . . . . . . . . . . . . . .  **21**
**22**  Enter the amount shown on Form 1040, line 36 . . . . . . . . . . . . . . . . . .  **22**
**23**  Combine lines 20, 21, and 22. If zero or less, enter zero . . . . . . . . . . . . . .  **23**
**24**  Enter the **smaller** of line 21 or line 23 . . . . . . . . . . . . . . . . . . . . .  **24**

**Section B.—Figure Your Short-Term Capital Loss Carryover**
(Complete this section only if there is a loss shown on line 8 and line 19. Otherwise, go on to Section C.)

**25**  Enter the loss shown on line 8 . . . . . . . . . . . . . . . . . . . . . . . . . .  **25**
**26**  Enter the gain, if any, shown on line 17 . . . . . . . . . . .  **26**
**27**  Enter the amount shown on line 24 . . . . . . . . . . . . . .  **27**
**28**  Add lines 26 and 27. . . . . . . . . . . . . . . . . . . . . . . . . . . . . . .  **28**
**29**  Subtract line 28 from line 25. If zero or less, enter zero. This is your **short-term capital loss carryover
from 1989 to 1990**. . . . . . . . . . . . . . . . . . . . . . . . . . . . . . . .  **29**

**Section C.—Figure Your Long-Term Capital Loss Carryover**
(Complete this section only if there is a loss shown on line 17 and line 19.)

**30**  Enter the loss shown on line 17 . . . . . . . . . . . . . . . . . . . . . . . . .  **30**
**31**  Enter the gain, if any, shown on line 8 . . . . . . . . . . . . . . . . . . . . . .  **31**
**32**  Enter the amount shown on line 24 . . . . . . . . . . . . . .  **32**
**33**  Enter the amount, if any, shown on line 25 . . . . . . . . . . .  **33**
**34**  Subtract line 33 from line 32. If zero or less, enter zero . . . . . . . . . . . . . .  **34**
**35**  Add lines 31 and 34. . . . . . . . . . . . . . . . . . . . . . . . . . . . . . .  **35**
**36**  Subtract line 35 from line 30. If zero or less, enter zero. This is your **long-term capital loss carryover
from 1989 to 1990** . . . . . . . . . . . . . . . . . . . . . . . . . . . . . . .  **36**

| **Part V** | **Complete This Part Only If You Elect Out of the Installment Method and
Report a Note or Other Obligation at Less Than Full Face Value** |

**37**  Check here if you elect out of the installment method . . . . . . . . . . . . . . . . . ▶ ☐
**38**  Enter the face amount of the note or other obligation . . . . . . . . . . . . . ▶ . . . . . . . . . . . . .
**39**  Enter the percentage of valuation of the note or other obligation . . . . . . . . . . ▶

| **Part VI** | **Reconcile Forms 1099-B for Bartering Transactions** | Amount of bartering income
from Form 1099-B or
equivalent statement
reported on form or schedule |
|  | (Complete this part if you received one or more Form(s) 1099-B or an equivalent
substitute statement(s) reporting bartering income.) |  |

**40**  Form 1040, line 22 . . . . . . . . . . . . . . . . . . . . . . . . . . . . . . .  **40**
**41**  Schedule C (Form 1040) . . . . . . . . . . . . . . . . . . . . . . . . . . . .  **41**
**42**  Schedule D (Form 1040) . . . . . . . . . . . . . . . . . . . . . . . . . . . .  **42**
**43**  Schedule E (Form 1040) . . . . . . . . . . . . . . . . . . . . . . . . . . . .  **43**
**44**  Schedule F (Form 1040) . . . . . . . . . . . . . . . . . . . . . . . . . . . .  **44**
**45**  Other form (identify) (if not taxable, indicate reason—attach additional sheets if necessary) ▶ . . . . . . . . .
. . . . . . . . . . . . . . . . . . . . . . . . . . . . . . . . . . . . . . . . . . . . . . . . . .
. . . . . . . . . . . . . . . . . . . . . . . . . . . . . . . . . . . . . . . . . . . . . . . .
. . . . . . . . . . . . . . . . . . . . . . . . . . . . . . . . . . . . . . . . . . . .  **45**
**46**  Total (add lines 40 through 45) . . . . . . . . . . . . . . . . . . . . . . . . .  **46**
  Note: *The amount on line 46 should be the same as the total bartering income on all Forms 1099-B and equivalent statements received.*

## CASE 3

**The Facts:** A homeowner purchased a home for $84,000. The home-owner runs a business out of one room, or 10% of the house, and claims depreciation. The house is sold one year later for $124,600, and a house costing $135,000 is purchased. How is the gain reported? How is the portion of the gain rolled over reported? How is the gain attributable to the home office that can't be rolled over reported?

**Comments:** Where a portion of a home is used for business or rental purposes, that portion of the gain on the sale cannot qualify for the favorable tax treatment afforded to the gain on the sale of a personal residence, which is rolled over. It's as if the seller sold two separate properties: a home and a business property. The home is 90% of the property. Thus the sales price of the personal portion of the home is 90% of the $124,600 sales price, or $112,140. This is reported on Line 4 of Form 2119. The 10% of the sales price that is applicable to the business use of the home, $12,460 (10% × $124,600), is reported on Form 4797, Part III, Line 20.

Case 3

| Form **2119** | **Sale of Your Home** | OMB No. 1545–0072 |
|---|---|---|

▶ See Separate Instructions.

Department of the Treasury
Internal Revenue Service (x)

▶ Attach to Form 1040 for year of sale.

**1989**

Attachment
Sequence No. **22**

| Please | Your first name and initial (If joint, also give spouse's name and initial.)                Last name | Your social security number |
|---|---|---|
| Type | Dr. Dee Goodon | 123 : 65 : 9876 |
| or | Present home address (no., street, and apt. no., or rural route) (or P.O. box no. if mail is not delivered to street address) | Spouse's social security number |
| Print | 1986 World Champion Way | : : |
| | City, town or post office, state, and ZIP code | |
| | Flushing, New York   11107 | |

### Part I    Facts About You and Your Home

**1a** Date former main home was sold ▶                    December 29, 1989

| | | | Yes | No |
|---|---|---|---|---|
| **b** | Enter the face amount of any mortgage, note (for example, second trust), or other financial instrument on which you will receive periodic payments of principal or interest from this sale. (See Instructions for line 1b.) ▶  $    – 0 – | | | |
| | Have you bought or built a new main home? . . . . . . . . . . . . . . . . . . . . . . | | X | |
| c | Are any rooms in either main home rented out or used for business for which a deduction is allowed? . . . . . .    (If "Yes," see Instructions.) | | X | |
| **3a** | Were you 55 or older on date of sale? | | | X |
| **b** | Was your spouse 55 or older on date of sale? . . . . . . . . . . . . . . . . . . . . . .    If you answered "No" to 3a and 3b, do not complete 3c through 3f or Part III. | | | |
| **c** | Did the person who answered "Yes" to 3a or 3b own and use the property sold as a main home for a total of at least 3    years (except for short absences) of the 5-year period before the sale? . . . . . . . . . . . . . . . | | | |
| **d** | If you answered "Yes" to 3c, do you choose to take the one-time exclusion of the gain on the sale? . . . . . | | | |
| **e** | At time of sale, who owned the home ?   ☐ you   ☐ your spouse   ☐ both of you | | | |
| **f** | Social security number of spouse, at time of sale, if different from above ▶    (Enter "None" if you were not married at time of sale.) | : : | | |

### Part II    Figure Your Gain (Do not include amounts that you deduct as moving expenses.)

| 4 | Selling price of home. (Do not include personal property items.) . . . . . . . . . . . . . . | 4 | 112,140 |
|---|---|---|---|
| 5 | Expense of sale. (Include sales commissions, advertising, legal, etc.) . . . . . . . . . . . | 5 | |
| 6 | Subtract line 5 from line 4. This is the amount realized . . . . . . . . . . . . . . . | 6 | 112,140 |
| 7 | Basis of home sold. (See Instructions.) . . . . . . . . . . . . . . . . . . . . . | 7 | 75,600 |
| **8a** | Subtract line 7 from line 6 (gain on sale). If zero or less, enter zero and do not complete the rest of    the form. Enter the gain from this line on Schedule D, line 3 or 10,* unless you bought another main    home or checked "Yes" to 3d. Then continue with this form . . . . . . . . . . . . . . | 8a | 36,540 |
| **b** | If you haven't replaced your home, do you plan to do so within the replacement period? . . . . . . . . .   ☐ Yes  ☐ No    (If "Yes," see Instructions under When and Where To File.) | | |

### Part III    If Age 55 or Older, Figure Your One-Time Exclusion   (Complete this part only if you checked "Yes" to 3d.)

| 9 | Enter the **smaller** of line 8a or $125,000 ($62,500, if married filing separate return) (See Instructions.) | 9 | |
|---|---|---|---|
| 10 | Subtract line 9 from line 8a (gain). If zero, do not complete rest of form. Enter the gain from this line    on Schedule D, line 10,* unless you bought another main home. Then continue with this form . . . | 10 | |

### Part IV    Figure Gain To Be Postponed and Adjusted Basis of New Home   (Complete this part if you bought another main home.)

| 11 | Fixing-up expenses. (See Instructions for time limits.) . . . . . . . . . . . . . . . | 11 | – 0 – |
|---|---|---|---|
| 12 | Subtract line 11 from line 6 (adjusted sales price) . . . . . . . . . . . . . . . . | 12 | 112,140 |
| **13a** | Cost of new home . . . . . . . . . . . . . . . . . . . . . . . . . . . | 13a | 135,000 |
| **b** | Enter the date you moved into your new main home ▶ ......January 5, 1990 | | |
| 14 | Subtract line 13a plus line 9 (if applicable) from line 12. If result is zero or less, enter zero. Do not    enter more than line 8a or line 10 (if applicable). This is the gain taxable this year. Enter the gain    from this line on Schedule D, line 3 or 10*. . . . . . . . . . . . . . . . . . . . | 14 | – 0 – |
| 15 | Subtract line 14 from line 8a. **However,** if you completed Part III, subtract line 14 from line 10. (This    is the gain to be postponed.) . . . . . . . . . . . . . . . . . . . . . . . | 15 | 36,540 |
| 16 | Subtract line 15 from line 13a (adjusted basis of new main home) . . . . . . . . . . . . | 16 | 98,460 |

*****Caution:** If you completed Form 6252 for the home in 1a, do not enter your taxable gain from Form 2119 on Schedule D.

| Please | Under penalties of perjury, I declare that I have examined this form, including attachments, and to the best of my knowledge and belief, it is true, correct, and complete. | | | |
|---|---|---|---|---|
| **Sign** | Your signature | Date | Spouse's Signature | Date |
| **Here** | | | | |
| ▶ | (If joint return, both must sign.) (Sign and date only if not attached to your tax return.) | ▶ | | |

**For Paperwork Reduction Act Notice, see separate Instructions.**                                        Form **2119** (1989)

307   10-89                                       Case 3                                            **2045-5**

| SCHEDULE D | **Capital Gains and Losses** | OMB No. 1545-0074 |
|---|---|---|
| (Form 1040) | **(And Reconciliation of Forms 1099-B)** | **1989** |

Department of the Treasury
Internal Revenue Service   (4)

▶ Attach to Form 1040.   ▶ See Instructions for Schedule D (Form 1040).
▶ For more space to list transactions for lines 2a and 9a, get Schedule D-1 (Form 1040).

Attachment Sequence No **12A**

| Name(s) shown on Form 1040 | Your social security number |
|---|---|
| Dr. Dee Goodon | 123 : 65 9876 |

1   Report here the total sales of stocks, bonds, etc., reported for 1989 to you on Form(s) 1099-B or on an equivalent substitute statement(s). If this amount differs from the total of lines 2c and 9c, column (d), attach a statement explaining the difference. See the Instructions for line 1 for examples . . . . . **1**

**Part I**   **Short-Term Capital Gains and Losses—Assets Held One Year or Less**

| (a) Description of property (Example. 100 shares 7% preferred of "Z" Co.) | (b) Date acquired (Mo., day, yr.) | (c) Date sold (Mo., day, yr.) | (d) Sales price (see Instructions) | (e) Cost or other basis (see Instructions) | (f) LOSS If (e) is more than (d), subtract (d) from (e) | (g) GAIN If (d) is more than (e), subtract (e) from (d) |
|---|---|---|---|---|---|---|
| **2a  Stocks, Bonds, and Other Securities (Include all Form 1099-B transactions. See Instructions.)** | | | | | | |
| | | | | | | |
| | | | | | | |
| | | | | | | |
| | | | | | | |
| | | | | | | |
| | | | | | | |
| | | | | | | |

| | |
|---|---|
| **2b** Amounts from Schedule D-1, line 2b (attach Schedule D-1) . | |
| **2c Total** (add column (d) of lines 2a and 2b). . ▶ **2c** | |

**2d  Other Transactions (Include Real Estate Transactions From Forms 1099-S.)**

| | | | | | | |
|---|---|---|---|---|---|---|
| | | | | | | |
| | | | | | | |
| | | | | | | |

3   Short-term gain from sale or exchange of your home from Form 2119, line 8a or 14 . **3**
4   Short-term gain from installment sales from Form 6252, line 22 or 30 . . . . **4**
5   Net short-term gain or (loss) from partnerships, S corporations, and fiduciaries. . **5**
6   Short-term capital loss carryover . . . . . . . . . . . . . . **6**
7   Add all of the transactions on lines 2a, 2b, and 2d and lines 3 through 6 in columns (f) and (g) . **7** ( )
8   Net short-term gain or (loss), combine columns (f) and (g) of line 7 . . . . . . . . . . . **8**

**Part II**   **Long-Term Capital Gains and Losses—Assets Held More Than One Year**

**9a  Stocks, Bonds, and Other Securities (Include all Form 1099-B transactions. See Instructions.)**

| | | | | | | |
|---|---|---|---|---|---|---|
| | | | | | | |
| | | | | | | |
| | | | | | | |
| | | | | | | |
| | | | | | | |
| | | | | | | |
| | | | | | | |

| | |
|---|---|
| **9b** Amounts from Schedule D-1, line 9b (attach Schedule D-1) . | |
| **9c Total** (add column (d) of lines 9a and 9b). . ▶ **9c** | |

**9d  Other Transactions (Include Real Estate Transactions From Forms 1099-S.)**

| | | | | | | |
|---|---|---|---|---|---|---|
| | | | | | | |
| | | | | | | |
| | | | | | | |

10   Long-term gain from sale or exchange of your home from Form 2119, line 8a, 10, or 14 . **10**
11   Long-term gain from installment sales from Form 6252, line 22 or 30 . . . . **11**
12   Net long-term gain or (loss) from partnerships, S corporations, and fiduciaries . . **12**
13   Capital gain distributions . . . . . . . . . . . . . . . . **13**
14   Enter gain from Form 4797, line 7 or 9 . . . . . . . . . . . . **14**    4353
15   Long-term capital loss carryover . . . . . . . . . . . . . . **15**
16   Add all of the transactions on lines 9a, 9b, and 9d and lines 10 through 15 in columns (f) and (g) **16** ( )    4353
17   Net long-term gain or (loss), combine columns (f) and (g) of line 16 . . . . . . . . . **17**    4353

For Paperwork Reduction Act Notice, see Form 1040 Instructions.                    Schedule D (Form 1040) 1989

**2045-6**                              Case 3                                307  10-89

| Schedule D (Form 1040) 1989 | Attachment Sequence No **12A** | Page **2** |
|---|---|---|
| Name(s) shown on Form 1040. (Do not enter name and social security number if shown on other side.) | | Your social security number |

### Part III    Summary of Parts I and II

18  Combine lines 8 and 17, and enter the net gain or (loss) here. If result is a gain, **stop here** and also
    enter the gain on Form 1040, line 13. If the result is a (loss), go on to line 19 . . . . . . . | **18** |

19  If line 18 is a (loss), enter here and as a (loss) on Form 1040, line 13, the **smaller** of:
  a  The (loss) on line 18; or
  b  ( $3,000) or, if married filing a separate return, ($1,500) . . . . . . . . . . | **19** |( | )

    **Note:** When figuring whether l9a or 19b is **smaller**, treat both numbers as if they are positive.
.   Go on to Part IV if the loss on line 18 is more than $3,000 ($1,500, if married filing a separate return),
    OR if taxable income on Form 1040, line 37, is zero.

### Part IV    Figure Your Capital Loss Carryovers From 1989 to 1990

#### Section A.—Figure Your Carryover Limit

20  Enter taxable income or loss from Form 1040, line 37. **(If Form 1040, line 37, is zero, see the
    Instructions for the amount to enter.)** . . . . . . . . . . . . . . . . | **20** |
    **Note:** For lines 21 through 36, treat all amounts as positive.
21  Enter the loss shown on line 19 . . . . . . . . . . . . . . . . | **21** |
22  Enter the amount shown on Form 1040, line 36 . . . . . . . . . . | **22** |
23  Combine lines 20, 21, and 22. If zero or less, enter zero . . . . . . . | **23** |
24  Enter the **smaller** of line 21 or line 23 . . . . . . . . . . . . | **24** |

#### Section B.—Figure Your Short-Term Capital Loss Carryover
(Complete this section only if there is a loss shown on line 8 and line 19. Otherwise, go on to Section C.)

25  Enter the loss shown on line 8 . . . . . . . . . . . . . . . . | **25** |
26  Enter the gain, if any, shown on line 17 . . . . . . . | **26** |
27  Enter the amount shown on line 24 . . . . . . . . . | **27** |
28  Add lines 26 and 27. . . . . . . . . . . . . . . . . | **28** |
29  Subtract line 28 from line 25. If zero or less, enter zero. This is your **short-term capital loss carryover**
    **from 1989 to 1990**. . . . . . . . . . . . . . . . . . . . . | **29** |

#### Section C.—Figure Your Long-Term Capital Loss Carryover
(Complete this section only if there is a loss shown on line 17 and line 19.)

30  Enter the loss shown on line 17 . . . . . . . . . . . . . . . . | **30** |
31  Enter the gain, if any, shown on line 8 . . . . . . . . . . . . . | **31** |
32  Enter the amount shown on line 24 . . . . . . . . . | **32** |
33  Enter the amount, if any, shown on line 25 . . . . . | **33** |
34  Subtract line 33 from line 32. If zero or less, enter zero . . . . . . . | **34** |
35  Add lines 31 and 34. . . . . . . . . . . . . . . . . . . . . | **35** |
36  Subtract line 35 from line 30. If zero or less, enter zero. This is your **long-term capital loss carryover**
    **from 1989 to 1990** . . . . . . . . . . . . . . . . . . . . | **36** |

### Part V    Complete This Part Only If You Elect Out of the Installment Method and
Report a Note or Other Obligation at Less Than Full Face Value

37  Check here if you elect out of the installment method . . . . . . . . . . . . . . ▶ ☐
38  Enter the face amount of the note or other obligation . . . . . . . . . . . ▶
39  Enter the percentage of valuation of the note or other obligation . . . . . . ▶

### Part VI    Reconcile Forms 1099-B for Bartering Transactions

| | Amount of bartering income from Form 1099-B or equivalent statement reported on form or schedule |
|---|---|
| (Complete this part if you received one or more Form(s) 1099-B or an equivalent substitute statement(s) reporting bartering income.) | |

40  Form 1040, line 22 . . . . . . . . . . . . . . . . . . . . . . | **40** |
41  Schedule C (Form 1040) . . . . . . . . . . . . . . . . . . . | **41** |
42  Schedule D (Form 1040) . . . . . . . . . . . . . . . . . . . | **42** |
43  Schedule E (Form 1040) . . . . . . . . . . . . . . . . . . . | **43** |
44  Schedule F (Form 1040) . . . . . . . . . . . . . . . . . . . | **44** |
45  Other form (identify) (if not taxable, indicate reason—attach additional sheets if necessary) ▶ . . . . . . . . .

    . . . . . . . . . . . . . . . . . . . . . . . . . . . . . . . . . . . . . . . . . . . . . . . . . . . . . . . . . . . .

    . . . . . . . . . . . . . . . . . . . . . . . . . . . . . . . . . . . . . . . . . . . . . . . . . . . . . . . . . . . | **45** |
46  Total (add lines 40 through 45) . . . . . . . . . . . . . . . . . . | **46** |
    **Note:** The amount on line 46 should be the same as the total bartering income on all Forms 1099-B and equivalent statements received.

11-7-89 | Case 3 | 4797 ¹

| Form **4797** | **Sales of Business Property** | OMB No. 1545-0184 |
|---|---|---|
| Department of the Treasury Internal Revenue Service (4) | (Also, Involuntary Conversions and Recapture Amounts Under Sections 179 and 280F) ▶ Attach to your tax return. See separate Instructions. | **1989** Attachment Sequence No. 27 |

| Name(s) shown on return | Identifying number |
|---|---|
| Dr. Dee Goodon | 123-65-9876 |

**Part I  Sales or Exchanges of Property Used in a Trade or Business and Involuntary Conversions From Other Than Casualty and Theft—Property Held More Than 1 Year**

1 Enter here the gross proceeds from the sale or exchange of real estate reported to you for 1989 on Form(s) 1099-S (or an equivalent statement) that you will be including on lines 2 or 10 (column d), or on line 20. (Form 1099-S is a Statement for Recipients of Proceeds From Real Estate Transactions.)

| (a) Description of property | (b) Date acquired (mo., day, yr.) | (c) Date sold (mo., day, yr.) | (d) Gross sales price | (e) Depreciation allowed (or allowable) since acquisition | (f) Cost or other basis, plus improvements and expense of sale | (g) LOSS ((f) minus the sum of (d) and (e)) | (h) GAIN ((d) plus (e) minus (f)) |
|---|---|---|---|---|---|---|---|
| 2 | | | | | | | |

3 Gain, if any, from Form 4684, Section B, line 21
4 Section 1231 gain from installment sales from Form 6252, line 22 or 30
5 Gain, if any, from line 32, from other than casualty and theft ... 4353
6 Add lines 2 through 5 in columns (g) and (h)
7 Combine columns (g) and (h) of line 6. Enter gain or (loss) here, and on the appropriate line as follows (partnerships see the Instructions for line references): ... 4353

If line 7 is zero or a loss, enter the amount on line 11 below and skip lines 8 and 9. (S corporations enter the loss on Schedule K (Form 1120S), line 5.) If line 7 is a gain and you did not have any prior year section 1231 losses, or they were recaptured in an earlier year, enter the gain as a long-term capital gain on Schedule D and skip lines 8, 9, and 12 below.

8 Nonrecaptured net section 1231 losses from prior years (see Instructions)
9 Subtract line 8 from line 7. If zero or less, enter zero

If line 9 is zero, enter the amount from line 7 on line 12 below. If line 9 is more than zero, enter the amount from line 8 on line 12 below, and enter the amount from line 9 as a long-term capital gain on Schedule D See Line-by-Line Instructions for line 9.

**Part II  Ordinary Gains and Losses**

| (a) Description of property | (b) Date acquired (mo., day, yr.) | (c) Date sold (mo., day, yr.) | (d) Gross sales price | (e) Depreciation allowed (or allowable) since acquisition | (f) Cost or other basis, plus improvements and expense of sale | (g) LOSS ((f) minus the sum of (d) and (e)) | (h) GAIN ((d) plus (e) minus (f)) |
|---|---|---|---|---|---|---|---|
| 10 Ordinary gains and losses not included on lines 11 through 16 (include property held 1 year or less): | | | | | | | |

11 Loss, if any, from line 7
12 Gain, if any, from line 7, or amount from line 8 if applicable
13 Gain, if any, from line 31
14 Net gain or (loss) from Form 4684, Section B, lines 13 and 20a
15 Ordinary gain from installment sales from Form 6252, line(s) 21 and/or 29.
16 Recapture of section 179 deduction for partners and S corporation shareholders from property dispositions by partnerships and S corporations (see Instructions)
17 Add lines 10 through 16 in columns (g) and (h)
18 Combine columns (g) and (h) of line 17. Enter gain or (loss) here, and on the appropriate line as follows:
  a  For all except individual returns: Enter the gain or (loss) from line 18 on the return being filed.
  b  For individual returns:
    (1) If the loss on line 11 includes a loss from Form 4684, Section B, Part II, column (b)(ii), enter that part of the loss here and on line 21 of Schedule A (Form 1040). Identify as from "Form 4797, line 18b(1)"
    (2) Redetermine the gain or (loss) on line 18, excluding the loss (if any) on line 18b(1). Enter here and on Form 1040, line 15

For Paperwork Reduction Act Notice, see page 1 of separate Instructions.                 Form **4797** (1989)

**4797** 2                                         Case 3

11-7-89

Form 4797 (1989)                                                                                          Page **2**

| **Part III** Gain From Disposition of Property Under Sections 1245, 1250, 1252, 1254, and 1255 | | |
|---|---|---|

| 19 Description of sections 1245, 1250, 1252, 1254, and 1255 property: | Date acquired (mo., day, yr.) | Date sold (mo., day, yr.) |
|---|---|---|
| A  10% of residence | 2/6/86 | 12/29/89 |
| B | | |
| C | | |
| D | | |

| Relate lines 19A through 19D to these columns ▶ | Property A | Property B | Property C | Property D |
|---|---|---|---|---|
| 20 Gross sales price . . . . . . . . . . | 12460 | | | |
| 21 Cost or other basis plus expense of sale . . . . . . . | 8400 | | | |
| 22 Depreciation (or depletion) allowed (or allowable) . . . . . . | 293 | | | |
| 23 Adjusted basis, subtract line 22 from line 21 . . . . . | 8107 | | | |
| 24 Total gain, subtract line 23 from line 20 . . . . . . . | 4353 | | | |
| 25 **If section 1245 property:** | | | | |
| a Depreciation allowed (or allowable) (see Instructions) . . . . . | | | | |
| b Enter the **smaller** of line 24 or 25a . . . . | | | | |
| 26 **If section 1250 property:** If straight line depreciation was used, enter zero on line 26g unless you are a corporation subject to section 291. | | | | |
| a Additional depreciation after 12/31/75 . . . . . | | | | |
| b Applicable percentage multiplied by the **smaller** of line 24 or line 26a (see Instructions) . . . . . . . . . | | | | |
| c Subtract line 26a from line 24. If line 24 is not more than line 26a, skip lines 26d and 26e. . . . . . . | | | | |
| d Additional depreciation after 12/31/69 and before 1/1/76 . . . | | | | |
| e Applicable percentage multiplied by the **smaller** of line 26c or 26d (see Instructions) . . . . . . | | | | |
| f Section 291 amount (for corporations only) . . . . . . . | | | | |
| g Add lines 26b, 26e, and 26f . . . . . . . . | | | | |
| 27 **If section 1252 property:** Skip this section if you did not dispose of farmland or if you are a partnership. | | | | |
| a Soil, water, and land clearing expenses . . . . . . . | | | | |
| b Line 27a multiplied by applicable percentage (see Instructions) . . | | | | |
| c Enter the **smaller** of line 24 or 27b . . . . . . . | | | | |
| 28 **If section 1254 property:** | | | | |
| a Intangible drilling and development costs, expenditures for development of mines and other natural deposits, and mining exploration costs (see Instructions) . . . | | | | |
| b Enter the **smaller** of line 24 or 28a . . . . . . . | | | | |
| 29 **If section 1255 property:** | | | | |
| a Applicable percentage of payments excluded from income under section 126 (see Instructions). . . . . . . . | | | | |
| b Enter the **smaller** of line 24 or 29a . . . . . . . | | | | |

**Summary of Part III Gains (Complete property columns A through D, through line 29b before going to line 30.)**

| | |
|---|---|
| 30 Total gains for all properties (add columns A through D, line 24) . . . . . . . . . . . . . . . . . . | 4353 |
| 31 Add columns A through D, lines 25b, 26g, 27c, 28b, and 29b. Enter here and on line 13. (see the Instructions for Part IV if this is an installment sale) . . . . . . . . . . . . . . . . . . . . . . | - 0 - |
| 32 Subtract line 31 from line 30. Enter the portion from casualty and theft on Form 4684, Section B, line 15. Enter the portion from other than casualty and theft on Form 4797, line 5 . . . . . . . . . . . . . . . . . . . . . . . . | 4353 |

| **Part IV** Complete This Part Only If You Elect Out of the Installment Method and Report a Note or Other Obligation at Less Than Full Face Value |
|---|

| | |
|---|---|
| 33 Check here if you elect out of the installment method . . . . . . . . . . . . . . . . . . . . . ▶ ☐ |
| 34 Enter the face amount of the note or other obligation . . . . . . . . . . . . . . . . . ▶............ |
| 35 Enter the percentage of valuation of the note or other obligation . . . . . . . . . . . . . . . ▶ |

| **Part V** Computation of Recapture Amounts Under Sections 179 and 280F When Business Use Drops to 50% or Less (See Instructions for Part V.) | | |
|---|---|---|

| | (a) Section 179 | (b) Section 280F |
|---|---|---|
| 36 Section 179 expense deduction or section 280F recovery deductions . . . . . . . . . . . | | |
| 37 Depreciation or recovery deductions (see Instructions) . . . . . . . . . . . . . . . | | |
| 38 Recapture amount (subtract line 37 from line 36) (see Instructions for where to report) . . . . . . | | |

# APPENDIX[1]

## SALES TIPS FOR HOME BUILDERS AND DEVELOPERS

Home builders and developers face similar problems to residential home sellers in selling houses. Thus, many of the steps recommended for them can prove instructive to the typical home seller. Developers and builders also face some special problems in that their houses are not occupied and some may not even be finished.

### INTERIOR MERCHANDISING

One of the most powerful sales tools home builders can use is an effective interior-merchandising program. Interior merchandising is the process of designing, furnishing, and finishing a model house.

Interior merchandisers meet these objectives using a very systematic approach. The first step is to conduct market research to see who the most likely buyers will be. They take into account not only the income level of expected buyers, but also the models of cars they drive, religious preferences, types of lifestyle, and so forth. Then they decorate the model homes to best appeal to this targeted profile.

The goal is to create an environment where the buyers can picture themselves living, where it feels like home to them. For example, if the target buyers are likely to have young children, one effective technique has been to set up a model train and leave it running in one of the children's bedrooms. For young families, one bedroom may be decorated as a nursery. For move-up home buyers, an extra bedroom or oversized landing may be turned into a home office.

---

[1] The authors would like to acknowledge the assistance of Mr. René Pabon, Jr., Senior Vice President and Partner in Norman Harvey Associates, based in Iselin, New Jersey; and Ms. Jean Zoller, A.S.I.D., M.I.R.M., Senior Vice President of JLD, Inc., based in Chicago, Illinois, in the preparation of this Appendix.

You will only get one chance to make a first impression, so it had better be good. Model homes should be designed and decorated so that visitors are drawn from the entrance foyer into interior rooms. The houses should show ample seating for the projected owners and their guests.

Most home buyers look for a light, clean look. Heavy draperies, dark wallpapers, anything that cuts down on the light in a room, should be avoided. Because many home buyers see homes in the evening, adequate artificial lighting is critical. Light tone-on-tone colors and several plants can enhance this effect.

In designing the finished homes, pay attention to the target price for offering—and selling—the houses. In many markets, house prices have declined. The key for new developments is to focus on what the market is likely to be when the houses are finished. One solution for unfinished housing is to downsize the houses to fit the budget buyers are likely to have. But the smartest approach is to be as flexible as possible. Therefore, a good strategy is the development of small villages within a larger development community, rather than developing the entire community at once in a uniform manner. If design, price requirements, or other aspects of the market change, new development can be changed because it will be in a separate village, set off from the prior village development.

This is also important because buyers won't pay $400,000 for a house sitting next to a $250,000 house. There's ego involved. When marketing houses at different price points, consider the psychology of the buyers. The more upscale buyer will want marble in the foyer, cedar shingles, and other amenities. The lower-scale buyer will be satisfied with less expensive tiling and aluminum siding.

The use of separate villages allows the developer to appeal to different markets within the same land area. Even where much of the property has already been developed, the village concept can still be implemented. Berms, shrubbery, and other natural barriers can be used to differentiate sections of a development.

Separation into different villages or neighborhoods can be a critically important marketing step.

# GLOSSARY

## A

*Abstract of Title.* A short summary reflecting the history of the ownership and title to a certain parcel of real estate. It should indicate all transfers, judicial proceedings, encumbrances, etc.

*Acceleration Clause.* A provision in a contract or loan agreement providing that when a specified event occurs, all payments due in the future become due and payable immediately. For example, in an installment-sale contract, a clause could provide that if the buyer is more than ten days late on three separate occasions, the seller can demand all payments on the installment note.

*Affidavit.* A written statement sworn to and signed before a notary public or other authorized person.

*Amortization.* The schedule of periodic (generally monthly) payments made to a bank or other lender on a mortgage. The amortization period (e.g., 30 years) is the number of years over which the mortgage principal will be paid off.

*Assessed Value.* The value of real estate as determined by the tax assessor. Often, it is some percentage of fair-market value.

*Assumption of Mortgage.* When a buyer purchases property and agrees to be personally liable for the mortgage that is on the property. Compare an assumption with the situation when a buyer simply purchases the property subject to the existing mortgage. In the latter case, the buyer acknowledges that the mortgage is a lien on the property; however, the buyer doesn't agree to become personally liable on the mortgage.

## B

*Bad Debt.* A loan that can't be collected. It may give rise to a deduction for tax purposes in the year in which worthlessness can be established.

*Balloon Payment.* The large balance due on a note and mortgage at a date (say, three years or five years from the date of sale) that is before the time when regular payments would have amortized (paid off) the loan.

*Basis.* Your investment in property for tax purposes. It includes the price you paid to purchase the property (including ancillary costs such as legal fees), increased by capital improvements (e.g., a new deck), and decreased by depreciation (e.g., on a home office or rental unit included in the home).

*Bill of Sale.* A written agreement that transfers ownership and title to personal property from the seller to the buyer.

*Binder.* Money paid by a buyer as a good-faith deposit to encourage the seller to take the property off the market. Another usage is in the context of insurance policies, where a binder, or temporary policy, is issued pending issuance of the actual policy.

## C

*Capital Improvement.* A permanent improvement or addition to real estate that will materially prolong the life of the property, change its use, or enhance its value. For example, patching 5 percent of a roof is a repair, but replacing the entire roof is a capital expenditure. Capital expenditures can't be deducted for tax purposes; they are added to your basis, or investment, in the property.

*Certificate of Occupancy.* Also called "C of O." This is an authorization or document issued by a local government body permitting the use of a property for a certain purpose. In some instances a certificate of occupancy must be obtained for the closing to be completed or for the buyer to move into the house.

*Closing.* The final meeting in a house sale transaction, where all checks are paid and the buyer is given title to the house.

*Condominium.* A system of separate ownership of individual units in a multi-unit real estate project. Each owner of an individual unit is a tenant-in-common in the common areas (halls, athletic facilities, parking, etc.).

*Consideration.* Something of value given in return for a promise to perform a certain act or contract. Some legal documents might say for "Ten dollars and other good and valuable consideration," or something similar.

## D

*Damages.* Money award that a court may give to redress a wrong and make the injured person whole.

*Debt.* Money or other valuable rights or property owing from one person to another.

*Deed of Trust.* In many states, particularly those located in the western half of the country, a deed of trust is used instead of a mortgage. Although there still may be differences between a deed of trust and a mortgage, the differences are primarily historical. (See Mortgage.)

*Default.* A failure to perform according to the terms of a contract. When a borrower violates a provision of a mortgage loan, or one of the parties to a contract violates a provision of the contract, a default may be triggered. A default will have the consequences that the contract or loan agreement provides when a default occurs. For a loan, this could mean acceleration (the entire loan balance becomes due and payable). In a sales contract, a default could excuse the other party from having to continue under the contract.

*Defect of Record.* A lien, encroachment, encumbrance, or other defect in the title to property, which is set forth in the public record. This means that the title search completed by the title company or the attorney will uncover the defect.

*Defective Title.* Title that is not marketable.

*Demand Note.* A loan evidenced by a note, which is due immediately upon an agreed-upon maturation, without requirement for further demand.


**E**

*Earnest Money.* A payment (and demonstration of good faith) that a buyer makes to a seller (often to the real estate broker to hold in escrow on the seller's behalf) to encourage the seller to take the property off the market and pursue a sale to that buyer.

*Easement.* The right of one person to make lawful use of another's land. For example, the electric company might have an easement to run wires along the back ten feet of your property. This is in contrast with an encroachment, which is an illegal use.

*Eminent Domain.* The right of a government body to take private property for public use.

*Encroachment.* An illegal intrusion on another's land—for example, when your neighbor's tool shed is on the last five feet of your property without your permission.

*Escrow.* The holding of monies and documents by an unrelated third party (escrow agent) pending the closing of the sale of the house. If the requirements and conditions to close are met, the monies in the escrow fund will be given to the seller, and the deed conveying title to the property will be given to the buyer.

*Execute.* To complete a legal agreement—for example, to sign a contract.

## F

*Fee Simple.* Absolute ownership interest in land.

*Fixture.* Personal (movable) property that has become permanently attached to the real estate. An example is a bookcase that is permanently nailed to the subwall. Fixtures will be sold automatically with a house unless they are excluded from the sale.

## G

*Grace Period.* A period of time beyond a due date during which a payment or other required action may be completed without penalty.

## I

*Imputed Interest.* Extra interest calculated by the IRS. In most sale transactions, if the seller and buyer don't set a reasonable, market-determined interest rate on deferred payments (as in an installment sale), the IRS can set a minimum rate and require the calculations to be made as if that rate of interest had been paid. This can have a significant effect on the tax results to be realized by the parties.

## J

*Judgment.* A determination of a matter by a court of proper or competent jurisdiction.

## L

*Land Contract.* A method of sale that permits the seller to retain title to the property until all amounts due are paid by the buyer. The seller's rights to repossess the property may be limited by local law.

*Lien.* A charge or claim on another's property as security for a debt due. A mechanic's lien is a lien for work performed and materials furnished to a property.

*Listing Broker.* The broker who signs the listing or brokerage contract with you to sell your house.

# M

*Marketable Title*. Ownership interest in the real property, which a buyer should be willing to take and a court should be willing to require a buyer to take.

*Mortgage*. Under the lien theory followed in many states, a mortgage is the legal document that gives the lender a lien on a house (or other real property) to secure a loan. In title theory states, a deed of trust is used. Under a deed of trust, an independent third party (someone other than the borrower and lender), called the trustee, holds title to the property, and when the debt is paid, the documents of title are returned to the owner/former borrower.

# N

*Note*. A document in which a borrower personally agrees to assume responsibility for the repayment of a loan. The difference from a mortgage is that a mortgage pledges the house (or other real estate) as collateral for repayment of the loan.

*Notice*. Information concerning a legal matter actually communicated to the party. Most contracts and agreements have provisions that specify how notice must be given.

# Q

*Quiet Enjoyment*. The unimpaired right to use and enjoy property purchased or leased.

# R

*Real Property*. Land and anything that is permanently affixed to land (e.g., house, garage, underground lawn sprinkler, etc.). Unlike personal property, which must be specifically included in a sale, all items constituting real property are considered part of the sale unless the sale contract specifically excludes them.

*RESPA*. A form required by the U.S. Department of Housing and Urban Development under the Real Estate Settlement Procedures Act.

*Restrictive Covenants*. Rules and regulations governing how property can be used. For example, when the subdivision in which your house is located was formed, all of the deeds for the houses might have included restrictions requiring a minimum lot size, etc.

# S

*Sale*. A contract by which one person transfers ownership in certain property to another person.

*Second Mortgage.* A loan that comes behind, or is second in priority, to the first mortgage on a house in the event of a foreclosure. Purchase-money mortgages—loans provided by sellers—are often second mortgages.

**T**

*Take-Back Mortgage.* Purchase-money financing. A loan that the seller agrees to extend to the buyer for part of the purchase price.

*Title.* The right to use and enjoy property.

*Transfer Taxes.* Taxes or fees required to be paid when title or ownership in property changes. For example, a cooperative corporation may require the payment of a transfer fee when a current owner sells. This won't qualify as a deductible tax for income tax purposes. A transfer tax paid to a county based on, for example, a percentage of the contract price may be deductible as a property tax.

# INDEX